ETHICAL LEADERSHIP

This book introduces readers to the moral dilemmas associated with business decisions, helping students to understand the moral and ethical considerations leaders face in the workplace, and providing a framework for balancing business demands with doing the right thing.

The author walks readers through the basics of Western moral philosophy before the 20th century and beyond it, covering Utilitarianism, Kantism, virtue ethics, and ethical pluralism as well as compelling Eastern moral philosophy to help readers link individual behavior to the larger scheme of corporate social responsibility. The text combines this with a survey of various leadership theories—including servant leadership, awakened leadership, authentic leadership, and spiritual leadership—to present a model that combines the strengths of each theory. Students will become familiar with the mind-sets behind moral pitfalls along with their potentially disastrous effects and how these can be overcome.

Chapter summaries and relevant cases, including studies on Fidel Castro, Wells Fargo, Mylan's EpiPen Price Gouging, and more, will help students to place theories in context, learning how to achieve success in business ventures successfully, compassionately, and ethically.

With an easy-to-grasp three-part progression and reflective questions for both chapters and cases, *Ethical Leadership* will benefit students of leadership and business ethics.

Joan Marques is Dean in the School of Business and Full Professor of Management at Woodbury University, USA. She is the author of several books published by Routledge, including *Business and Buddhism* in 2015, and *Leadership* in 2016.

ETHICAL LEADERSHIP

Progress with a Moral Compass

Joan Marques

Routledge
Taylor & Francis Group

NEW YORK AND LONDON

First published 2018
by Routledge
711 Third Avenue, New York, NY 10017

and by Routledge
2 Park Square, Milton Park, Abingdon, Oxon, OX14 4RN

Routledge is an imprint of the Taylor & Francis Group, an informa business

Library of Congress Cataloging-in-Publication Data
Names: Marques, Joan, author.
Title: Ethical leadership: progress with a moral compass / Joan
Marques.
Description: 1 Edition. | New York: Routledge, 2017.
Identifiers: LCCN 2017022218 | ISBN 9781138636538 (hbk) |
ISBN 9781138636552 (pbk) | ISBN 9781315205946 (ebk)
Subjects: LCSH: Business ethics. | Leadership—Moral and ethical
aspects. | Social responsibility of business.
Classification: LCC HF5387 .M34637 2017 | DDC 174/.4—dc23
LC record available at https://lccn.loc.gov/2017022218

ISBN: 978-1-138-63653-8 (hbk)
ISBN: 978-1-138-63655-2 (pbk)
ISBN: 978-1-315-20594-6 (ebk)

Typeset in Bembo
by codeMantra

CONTENTS

LIST OF FIGURES AND TABLE

Figures

Table

PART I

Changing Paradigms about Moving Forward

1

THE NOTION OF PROGRESS IN THE PAST

Abstract

Laying the foundation for moral thinking as it has progressed over the past century, this chapter initiates the discussion about the discrepancy in perceiving progress as it happened in much of the 20th century and before, compared to contemporary insights. In previous centuries, humanity focused on growth and innovation without considering the long-term (and sometimes even the short-term) effects on nonhuman life or the environment. Even human well-being was considered within specific parameters, whereby the powerful ones were held to different standards than those who were assigned to hard labor.

Introduction

Every era in history deserves its own credit for the progress it brought. Although we may look back today and wonder how the people in previous centuries managed to get by, it remains important to understand that for them, those were critical times of newness, immense challenges, and progress.

Considering the fact that management was still in a developmental stage as a way of guiding people by rules, the 20th century displays numerous learning opportunities to us through the poor management that was exerted, especially in its first half. With the industrial revolution fully in operation, the emphasis was more on output and quality control, and less or not at all on employee satisfaction. Oftentimes, there was one single style implemented and, usually, that style was heavily task oriented and not so much people oriented. It was like being forced only to waltz while the world played many kinds of music.[1]

One of the most prominent concerns with the 20th-century way of managing and leading people is that it has established itself as a status quo, and many work-based entities still don't question its foundations or whether this trend is still working today. In other words, the ways of moving through a collective task are still approached from an industrial-era perspective, even though these ways have since shifted to a knowledge- and technology-based era: organizations are still run as if they harbor mechanistic operations and functions; as if processes, occurrences, and challenges are still predictable and measurable; as if our expectations can easily be realized through calculations and predications; and as if there is one single best way to advance.[2] Unfortunately, these are outdated strategies that did not even work well in the previous century. The only reason why these strategies seemed to make sense in the previous century is that there were continuously new inventions and instruments, and theories were continuously adapted, so the distraction was sufficient to refrain from focusing on the challenge that managing and leading people were becoming.[3]

A Booming Century with Numerous Changes

With the second industrial, also known as technological, revolution in full swing, the 20th century brought us a wide range of developments. Some were constructive, such as colored photographs, penicillin, car radios, airplanes, radar, television, computers, and the Internet, and some destructive, such as massive deforestation, depletion of natural resources, uncontrolled waste, the Holocaust, the Berlin Wall, and multiple wars.

In many regards, the 20th century set a speed of development in motion that was unheard or unthought of in previous centuries. Mass communications were definitely a major pillar of this century, as a variety of media outlets, such as newspapers, radio, television, and, in the last decades of the century, the Internet, enabled people to learn from other cultures and see places they never knew existed.

The learning curve was also high for those who lived and worked in the 20th century, as disruptive change seemed to be part of a frequent mental menu. This was the century in which generations became classified (perhaps even "stereotyped"), particularly in the US:

- *The GI Generation*, born between 1901 and 1924, lived through the Great Depression and lived through World Wars I and II. Actually, members of the GI Generation went to war four times, when also including the Russian civil war and the Korean War. Through war, they learned about life and developed their view of the world. *GI* is an acronym for "government issue," reflecting the uniforms these people wore. GI members had great respect for structure, rules, and regulations. They formed bonds that would never break. They strongly believed in team performance and group strength. They were extremely loyal.[4]
- *The Silent Generation*, born between 1925 and 1942, was too young to be personally traumatized by the pressures of World War II, but may have suffered from the loss of fathers, brothers, and uncles, and from the deprivations of living with war. Members of the Silent Generation were rather

patient, sometimes even resigned. They were not loudmouths, but quiet endurers of their circumstances. They were supportive of anything that would make their environment and country a better place to live.[5]

- *The Baby Boomers*, born between 1943 and 1964, are a lively bunch born right after World War II and highly vocal against the Vietnam War and civil injustice. Members of the Baby Boomers are part of a large crowd: between 1943 and 1964, a child was born in the US every seven seconds. Very self-aware, Baby Boomers expanded on their parents' notion of striving for improvement, only they took it a step further: rather than caring solely about improvement in their country, they desired betterment of the entire world.[6]

- *Generation X*, born between 1965 and 1979, is a generation that was confronted with the AIDS epidemic and the fall of the Berlin Wall, and which refused to be labeled (hence, "X"). As children, the members of this generation were often left alone, due to both parents working. It may be no wonder, then, that Gen-X-ers have been labeled as being rather self-centered. Other labels that have been placed on members of this generation are "authority-adverse, motivated by personal gain, poor listeners, disloyal to the organization, and focused on having fun."[7]

- *The Millennials* (sometimes also listed as Generation Y), born between 1980 and 2000, are big on the Internet, and technology in general.[8] Many of the labels of Gen-X have also been slapped on this generation. Millennials have also been called over protected, and ego driven. Yet, authors William Strauss and Neil Howe predict that Millennials will become more like the "civic-minded" GI Generation, with a strong sense of community, both local and global.[9] Strauss and Howe also describe the Millennials as a generation that is on track to become a forceful one, beset with technology planners, community shapers, institution builders, and world leaders, potentially turning into the principal generation of the 21st century, just as the GI Generation was in the 20th century.

As can be derived from the brief descriptions above, each generation faces its own set of challenges and advantages, and represents its own identity, to which leaders must adapt in order to get results.

Management in the 20th Century

In regards to management and leadership, the 20th century was also a fertile era, as it presented us a mosaic of insights and factors, initially to safeguard productivity, and later also to ensure proper treatment of people in work processes. From the earliest days of the 20th century, theorists have endeavored to define models and concepts that would improve efficiency and effectiveness in work environments. A series of management trends were introduced to the practical and academic field, varying from scientific management to administrative theory, and from bureaucratic theory to human relations and human resources. As indicated earlier, most of these theories were initially developed to ensure effective performance in work settings in order to safeguard profits. However, as the 20th century progressed, awareness heightened, and the well-being of workforce members also became a critical focus point.

As a result of the maturing industrial era, the performance focus in the 20th century was fixated on continuously multiplying levels of output and performance. Corporate leaders found themselves dealing with increased pressure to rapidly convert ailing corporations into profitable ones. The importance of *time* as the core performance factor skyrocketed.

Management, a phenomenon that has been around since human civilizations began, rose to the highest echelons as a study topic in the late 19th century. Thanks to the industrial revolution, humanity had arrived at a stage where a more systematic approach was needed to ensure proper alignment of material and human resources. When considered in that regard, the theoretical foundation of management started at the dawning of the 20th century.

The scientific era: As the 19th century was reaching its end, managing corporations rose in prominence and the need emerged to put some structure to this trend. Manufacturing was still a core work process in the United States at the time, so theorists were fixated on the possibility of improving work-related efficiency. One of those theorists was Frederick W. Taylor, who became a significant contributor to management thought in its foundational aspects.[10] Taylor, a mechanical engineer, studied motion studies and efficiency, as he wanted to ensure a more economical use of resources in manufacturing processes. His "scientific management" theory focused on efficient performance of tasks, matching the most appropriate worker for the task at hand, and developing a reward system that would result in optimal performance—a triangular approach of effort, performance, and reward.[11]

Taylor felt that individual evaluation and rewards would lead to greater passion and input than would group-based rewards. His intention was for managers to select the proper employee for a job, but this intention ignited major criticism, because it soon led to partiality and exploitation. This was not necessarily due to Taylor's theory, but to the way it was implemented. Over time, scientific management gained a poor reputation on basis of the manipulative implementation of the theory by managers. Taylor and others, such as Frank and Lillian Gilbreth, who were trying to include engineering techniques in work performance, may have assumed that employee remuneration would be determined on an individual basis, with consideration of the difficulty of the task and the employee's output. "The principal object of management, according to Taylor, should be to secure the maximum prosperity for the employer, coupled with the maximum prosperity for each employee."[12] Unfortunately, this assumption did not materialize, and the scientific approach led to strikes in several production factories after the first decade of the 20th century.

One justified criticism of scientific management is that it was not concerned with the feelings of employees. It focused on managerial decision-making and not on employee concerns.[13]

The administrative era: As the 20th century progressed, another engineer, Henry Fayol, presented the world with a process-based notion of management. Fayol's initial idea of management functions was a six-step process: (1) forecasting and planning, (2) organizing, (3) commanding or directing, (4) coordinating, (5) developing output, and (6) controlling. Over time, these six steps were consolidated into a four-tiered concept: POLC, which stands for Planning, Organizing, Leading, and Controlling.

As the industrial revolution was in full swing, and competition was continuously increasing, thinkers such as Fayol and his contemporaries wanted to establish universal structures to enhance efficiency in workplaces. In order to do so, they developed the Administrative Theory, which focuses on departmentalization of actions. In this theory, different activities that contribute to the common purpose of the organization, have to be identified and classified into different groups or departments, in such a way that the task can be accomplished effectively.

Just like Taylor, the Administrative Theory was not concerned with social or human constraints, but focused mainly on economic needs, which promptly ignited criticism from later management theorists. In the Administrative Theory, managers were again treated as the sole determinants in the work process, leaving the same room as in Scientific Management Theory (the earlier-explained motion studies) for manipulation and partiality.[14]

The bureaucratic era: Another angle that gained much acclaim in the first half of the 20th century was the bureaucratic approach, developed by German scholar Max Weber. Even though we may not think of "bureaucracy" as an effective approach these days, the concept was not designed with slow-moving processes in mind. Weber's intention with the bureaucratic approach was to create a system with clear reporting lines, so that managers would have less power and influence outside their immediate area of responsibility. He wanted to create a system with legitimized authority and impersonal rules.[15]

Weber's concept was inspired by the desire to establish fairness in workplaces through a strict hierarchy, with clear reporting lines. The rules and documents that came with this strict reporting process were intended to safeguard the element of fairness, and minimize the influence of politics. Unfortunately, it has been proven that the organic nature of human beings is averse to rules that are too rigid and too numerous. Due to the many strict rules of the bureaucratic approach, progress in any action slowed down tremendously, and irritated rather than satisfied stakeholders.

The behavioral and human relations era: As the 1920s transitioned into the 1930s, and the Great Depression crippled workplaces left and right, the human aspect started shifting toward the forefront of business systems. A social worker named Mary Parker Follett took the lead in provoking the paradigm shift of seeing and treating employees as active members in the work process, and involving them in strategic thinking, which could contribute to better workflows and help workers feel more appreciated.[16]

The 1920s and 1930s were also the formation years for the research projects of Elton Mayo, an industry researcher and organizational theorist, to develop the "Hawthorne effect." This phenomenon was based on a test that found employee performance increases through psychological stimuli. The Hawthorne effect maintained that employees who are positively singled out and treated as more important than others, either through better accommodation (office, lights, surroundings) or better treatment (work schedule, breaks, leadership), display higher productivity levels than do those who are not singled out.[17] While opinions about the validity of the Hawthorne effect have differed widely since then, it nevertheless brought some important insights to light, such as the fact that it is hard to predict precise outcomes, even when providing special accommodation; interpersonal relationships between employees among one another, and among employees and their managers may contributed to the outcome; the norms in working groups determine workers' notions about their workload and therefore also their productivity levels; and workplaces are social systems, consisting of interdependent parts.[18]

Unlike other theories, the behavioral theories don't consider informal relationships between employees as a negative, but rather as a positive influence to work performance. When people trust each other, they are more willing to assist one another and ensure better overall performance.

Behavioral theories were further polished by later theorists, such as Chris Argyris, Frederick Herzberg, Douglas McGregor, and Victor Vroom, who underscored that employees should not be treated as a means to an end.

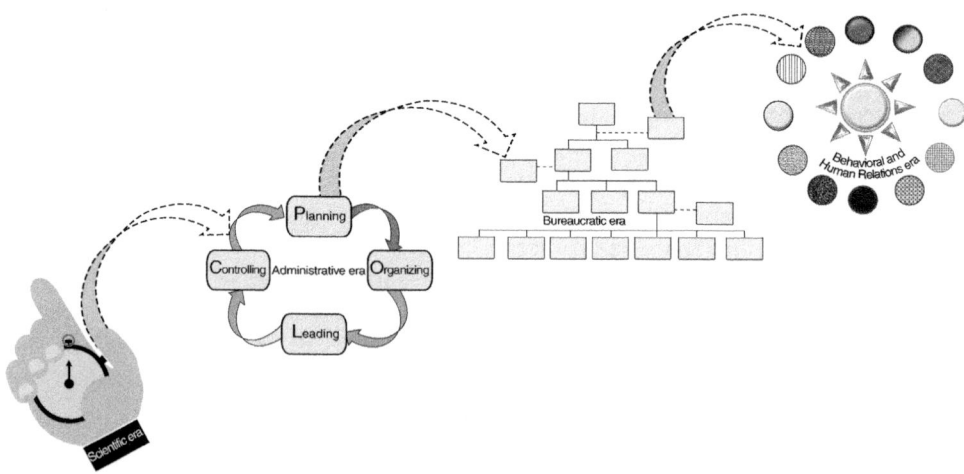

FIGURE 1.1 Management in the 20th Century.

McGregor's Theory X and Theory Y, for instance, maintain that employees' behaviors are mostly a response to their managers' attitude. Additionally, employees will seek a connection between their efforts and their rewards, and will start withholding their input if they feel that they are being taken advantage of.[19]

Progress in the 20th Century

The 20th century was an impressive one in many ways. In none of the centuries before, over the entire course of human civilization, had there been so much change and progress as in that one. The 20th century brought us massive diversity in engineering and appliances, but also destructive world wars, immense growth, and overwhelming losses of human lives. As for the population growth: while it took our entire human history up to the year 1804 to reach a global human population of 1 billion, we managed to create the next billion in only 100 years: by 1927, the world had 2 billion people. From there on, the growth further accelerated, bringing the human cohort to 3 billion in 1959, 4 billion in 1974, 5 billion in 1987, 6 billion in 1999, and 7 billion in 2011.[20] In spite of wars, mass disasters, epidemics, and other types of death, the human race has been adding a billion population every 12 years or so. While the term *growth* generally implies a positive trend, we can safely state that this particular growth is extremely concerning, because we are reaching the point where there will be more human beings than the resources needed to sustain them[21].

As for the tragic instances of massive loss of human lives, Charles Tilly, an American sociologist and political scientist, asserts that "about 100 million people died as a direct result of action by organized military units backed by one government or another over the course of the century. Most likely a comparable number of civilians died of war-induced disease and other indirect effects."[22] Some other instances in the 20th century that led to major loss of human lives are "Stalinist Terror" in the Soviet Union between 1922 and 1935, in which 10 to 43 million people perished through famine; purges; labor camps; population transfer; deportations; and massacres. Multiple catastrophes under Mao Zedong's leadership in China include "The Great Leap Forward," slave labor, violent political purges, and class exterminations, in which between 32 and 70 million people lost their lives between 1946 and 1976. Nonetheless, comparing the magnitude of human growth with the losses that occurred, we are still looking at a tremendous surplus in the overall human population over time.

The 20th century gave rise to emotions, trends, phenomena, and cultural shifts unknown to humanity before. The tremendous expansion of global involvement provoked major senses of national pride, with all the rewards and drawbacks thereof. On the positive side, all of these developments prompted movements of a kind that had been nonexistent before, such as decolonization and regional and global alliances as well as conflicts.

Because individual progress was considered to be hugely important, especially in the Western world, the term *Social Darwinism* was frequently used by scholars to capture social trends. Social Darwinism is a collective name for several theories of society emerging in the United Kingdom, North America, and Western Europe in the late 19th century, and claiming to apply biological concepts of natural selection and survival of the fittest to sociology and politics. In its simplest form, Social Darwinism adheres to the notion that "the strong survive" or "kill or be killed" in general, including human issues.[23] Merriam Webster defines it as "a sociological theory that sociocultural advance is the product of intergroup conflict and competition and the socially elite classes (as those possessing wealth and power) possess biological superiority in the struggle for existence."[24] Over time, Social Darwinism became interpreted by a broad variety of groups to support their own beliefs. For instance, in one of its most radical interpretations, the theory was used to promote the idea that the white European race was superior to others and, therefore, destined to rule over them.[25]

Social Darwinism is also labeled as an anti-philanthropic theory, and many business moguls of the 20th century openly rejected this stance by granting millions to social institutions, such as schools, colleges, hospitals, parks, art institutes, and more. However, a degree of caution is necessary here, to be illustrated with this example:

> In the early 20th century, new medical treatments emerged, and the awareness of their profitability entered the radars of the wealthiest business people of those days, such as [John D.] Rockefeller, [John Pierpont] Morgan, and [Andrew] Carnegie. These wealthy individuals expressed interest in joining forces with the American Medical Association, and became the financiers of the new medical economy. In return for their major donations, they requested a presence of their representatives on the boards of the organizations they supported, thus shrewdly taking control of the universities and medical institutions that benefited from their money. This presence of heavily capitalist minds in a health-based industry provoked a complete shift in the way medicine was taught and practiced. Medical doctors were less educated about actually healing health issues, but more in prescribing drugs to reduce or eradicate symptoms. The emphasis became more on teaching medical doctors [about] pharmaceutical drugs than on training them in actual health-restoration. As a result, the medical industry became a booming one, making billions of dollars on major diseases such as cancer, for which legally only three cures have been listed as acceptable: surgery, radiation, and chemo therapy. Throughout the 20th century, several individuals claimed different degrees of success with natural cures for this disease, but neither of these cures were ever formally examined by the existing medical order, because most of these newly claimed cures were readily available in nature,

and would therefore not be patentable. Besides, there was simply too much money made with "curing" cancer in the current situation. Till today, no new cure for cancer has been invented, in spite of the countless large donations allocated to research on this disease. Sceptics believe that there is a vested interest in keeping matters as they currently are, since cancer remains to be the biggest industry in the USA.[26]

The above example serves to show that, oftentimes, philanthropic gestures are not made for selfless reasons, but to promote one's position, beliefs, or perspectives on future gains, which feeds right back into the Social Darwinist mind-set of condoning superiority and advancement for the "strong" ones.

Progress in the 20th century meant moving forward, but moving forward did not always happen with long-term or even short-term advancements for others in mind. Progress pertained to economic and technological advancement without consideration of moral, environmental, or societal consequences. Due to the numerous scientific and technological leaps that were made, shifts happened at a multitude of levels, from political climates and relationships, to ideological, economical, and social shifts. This was the century of Willis Carrier, who brought us the air conditioner; the Wright brothers, Wilbur and Orville, who developed the first practical fixed-wing aircraft; Albert Einstein and his relativity theory; Adolf Hitler and his ideas of ethnic cleansing and the Holocaust; Mahatma Gandhi and his nonviolent civil disobedience movement toward independence for India from the UK; Vladimir Ulyanov (Lenin), communist revolutionary and founder of the Soviet Union, and Joseph Stalin, his ruthless successor; Nelson Mandela and his stride for equal rights between blacks and whites in Africa; Martin Luther King Jr. and the civil rights movement in America; David Ben-Gurion and his actions toward independence for the Jewish state of Israel; Cuban revolutionary Fidel Castro and Argentinian revolutionary Ché Guevara; Tim Berners-Lee and his World Wide Web; Bill Gates, Steve Jobs, and the rise of personal computers as the dominant way to access almost anything; and so many more.

It was also the century where transportation metamorphosed from horseback riding, simple automobiles, and lengthy sea journeys, to high-speed trains, commercial air travel, and space explorations; the century that saw the first man stepping on the moon, and had the scientific world realizing that the universe was far more complex than initially estimated. Global communication shifted from slow-traveling letters, expensive telephone calls, and telegrams for critical issues, to instantaneous information exchanges, first through facsimiles, and then through Internet-based software (email, chat programs, and visual communication formats). Yet, while a string of inventions succeeded each other and knowledge became more readily available, humanity was also confronted with a wide range of new concerns, such as depleting natural resources, disappearing forests and wildlife, as well as the surfacing of new terms, such as world war, ideology, nuclear war, fossil fuels, quantum physics, and carbon footprint.

Interestingly, several positive developments had negative effects, and negative developments had positive effects:

- An example of positive developments sorting negative effects is the fact that science made several medical breakthroughs, enabling human life expectancy to increase in a world that was becoming saturated, or even overpopulated, at an accelerated pace (Most contemporary estimates for the carrying capacity of the Earth under existing conditions are between 4 billion and 16 billion. Depending on which estimate is used, human overpopulation may or may not have already occurred).[27] So, while medical breakthroughs are positive trends, they also caused a surge in human population and augmenting pressure on available resources.
- Another example are the technological inventions. While such inventions generally led to greater comfort levels, increased productivity, and improved social standards, they also immensely increased the use of depleting natural resources, such as fossil fuels for different forms of transportation, railways, and aircraft. Similarly, some inventions entailed the development of mass-killing devices, resulting in disastrous occurrences such as the 60 million deaths in World War II,[28] including the atomic bomb killings (129,000 people) in Hiroshima and Nagasaki.
- An example of negative developments having positive effects is the fact that the two world wars in the 20th century helped disintegrate kingdoms, empires, and the general trend of colonization, leading to a world with more independent nations that were no longer limited to the suppression of colonizing nations, which were oftentimes located in entirely different continents. This was most clearly the case after World War I, when national awareness reached levels that instigated the creation of many new countries, particularly in Eastern Europe. For instance, the new nation of Czechoslovakia emerged, comprising the former kingdom of Bohemia and parts of the Hungarian kingdom. Russia transformed into the Soviet Union, with Finland, Estonia, Lithuania, and Latvia becoming independent nations in 1917 and 1918.

Moral Mind-sets in the 20th Century

Being the bedrock of so many inventions, new trends, and developments, the 20th century epitomized a major turnaround in the way humanity worked, thought, traveled, shopped, communicated, and perceived power. As new possibilities and swifter actions emerged, new threats surfaced as well, and it took some time for some of these threats to become clear. A good example is the use of depleting natural resources. Not only did this new way of consuming cause concern of goods that were now becoming scarcer, but it also brought health and sustainability threats to the forefront, such as air pollution, global warming, and global climate change.

Case 1.1 Jack Welch: Revered Leadership of the 20th Century

Starting his 20-year leadership journey at General Electric in 1981, John F. Welch, popularly referred to as "Jack Welch" became one of the epitomic leaders of this century. Throughout the first decade of his leadership tenure, he implemented extensive cost-cutting plans, among which were some controversial divestitures of GE subsidiaries. Once he felt that the company was streamlined, Welch upheld a policy in which employees had to focus on making GE products and services number one or number two in their respective industries. This task-and-output-oriented strategy was powerful, propelling GE to become one of the most efficient conglomerates of its time, and an industry leader in everything from aircraft engines to television (NBC).[29]

Admittedly, GE's stock was doing poorly and had lost half its value over the previous ten years before Jack took over the reins. His aggressive approach was needed to ensure a turnaround of the company.[30] Focusing on shareholder's value, as was the dominant approach of the century, Jack increased GE's market value from $12 billion to $280 billion. In an effort to enhance entrepreneurial spirit among his workforce, he established *skunkworks*, which were small entrepreneurial units within the larger corporation. He popularized the "rank and yank" policy, which has since been adopted by other corporations. This was a system in which, annually, the bottom 10 percent of the company's managers were fired, regardless of their absolute performance. Conversely, he rewarded the ones in the top 20 percent with bonuses and stock options. His eliminating approach of employees earned him the name "Neutron Jack." Welch proudly wrote in his book *Jack: Straight from the Gut* that, from 1980 to 1985, he reduced his workforce by about 27 percent—from 411,000 to 299,000 employees—while exponentially increasing GE's market capital.[31] In 1999, the company's market capitalization was estimated at $400 billion, making it one of the most valuable companies on earth, second only to Microsoft.[32]

There is a lot to be said about Welch's leadership: he definitely got rid of useless baggage, and placed the company on a more contemporary track, rather than on the obsolete path it had previously been treading. His implementations were swift, and his decisions ruthless. When asked if he considered this cruel, he refuted that cruelty is when you let someone believe they are doing well for years and then fire them when they are too old and slow to improve. He challenged his managers to shift to the limits of their perceptions and to take ownership of progressive trends. He stepped away from the previous trend of acceptable incrementalism (minuscule progress as long as it was moving ahead), and embraced radicalism: a do-or-die mentality of proposing creative changes, based on proactive measures or benchmarking.

Several sources emphasized a mellowing shift in Welch's approach toward his employees in the 1990s, but whether or not his approach toward some of the company's most important stakeholders—its employees—was morally sound remains in question. Evaluating business leadership from a Kantian perspective, Norman Bowie explains that Immanuel Kant, the German philosopher who laid the foundations of this moral theory, established that every person should be treated as an end unto himself or herself, and not as a means toward others' ends.[33] Each person, according to Kant, is a rational creature, entitled to dignity and respect. Kant argues that in organizations or communities, we should adhere to rules that we would also accept if we were the legislators. Leadership, then, cannot be considered from an instrumental perspective when we consider Kantian morality, because an instrumental view entails that we would use our workforce, as our most efficient means, toward our own or the company's ends. Bowie goes on to present Jack Welch as a typical business leader who utilized an instrumental view, and would therefore not be seen as a moral leader from a Kantian viewpoint. Especially in the first decade of his leadership over GE, Welch was fixated on strict financial goals, expecting his managers to either meet those goals or forfeit their positions. He was so demanding that in those years, he regularly landed on *Fortune's* list of the most difficult bosses to work for. He obviously used subordinates as a means for his own end or as a means to increase the wealth of GE shareholders.

Even when Welch changed his approach toward greater moderation and more-human respect and empathy in the 1990s, he admitted that he would only use enlightened management techniques if they contributed to the bottom line. If they did not, he would cease using them. Within the Kantian moral construct, Welch would, therefore, not be considered a morally responsible leader.[34]

Reviewing in a more specific light some of Welch's troubles in the 1990s, Greenwald et al. (1994) point out the slippery moral slope that an excessive bottom line approach could cause.[35] Even though Welch liked to boast about GE's minimal criminal convictions during his years at its helm, some of the companies he acquired in the late 1980s turned out to be moral lemons, bringing to light ethical violations that required immediate and harsh action on Welch's part. One such scandal pertained to a whistle-blower case regarding GEs conspiracy with South Africa's De Beers Group mining company, involving price fixing of industrial diamonds. The whistle-blower brought a multimillion-dollar lawsuit against GE, and the US Department of Justice was considering bringing its own charges, as well. Aside from the De Beers case, there were several other troubles on the legal and ethical horizon for GE, and management analysts started questioning Welch's driving motives for wanting to be number one or number two in the market for any business the company was involved in. Some of these analysts considered Welch's purpose hollow, as it had no foundation other than an excessively competitive performance modus operandi for division managers to become ruthless competitors, cut corners, and do whatever they had to do to win the desired place in the market. The criticizing management analysts expressed their concern for the moral downfall that this approach could cause.[36]

As Welch moved on to become a prominent management analyst himself after his retirement from GE, his performance as CEO of this global giant continued to be evaluated. Phillip Thompson (2004) specifically criticized Welch's strong bottom-line focus, which affected the option of leading through a broader and more humane moral horizon.[37] As indicated in the introduction of this case, Welch was hailed by several business sources as the quintessence of 20th-century business leadership. He was listed as *Fortune Magazine's* "Manager of the 20th Century" and ranked no. 7 on *Fast Company's* list of greatest business leaders for the same era. Welch's primary focus on profitability, market share, and productivity went hand in hand with hardnosed dismissal of employees in less-profitable sections of GE, and reward to those who were able to improve the bottom line.[38] Thompson analyzes Welch's leadership from a religious perspective and concludes that Welch's notions of God were limited to what this phenomenon could do for or did to him, and not beyond that. Welch, asserts Thompson, grew up with a chip on his shoulder, along with a bloated sense of confidence and determination.

While these last two qualities can be good leadership assets, an overdose of them can lead to what Welch became: a person void of compassion or empathy, detached from the effects of his massive layoffs, and only pushing for results at any cost, thereby nurturing an environment in which ruthless competition is endorsed. As a result, moral frameworks remained minor to nonexistent in this picture, and Welch's notion of values turned out to be centered on bottom-line-rising concepts, such as "aggressive targets," "excellence," "team building," "competitive advantage," "customer focus," "change," and "energy." While, on one hand, the company's public relations campaign touted team spirit and ownership, on the other hand, the reality promoted harshness, callousness, excessive work-priority, and Machiavellian behavior.[39] A string of confessions from former GE employees suggests that success rather than integrity were the foundational drivers of GE during Welch's leadership years. This focus sometimes resulted in questionable accounting practices to keep the desired image of consistent profitability intact, underpaid employees in the company's external manufacturing operations, and multiple legal actions in which the company was accused of unlawful practices. In sum, states Thompson, Welch's "glorious" growth of GE happened at the massive expense of human livelihood, dignity, and moral values, as well as inconsiderate environmental exploitation. Thompson equates Welch's practices as one of a crude utilitarian nature, stating that employees, stockholders, and consumers who remained involved were rewarded at the expense of those who had to go. Thompson concludes that it is fortunate, then, that Welch's influence has declined in recent years.

Questions

1. Do you believe Jack Welch was a morally responsible leader? Please explain your answer.
2. Upon reading this case, what do you consider are Jack Welch's greatest strengths and weaknesses as a leader?
3. Do you think Welch would be as successful a leader in our current era, as he was in the 20th century? Why or why not?

The 20th Century and Future Considerations

In the last few decades of the 20th century, change emerged in one of the most powerful concepts in business. Workforce members were made aware that change was the only constant, and that it was occurring at an ever-increasing pace. Every member and every aspect of the corporate chain was subject to speed: speed in innovating to surpass competitors, speed in output to expand market share, and speed in profit generation to keep shareholders satisfied. The quicker a manager could demonstrate an upward trend in the corporation's performance, the more heroic he was considered to be.[40]

In general, aspects of change and speed cannot be disregarded as being inferior, as they make increasing sense in our world today. Being comfortable with change and flexible to speed is a winning concept in the aggressively competitive environment that is the contemporary work climate. Yet, both change and speed are worth little if not considered within the parameters of well-being for current and future generations of living beings on our planet.

Until the last few decades of the 20th century, few people were concerned about the impact of their actions on future generations. Corporations were mainly focused on growth and outperforming competitors, which oftentimes meant finding the most inexpensive resources for the highest possible production in order to increase market share. Whether or not this trend happened at the expense of human well-being, distinction of species, rainforest destruction, air pollution, or ocean contamination was not really on anyone's radar, at least not for the first half (or more) of the 20th century. In the mid-20th century, an environmental movement emerged, announcing that there were environmental costs associated with the many material benefits the human population was enjoying. Then, in the late-20th century, environmental problems became more apparent. Books were published on a topic that had not been of much interest to many: the cost of unrestricted growth. Donella Meadows, an environmental scientist, was among the first to raise global awareness on humanity's dangerous behavior. Her book *Limits to Growth* became a landmark work in this regard, an eye opener to some, yet a source of outrage to others. Especially those who were profiting from the unbridled actions of corporate and production expansion were unhappy or skeptical about awareness trends of this kind.

In an updated version of this book,[41] Meadows explains that the problems we are facing today are an immediate consequence of our tendency to overshoot. *Overshooting* is the act of surpassing our limits. It happens on a small scale, for instance, when we digest too much alcohol and wake up with a mean headache, or when we turn the hot water faucet in the shower too far, causing the danger of getting blistered. It also happens on a large scale, such as when fishing fleets grow too large and catch more than the sustainable harvest, or when chemical companies produce more chlorinated chemicals than the atmosphere can safely assimilate. Summing up the problem, Meadows explains that overshooting, as humanity has done to the ecosystem, is always manifested in three stages: (1) growth, acceleration, and rapid change; (2) a limit beyond which one should not proceed without effecting safety measures; and (3) perceptional error or mistaken judgment in efforts to keep matters within limits.

Shortly after the first edition of Meadows's book was published, the world was confronted with major energy crises, in 1973 and 1979, which painfully underscored how dependent the global community had become on non-renewable energy resources. Yet, it would take another quarter of a century before the awareness of mindful and morally responsible corporate behavior would become an issue that demanded true global attention, and forced corporate leaders to take a hard look at their processes and the doom they were bringing upon future generations.

Time and again, major corporations have demonstrated their negligence when it came to moral responsibility and sustainable performance. A quick glance yields the following small overview:

- Abbott Labs was charged with a $500 million fine and $198.5 million forfeiture for illegal marketing in 2012. With that, the company was assessed the second-largest criminal fine in US history for a drug company. Abbott's had engaged in unlawful promotion of Depakote®, one of their drugs aimed at controlling behavioral disturbances for patients with dementia and schizophrenia. The FDA approved Depakote for only three uses: epileptic seizures, bipolar mania, and the prevention of migraines.

The FDA never approved the drug as safe and effective for the off-label use of controlling behavioral disturbances in dementia patients.[42]

- Barclays, a British multinational banking and financial services company headquartered in London, and with operations in more than 50 countries, was fined $450 million for illegally altering interest rates to increase profits.
- GlaxoSmithKline plc (GSK), a British pharmaceutical company, and the world's sixth-largest pharmaceutical company as of 2015, pleaded guilty in 2012 to promotion of drugs for unapproved uses, failure to report safety data, and kickbacks to physicians in the United States. The company agreed to pay a $3 billion (£1.9 bn) fine, which was thus far the largest settlement in the country by a drug company.
- Johnson & Johnson, an American multinational manufacturer of medical devices, pharmaceutical, and consumer packaged goods, has been fined multiple times for unethical practices over the past decades: the company had to pay $2.2 billion dollars for illegal sales practices, including paying doctors and manipulating research for the diabetes drug Avandia.
- BP, also known as British Petroleum, is a British multinational oil and gas company headquartered in London, and one of the world's seven oil and gas "supermajors." BP has operations in more than 70 countries. In 2005, 15 workers were killed and more than 170 injured in the Texas City Refinery explosion. In 2010, the Deepwater Horizon exploded in the Gulf of Mexico, and a huge oil spill resulted in an onslaught of litigation. BP has agreed to pay a record environmental fine of $18.7 billion to settle legal actions brought by the US and several states over the fatal oil spill.
- Halliburton, an American multinational corporation, and one of the world's largest oil field services companies, with operations in more than 80 countries, has been involved in many controversies, including the Deepwater Horizon explosion, for which Halliburton settled legal claims paying litigants about $1.1 billion. In addition, Halliburton, accused of bribing Nigerian officials, ultimately paid $177 million to settle allegations by the US Securities and Exchange Commission.
- General Electric also had its share of ethical infringements and resulting litigations. In 1999, the company agreed to pay a $250 million settlement in connection with claims it polluted the Housatonic River (Pittsfield, MA) and other sites with polychlorinated biphenyls (PCBs) and other hazardous substances.
- Intel Corporation is an American multinational technology company headquartered in Santa Clara, CA. Intel is one of the world's largest and highest-valued semiconductor chip makers, based on revenue. The company was fined €1.06 billion (about $1.45 billion) for engaging in unfair competition practices in Europe. This fine is in addition to an earlier paid settlement of $1.25 billion, which Intel had to pay in 2009 after the US Federal Trade Commission completed an investigation in the US.

- Pfizer, an American global pharmaceutical corporation headquartered in New York City, agreed to a $2.3 billion settlement—at that time the largest health care fraud settlement—for illegally marketing the arthritis drug Bextra for uses unapproved by the US Food and Drug Administration (FDA).[43]

The list could go on for the rest of this book. Unfortunately, many of these fines were not limited to the 20th century, but manifested themselves well into the 21st century. This indicates that, while there has been increased awareness among the global community—a topic we will address in more detail in later chapters—the tendency of overruling moral behavior for profit purposes is still a strong determinant in business decisions. This is further enforced by the fact that these fines, as substantial as they may seem, are often a small amount of the revenue of these companies. The pure economic consideration becomes, then, that doing the right thing, which often costs money and requires a longer time to generate earnings, is not as desirable as doing the wrong thing, generating huge revenues, and then paying a relatively small fine in comparison to the revenues when caught. In upcoming chapters, we will address this moral dilemma in more depth.

Summary

- The 20th century displays numerous learning opportunities to us through the poor management that was exerted in the workplace, especially in the first half of the century. With the industrial revolution fully underway, the emphasis was more on output and quality control and less, or not at all, on employee satisfaction.
- The 20th-century way of managing and leading people has established itself as the status quo, and many work-based entities still do not question its foundations or whether this trend is still working today.
- In many regards, the 20th century set a speed of development in motion that was unheard or unimagined in previous centuries. Mass communications were definitely a major pillar of this century, as a variety of media outlets, such as newspapers, radio, television, and, in the last decades of the century, the Internet, enabled people to learn from other cultures and see places they never knew existed.
- In the 20th century, the following generations became classified, particularly in the US:
  - *The GI Generation*, born between 1901 and 1924. They were extremely loyal.
  - *The Silent Generation*, born between 1925 and 1942. They were supportive of anything that would make their environment and country a better place to live in.

- *The Baby Boomers*, born between 1943 and 1964. They expanded on their parents' notion of striving for improvement.
- *Generation X*, born between 1965 and 1979. They were often left alone, due to both parents working, and have been labeled as being rather self-centered.
- *The Millennials*, born between 1980 and 2000. They seem to be on track to become a forceful generation.
- The theoretical foundation of management started at the dawning of the 20th century:
  - *The scientific era* studied motion and efficiency, focused on ensuring a more economical use of resources in manufacturing processes.
  - *The administrative era* presented the world with a process-based notion of management, aimed at establishing universal structures to enhance efficiency in workplaces.
  - *The bureaucratic era* was aimed at creating a system with clear reporting lines, so that managers would have less power and influence outside their immediate area of responsibility.
  - *The behavioral and human relations era* endeavored to see and treat employees as active members in the work process, and involve them in strategic thinking, which could contribute to better workflows and help workers to feel more appreciated.
- The 20th century brought us massive diversity in engineering and appliances, but also destructive world wars, immense growth, and overwhelming losses of human lives amid an unprecedented global population increase.
- Because individual progress was considered to be hugely important, especially in the Western world, the term *Social Darwinism* was frequently used to capture social trends. Social Darwinism adheres to the notion that "the strong survive" or "kill or be killed" in general, including human issues. Social Darwinism is also labeled as an anti-philanthropic theory, and while many business moguls of the 20th century openly rejected this stance, the immense increase in wealth from these very philanthropists could pose conscious questions.
- Progress in the 20th century oftentimes pertained to economic and technological advancement without consideration of moral, environmental, or societal consequences. Interestingly, several positive developments had negative effects, and negative developments had positive effects. For instance,
  - Science made several medical breakthroughs, enabling human life expectancy to increase in a world that was becoming saturated, or even overpopulated, thus increasing pressure on available resources.
  - The two world wars in the 20th century helped to disintegrate kingdoms, empires, and the general trend of colonization, leading to a world

    with more independent nations that were no longer limited to the suppression of colonizing nations.

- Being the bedrock of so many inventions, new trends, and developments, the 20th century epitomized a major turnaround in the way humanity worked, thought, traveled, shopped, communicated, and perceived power. As new possibilities and swifter actions emerged, new threats surfaced as well, and it took some time for some of these threats to become clear.

- Until the last few decades of the 20th century, few members of the human race were concerned about the impact of their actions on future generations. Corporations were mainly focused on growth and outperforming competitors. Then, in the late 20th century, environmental problems became more apparent. Books were published on a topic that had not been of much interest to many: sustainability. Since then, many major corporations have demonstrated their negligence when it came to moral responsibility and sustainable performance.

Reflective Questions

1. The introductory part of the chapter states that the 20th century set the trend for management decisions as they are made today. This is not presented as a positive aspect. Why not?

2. Reflect on the population generations presented in the chapter. Now, consider a family member, a friend, or someone in your work circle and what generation he or she belongs to. Can you see in this person some of the described traits of that generation? Please explain.

3. Mary Parker Follett took the lead in provoking the paradigm shift of seeing and treating employees as active members in the work process, and involving them in strategic thinking, which could contribute to better workflows and help workers feel more appreciated. Please conduct a brief research on Mary Parker Follett and explain some more about her viewpoints in regards to management in a brief essay (about 300–400 words). Don't forget to cite your resources copiously.

4. In discussing Social Darwinism, the chapter presents an example of wealthy business people who became the financiers of the new medical economy and changed the medical landscape of the US. Please engage in some additional research on this topic and share your own opinion about this? Do you agree or disagree with the stance presented in this chapter?

5. In the final section of the chapter, Donella Meadows's book *Limits to Growth* is briefly discussed, in which Meadows explains that the problems we are facing today are an immediate consequence of our tendency to overshoot:
   (a) How do you overshoot in your day-to-day activities?
   (b) How is humanity overshooting in our day and age?

Notes

1 Crosby, P. B. (1992). 21st century leadership. *The Journal for Quality and Participation 15*(4), 24.
2 Stumpf, S. A. (1995). Applying new science theories in leadership development activities. *The Journal of Management Development 14*(5), 39–49.
3 Ibid.
4 Wood, S. (2005). Spanning the generation gap in the workplace. *American Water Works Association Journal 97*(5), 86–87, 89.
5 Ibid.
6 Ibid.
7 Ibid.
8 Timeline: American Generations since 20th Century. July 31, 2016, http://projects.scpr.org/timelines/american-generations-timeline
9 Strauss, W., & Howe, N. (2000). *Millennials Rising: The Next Great Generation.* Cartoons by R. J. Matson. New York: Vintage Original, 370.
10 Wren, D. A. (2011). The centennial of Frederick W. Taylor's the principles of scientific management: A retrospective commentary. *Journal of Business & Management 17*(1), 11–22.
11 Van Buren III, H. J. (2007). Fairness and the main management theories of the 20th century: A historical review, 1900–1965. *Journal of Business Ethics 82*, 633–644.
12 Petersen, P. B. (1991). Scientific management: An opposing point of view by management in 1911. *Academy of Management Best Papers Proceedings*, 137.
13 Van Buren, 633–644.
14 Ibid.
15 Ibid.
16 Hartman, S. W. (N/A). Management theory. October 10, 2013, http://iris.nyit.edu/~shartman/mba0120/chapter2.htm
17 Franke, R. H., & Kaul, J. D. (1978). The Hawthorne experiments: First statistical interpretation. *American Sociological Review 43*, 623–643.
18 *Hawthorne Effect* (2013). Updated September 24, 2010. Created July 13, 1995. www.nwlink.com/~donclark/hrd/history/hawthorne.html
19 Van Buren, 633–644.
20 PBS Newshour. (October 27, 2011). World Population to Hit Milestone with Birth of 7 Billionth Person. www.pbs.org/newshour/bb/world-july-dec11-population1_10-27
21 Dimick, D. (Sept. 21, 2014). As World's Population Booms, Will Its Resources Be Enough for Us? *National Geographic.* Retrieved from http://news.nationalgeographic.com/news/2014/09/140920-population-11billion-demographics-anthropocene/
22 Tilly, C. (2003). *The Politics of Collective Violence.* Cambridge, UK: Cambridge University Press, 55.
23 *What Is Social Darwinism* (ND). AllAboutScience.org. September 17, 2016, www.allaboutscience.org/what-is-social-darwinism-faq.htm
24 *Social Darwinism* (ND). Merriam-Webster.com. September 17, 2016, www.merriam-webster.com/dictionary/social%20Darwinism
25 *What Is Social Darwinism* (ND).
26 Griffin, G. E. (2010). *World without Cancer: The Story of Vitamin B17.* 2nd Edition. New York: American Media.
27 Human Overpopulation. *Wikipedia.* Retrieved from https://en.wikipedia.org/wiki/Human_overpopulation
28 World War II casualties. *Wikipedia.* https://en.wikipedia.org/wiki/World_War_II_casualties
29 Harvard Business School (ND). Great American Business Leaders of the 20th Century. August 28, 2016, from www.hbs.edu/leadership/20th-century-leaders/Pages/details.aspx?profile=john_f_welch_jr.

30 Colvin, G. (1999). The Ultimate Manager in a time of hidebound, formulaic thinking, General Electric's Jack Welch gave power to the worker and the shareholder. He built one hell of a company in the process. *FORTUNE Magazine.* August 28, 2016, from http://archive.fortune.com/magazines/fortune/fortune_archive/1999/11/22/269126/index.htm

31 Welch, J., & Byrne, J. (2003). *Jack: Straight from the Gut.* New York: Grand Central Publishing.

32 Colvin, G. (1999). The Ultimate Manager.

33 Bowie, N. (2000). A Kantian theory of leadership. *Leadership & Organization Development Journal 21*(4), 185–193.

34 Ibid.

35 Greenwald, J., Castro, J., McCarroll, T., Moody, J., & McWhirter, W. (1994). An interview with Jack Welch: Jack in the Box. *Time 144*(14), 56.

36 Ibid.

37 Thompson, P. M. (2004). The stunted vocation: An analysis of Jack Welch's vision of business leadership. *Review of Business 25*(1), 45–55.

38 Ibid.

39 Ibid.

40 Tilly, *The Politics of Collective Violence,* 55.

41 Meadows, D., Randers, J., & Meadows, D. (2004). *Limits to Growth: The 30-Year Update* (3rd Ed.). Vermont: Chelsea Green Publishing.

42 Department of Justice. (2012). Abbott Labs to pay $1.5 billion to resolve criminal & civil investigations of off-label promotion of Depakote. *Justice News.* Retrieved from www.justice.gov/opa/pr/abbott-labs-pay-15-billion-resolve-criminal-civil-investigations-label-promotion-depakote

43 Punytive Damages: Largest corporate fines & settlements ($250m+) of the last seven years. *Information Is Beautiful.* (Oct. 17, 2016), www.informationisbeautiful.net/visualizations/punytive-damages-biggest-corporate-fines

2
THE NOTION OF PROGRESS TODAY

Abstract

In our day and age, progress is increasingly perceived as growth with consideration of the well-being of stakeholders: immediate and distant, human and nonhuman. Awareness about carbon footprints, environmental responsibility, and spiritual behavior, as advancement strategies, is rapidly winning ground in the aftermath of a turbulent first decade of the 21st century, with numerous exposures of those who engaged in self-centered progress. This chapter will lay the foundation toward linking the notions of (individual) moral behavior to the larger scheme of (corporate) social responsibility. The global context and cross-cultural issues will be observed within the discussion.

The Need for a Shift to Well-Being Focus

The 21st century started with a sequence of national and global economic upheavals, prompted by corporations that were led by self-centered leaders, who were corrupted by a mind-set of personal and shareholder focus, and a blatant disregard of stakeholder well-being. The disturbing stories still ring in the ears of those who were part of the workforce in those early days of the century: Enron, where they shrewdly kept huge balances off the balance sheet until the house of cards collapsed in 2001; Tyco, where money was siphoned through unapproved loans and fraudulent stock sales until the US Securities and Exchange Commission (SEC) uncovered the questionable practices in 2002; WorldCom, where revenues were inflated with fake accounting entries until their internal auditing department uncovered the fraud in 2002; HealthSouth, the largest publicly traded healthcare company in the US, where numbers and transactions were fabricated, until their strange practices raised suspicion from the SEC in 2003; Freddie Mac, the mortgage financing giant, where they intentionally misstated and underrated their earnings until the SEC became suspicious in 2003; American Insurance Group, where they booked loans as revenue and coaxed clients to insurers with whom they had payoff agreements, until the SEC was tipped off by a whistle-blower in 2005; Lehman Brothers, an expansive global bank, where they hid more than $50 billion in loans disguised as sales, until they went bankrupt in 2008.[1] There were more cases, but the above examples paint a solid picture of the problem: lack of consideration about the well-being of stakeholders, and an overemphasis on personal gain.

It was particularly the collapse of Lehman Brothers that prompted the now-infamous financial meltdown in 2008: an episode that entered the annals of history as the worst recession in 80 years,[2] and required immense taxpayer-financed bailouts to restore some balance in the financial environment. The ascent to economic restabilization was challenging, but it created more awareness among the members of society. Although this awareness may have been reactive rather than proactive, it is better than nonexistent.

It seems as if humanity is slowly becoming aware of the fragility and exhaustion of the planet that is our common home. Gradually, the understanding is trickling in that the economic foundations of business, as held thus far, are unsustainable. Continuous expansion is impossible when you have finite resources. The consideration of unlimited growth, which propelled so many corporations and their leaders forward in their decision-making processes, has come under rigid scrutiny. The unlimited-abundance mind-set of the past is now making place for the wakeful, yet chilling, paradigm of shrinking resources that must be used by a continuously increasing global human population. And yet, while there are undeniable signs and numerous reports about the resource impasse in which we find ourselves, only a handful of corporations take actual actions toward a more responsible approach. Some of the world's corporate giants, such as Wal-Mart, Unilever, Coca-Cola, and Nestle, have acknowledged our problems of water shortages, scare resources, climate change, and even social issues, such as child labor and inequity in health and education access, but their actions have remained minimal.[3] It remains suspiciously quiet in that regard in most corporate boardrooms, with only a minority of corporations actually explaining their actions toward a more moral, sustainable, and responsible approach.[4]

What Matters Today

In our day and age, progress is increasingly perceived as growth with consideration of the well-being of stakeholders: immediate and distant, human and non-human. Awareness about carbon footprints, environmental responsibility, and spiritual behavior, as advancement strategies, is rapidly winning ground in the aftermath of a turbulent first decade of the 21st century, with numerous exposures of those who engaged in self-centered progress. What is definitely rising in importance is the need to become more value centered. The entire notion of corporate excellence has shifted from the old perception of ever-expanding in size and profits, to one in which clarity, focus, and connection are critical.[5] Clarity, in this case, is the understanding of the goal that has been set and the decisions that must be taken in unforeseen circumstances to remain afloat. *Focus* is explained here as maintaining connection with those who are attaining the goals, and acknowledging their input. *Connection* is referred to as the ability to maintain ongoing, honest, and clear communication lines with stakeholders.[6]

Considering the trends and behaviors that matter today, in a world of accelerating awareness, increased exposure to other cultures, expansions of boundaries and horizons, augmented speed, and understanding the unique reality of having four generations (Baby Boomers, Generations Y and X, and Millennials) simultaneously operating in the workforce, the following behavioral skills matter today:

Connection: The will and insight to connect with people and other beings outside of our comfort zone, so that we can learn to understand, respect, and appreciate them, and elevate our readiness to work toward a collaborative coexistence.

Pillay (2016) explains the process of connecting as an act of brain wave synchronization with others through conversations. What it entails is that leaders adjust their brain waves in order to get on the same "page" as their followers, thus increasing their collective levels of understanding, cooperation, task completion, and creative expression. Synchronizing the brain in order to truly connect with others seems simpler than it is. A leader must be mentally present and must resonate with the followers' viewpoints, so that the leader can mindfully empathize with followers' feelings. This, in turn, requires motivation from the leader's side. If the leader lacks the motivation to "connect," then there will be little or no effort to synchronize with others.[7] The level of motivation, presence, and resonance in a leader is enhanced by his or her self-knowledge. Understanding our own drives and motives can be instrumental in wanting to understand those of others. We can enhance our self-knowledge in various ways, such as through deep contemplation, or engaging in relaxing, non-work-related activities, such as walking, gardening, or knitting. All these processes, which are unrelated to our work, help increase our sense of wholeness, thus our self-knowledge, and, therefore, our readiness to connect with others: we merge impressions of the past into ideas about the future, and become better able to relate to others.[8]

Communication: The ability to find ways to learn from and share with others, so that broader awareness arises. Communication does not only happen in verbal ways, but very often even more in nonverbal ways, through which deeper understanding and acceptance can be attained.

Everse (2011) highlights some proven communication strategies that will establish better relationships and understanding with employees:[9]

- Keep the message simple, but don't infringe on the meaning. Maintain the inspirational core, so that people remain aware of why they are doing what they are doing.

- Convert developments about the environment and stakeholders' needs into your stories, so that a greater sense of responsibility and more ownership can be generated among your workforce.
- Build a framework for your communication strategy. A good one is "inspire, educate, and reinforce," whereby *inspire* represents the communication of meaningful progress, *educate* represents the process of enabling employees to do what is expected from them, and *reinforce* stands for regularly repeating the reasons behind the collective actions, including rewards to those who excel in their efforts.
- Enable two-way communication. This means that leaders should overcome the urge to simply convey their visions and then leave, rather that they should establish rotating employee-teams that keep in communication with the leaders.
- Be real. Step away from excessively formal language and keep messages authentic.
- Tell a story. Very few people are interested in charts and numbers. They remember stories much better. Give compelling examples.[10]
- Make your messages timely and appealing. Use the media-styles that employees are familiar with and not those stuffy ones that were in use 20 years ago.
- Be prepared to invest in employees to demonstrate your awareness of their importance as the main liaison with customers.[11]

Consideration: The will to internalize and interpret the communication from fellow beings. In more spiritual terms, it might be phrased as "opening our hearts" so that we may understand what we see, hear, and feel.

The quality of communication between leaders and employees is enhanced through the leaders' wisdom, which can be seen as a blend of deep comprehension and acceptance of life and human nature, the ability to engage in deep self-inspection, and consideration, care, and compassion for others.[12] Earlier, this blend was phrased as "self-knowledge" (see under "Connection" above). Thus, the role of consideration should not be underestimated. Through intellectual stimulation and individualized consideration, relationships deepen, and a transformational effect is established.[13] If a leader has a strong ethical orientation, then this transformational effect can even contribute to an improved ethical culture in the organization.[14] Leaders can also use intellectual stimulation to fuel ownership and creativity among followers, while their individualized consideration conveys their care and support for employees' personal development.[15]

Cooperation and collaboration: The stage where we find ways, based on our connection, communication, and consideration, to undertake constructive action toward betterment for all. It must be emphasized here that actions don't always lead to success, and that they may sometimes need to be undertaken at a small level for some time before others will decide to follow.

Ashkenas (2015) alerts us to the difference between cooperation and collaboration. Through examples of companies that experienced failures in product development and customer service, he emphasizes that, while *cooperation* gets people together to work on a common goal, it is *collaboration* that will enhance efficiency through streamlined and well-attuned operations.[16] Cooperation can be explained as the pleasant, positive intention to realize a vision, yet collaboration is the monitoring process that ensures that the various parties don't work against one another without being aware of doing so. Collaboration goes beyond merely keeping one another informed, or passing a product from one department to another: it requires a joint effort in which the responsible team ensures that there are no counter-activities in which one party undoes the work of another, and thereby—unwillingly—derails the entire project.

Collaboration entails alignment of goals and resources while the process unfolds. Collaboration can be enhanced by creating a clear map from initiation to realization, in order to make the plan visible and comprehensible to all parties, and communicating this map to all parties involved at the same time, and not in a sequence, because that is where disjointed sequencing has the greatest chance to occur. With all important parties together, there is more room for complete understanding, and less chance for frustration at the end.[17]

Courage: Undertaking action, especially when others don't follow or understand immediately, requires courage. Doing the right things definitely does. Being morally responsible and making strides toward doing the right thing is not always a popular task.

Pfeffer (2011) shares a story of a CEO who experienced this need for courage: it required two months to work toward layoffs, two weeks to implement them, and two years to recover.[18] In hindsight, the layoffs seemed unnecessary in this particular company, but the CEO explained that it was generally expected for him to do what he did. Pfeffer uses this example to demonstrate how tough it can be to act against the status quo. It requires courage to be different. Pfeffer presents another example pertaining to the financial recession caused by poor loans, which were granted by so many established financial institutions. A similar dynamic was at work here: all other institutions did it, so the people from some of the major banks did it, too, even though they saw the writings on the wall and were well aware that the loans they were making were unsubstantiated.

Yet, just as there are many CEOs who prefer to follow the trend in spite of knowing better, so there are also those who muster the courage to be different. For instance, in 2001, Southwest Airlines resisted massive layoffs, in contrast with its competitors. This employee-saving strategy became a major advantage for the company and its performance record. Similarly, Steve Jobs of Apple withstood the criticism of holding too much cash on hand, but this enabled him to engage in innovative projects when others were unable to. Courage, advises Pfeffer, is built on a long-term focus on stakeholder well-being, with values and ethics as underlying guides.[19]

Confidence: A phenomenon that grows with experience. It also grows when you engage in courageous acts. The great thing with confidence is that it is contagious, not only toward others, but first and foremost toward yourself.

Moss Kanter (2014) explains confidence as an expectation of a positive outcome.[20] Confidence sparks motivation and enhances perseverance toward achieving your goal. Confidence is an instigator of qualities that get the job done, such as investment and effort. Converted from Moss Kanter's eight traps to avoid, we now present eight actions to muster confidence in working toward your goals:

1. Develop and keep self-promoting assumptions. You can only do something if you think you can. The people who progress in life are those who aspire to do so.
2. Keep goals small and not too distant from one another. This doesn't mean that the ultimate goal shouldn't be a prestigious one, it only means that there should be intermediate steps to be celebrated, so that the too-distant end goal does not lead to discouragement.
3. Be cautious with the notion of winning. Don't start claiming victory after a few steps in the right direction: there will always be unexpected hurdles to overcome.
4. Create a support system: none of us is an island. We will always need others to support us in our actions. It's not always easy to share responsibility, but if you can build the confidence of others along with your own, then you have an entire winning team on your side.
5. Maintain an internal locus of control: it's no use to blame others for what went wrong. It demoralizes others, and undermines confidence. Rather, analyze what went wrong, learn from it, and move on.
6. Lead with your strengths, and accept criticism graciously. Just don't see criticism as a personal attack, but rather, as an opportunity to improve.
7. Be prepared for setbacks. Being a confident person doesn't mean that you should lose your sense of realism. The obstacles on your path are only there to provide opportunity for strengthening, improving, and sharpening focus.
8. Keep the balance: confidence, like every good quality, is a point of balance between two other characteristics. Too much confidence can lead to arrogance, too little confidence to despair. Remain humble, but also celebrate your achievements.[21]

Creativity: The need for original thinking to successfully reach set goals. Moving toward a set goal enhances confidence, which, in turn, can have a positive effect on coming up with creative solutions to unexpected issues. Yet, goals have increasingly become moving targets in our world of rapid changes, continuous surprises, and disruptive trends.

Creativity remains a much-praised word, yet a challenging reality in many work settings. Once processes have been put in place, and people have become comfortable within them, it becomes a great challenge to convince them of creative shifts, regardless of their potential. And yet, punishment for failure is harsher now than ever before.[22] Whether we like it or not, creativity has emerged into a core survival tool of our times. The rise and fall of ventures has never happened at such an accelerated pace as today. At the same time, we find that we also must think creatively about the way we manage our businesses, because the old ways that used to be successful no longer are. What worked in the past has become obsolete today. Efficiency is still important, but creativity is equally critical in growing a venture.[23] We find ourselves continuously confronted with new ways of communicating, measuring, employing, marketing, and producing. The parameters of what works in today's performance environment are entirely different from those in the past. The time has passed when hard skills could do the job of keeping a company afloat. Today, creativity is required, and in order to achieve creativity, soft skills and a nurturing approach are critical.

In order to lead an organization that is creatively competitive, one must be able to lead from multiple angles:

- from the front, not in the old-fashioned, demanding, and controlling way, but more as a purposeful explorer, in search of new trends and opportunities;
- from behind, in order to observe where the need arises for support, training, and tools, in order to foster creative skills; and
- from the side, which requires the leader to be confident enough to innovate and remove unexpected obstacles without running the entire show.[24]

Candidness: The ability to be open and frank in sharing one's viewpoints. Candidness is sometimes unjustly considered to be the gateway to saying hurtful things and damaging relationships. Yet, when people who work together have developed a relationship of trust and constructive interaction, candidness can be a major leap toward progress without barriers.

Whether or not candidness is a good practice in work environments is still a point of discussion. While, on one hand, organizational leaders feel that employees should maintain a positive demeanor at work, on the other hand employees often feel that they should have the opportunity to express their discontent. In fact, both perspectives make sense, which is why a golden middle path should be tread here. One of the newer trends that has emerged is that of *front-stabbing,*[25] where people feel that they should be able to provide unabashed, uncensored feedback to others. Whether that makes for a constructive work environment, however, remains to be seen. It is not hard to envision that many employees will feel hurt and demoralized if their supervisors start front-stabbing them with uncoated criticism.

Candidness is an example of a quality that can be used in both constructive and destructive ways, and those who apply a candid approach should remain mindful of others' emotions, feelings, and dignity. When candid feedback is given in a constructive way, it will boost motivation and, hence, performance.[26] When it is given in a destructive way, it will demoralize employees and lead to poorer or fear-driven performance, fueled by resentment. When a leader or supervisor has proven himself or herself as an authentic, well-intentioned, and supportive person, then candidness will be more accepted from him or her, as employees understand the constructive stance it comes from. Three strategies to keep in mind when aiming at giving candid feedback are:

1. Deliver more positive than negative feedback. Negative feedback lingers longer and settles deeper in one's mind than does positive feedback. To create a constructive work environment, it is, therefore, better to insert more instances of positive feedback.
2. Focus more on the strengths, and don't spent more time on negative criticism than on positive criticism. Illustrate your positive criticism with illustrative examples.
3. Keep an objective stance when providing the negative feedback, and leave personal feelings out. Also, suggest constructive alternatives.[27]

Compassion: The ability to place oneself in others' shoes. Compassion remains an ambiguous topic in relationship to leadership. Some feel that compassion should be kept outside organizational doors, because it creates weakness and too much surrendering to employees' needs. Others feel that compassionate leaders get more done, due to their ability to relate to their employees.

Cramm (2010) emphasizes how easy it is for us to fall back into old family or group roles, roles we consider expected of us.[28] Similarly, she warns of the tendency to mentally label others within certain roles without considering these others more deeply and thoroughly. Yet, while it takes conscious effort to see others as they really are, strengths and weaknesses included, such effort can result in a positive improvement in mutual relationships.

Cramm suggests five action patterns to consider:

1. Assuming the best in others, which entails understanding that their differences from us don't make them bad team players or unmotivated employees, just different people.
2. Understanding their passions and perspectives, which requires a decent interest in their background.
3. Serving their needs, which means that you must consider and include their perspectives in your leadership agenda.
4. Accepting responsibility, which means that you ask for feedback in order to improve, and take ownership when problems must be resolved.
5. Assuming the best intentions, which entails consistency in approach toward diverse groups of stakeholders, so that your authenticity is solidified.[29]

Caution: with the ability to engage in responsible decision-making. When leaders perform in a cautious way, they consider all their stakeholders, and keep in mind that decisions are always made with incomplete information at hand. They, therefore, ensure that the follow-up to every decision is well monitored, in order to apply adjustments where needed.

Caution is one of the important behaviors that leaders acquire as they mature. In a reflective piece about advice that leaders would have liked to give to their younger selves, Sturt and Nordstrom (2016) underscore that wisdom and insight come with experience and not necessarily from formal education.[30] They mention some of those interpersonal qualities that we often underestimate when we assess what is valuable in leadership, such as building strong relationships, honing trust, and applying a responsible degree of risk-taking. Breaking their message down into six lessons, they assert that:

1. Relationships are an important part of one's career, and they are useful in the most unexpected moments of our lives.
2. Trust is developed when we show respect to and learn from other people, remain humble and caring, and are honest and accountable.
3. Chances should not be wasted, but utilized in a responsible, cautionary manner.
4. Fear should not be the main driver in our career. Courage is a better guide.
5. Seeking advice from others is not a sign of weakness, but of strong leadership.
6. Appreciate yourself as a leader. This often takes courage, because many leaders are their own worst critic. While healthy self-examination is a great way to keep ourselves grounded, we can only earn the appreciation of others when we appreciate ourselves.[31]

Care: The ability to show interest in the whereabouts of others. One of the highest and most frequent desires of employees is care from their leader. Caring leaders are valued, even though some sources feel that, like compassion, care should not have a significant place in work environments. Nonetheless, a caring leader can count on his or her employees in challenging times. This should not be underestimated as a convincing, albeit not the main, reason to care about those we work with.

Wager (2011) considers caring one of the foundational pillars in inspiring teams, along with passion, honesty, vision sharing, storytelling, performing, and being responsible.[32] He reflects on the fact that care is something we all want to experience. Wager reasons that if we admit the need for care, then we should also understand how important it is to demonstrate our care toward those who report to us. When we feel cared for, we feel valued. Simply asking our employees how they are feeling may be a nice start of a conversation that demonstrates our interest and care for their well-being, but when people feel that they are appreciated beyond merely what they do, a foundation is established for a constructive, mutually appreciative, and trusting relationship.

Consciousness: Consciousness is often equated with awareness. It is frequently described as the ability to subjectively experience wakefulness. Yet, when considered within the realm of a leader's performance, consciousness reaches beyond a mere awareness of "being there." Rather, consciousness has to do with the leader's ability to observe, digest these observations through the lens of experience, stakeholder consideration, and moral reflection, thus arriving at a mode of action that seems the most acceptable given the circumstances.

Consciousness is a difficult subject to define, because different people have different opinions about what it entails. Among the many definitions that exist, consciousness has been described as, "The function of the human mind that receives and processes information, crystallizes it or rejects it with the help of the following: 1. The five senses; 2. The reasoning ability of the mind; 3. Imagination and emotion; [and] 4. Memory."[33] Conscious leaders have been described as those who focus on their surroundings, environment, and stakeholders, rather than making decisions from a selfish viewpoint. And because they act this way, they earn trust and inspire a positive transformation in those around them (Figure 2.1).[34]

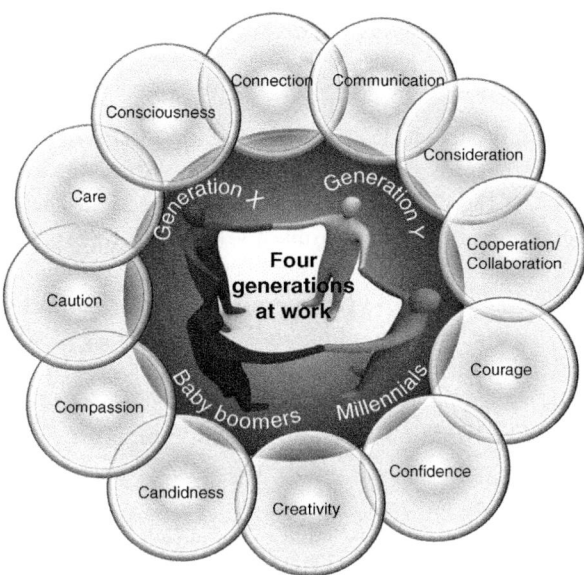

FIGURE 2.1   What Matters in Today's Work Environments.

A Brief Look at Some Moral Theories

Ethics is as broad and divergent a concept as leadership, success, or happiness. There is no single perception about ethics that holds the entire truth. Moral theories are known to be abundant in concept and context, with some of the better-known ones oftentimes leading to divergent decisions. Moral standards are personal. Ethical behavior cannot be taught. People can only learn about moral concepts, but they will ultimately make up their own mind, influenced by what they have formally learned, along with a plethora of explicit factors, such as their upbringing, culture, religious convictions, living circumstances, and character. Most people end up using different moral considerations at different times, depending on what is at stake. They may, for instance, believe that lying is unethical, but will decide that lying to save someone's life is not immoral. Similarly, they may decide that the life of a homeless person is worth less than that of a well-situated, tax-paying citizen, and therefore apply different moral value to the life of the homeless person compared to the life of the law-abiding citizen. Some moral theories call for one line, and for making decisions without any regard to who is involved. Others demand a closer look at the consequences of an act, and invite us to base our decisions on the desired outcomes. Some moral theories are so old that their content must be considered against the background of the times in which they were formulated.

To clarify the divergence of moral theories, we will present some of the most commonly discussed ones in the following sections, but underscore that there are many more than those discussed in this chapter.

Universalism

The Universalist approach, as it is most frequently discussed in our times, was mainly developed by Immanuel Kant, a German philosopher who lived in the 18th century (1724–1804). Universalism is considered a *deontological*, or duty-based, approach.[35] Strict and responsible by nature and through education as well as the way he was raised, Kant based his philosophy on human autonomy. The notion of autonomy should be interpreted here as formulating our own law on the basis of our understanding and the framework of our experiences. Being self-conscious, thus aware of the reasons behind our actions, is one of the highest principles of Kant's theoretical philosophy.[36] Kant felt that one's moral philosophy should be based on autonomy. In his opinion, there should be one universal moral law, which we should independently impose onto ourselves. He named it the *categorical imperative*.

The categorical imperative holds that every act we commit should be based on our personal principles or rules. Kant refers to these principles or rules as *maxims*. Maxims are the *why* behind our actions. Even if we are not always aware of our maxims, they are there to serve the goals we aim to achieve.

In order to ensure that our maxims are morally sound, we should always ask ourselves whether we would want our maxims to be universal laws. In other words: would our maxim pass the test of universalizability? Within the framework of the categorical imperative, a maxim should only be considered permissible if it could become a universal law. If not, it should be dismissed.[37] "Kant also emphasized the importance of respecting other persons, which has become a key principle in modern Western philosophy. According to Kant, 'Act so that you treat humanity, whether in your own person or that of another, always as an end and never as a means only.'"[38]

Shining some clarity on the above, the categorical imperative can be divided in two parts[39]:

• We should only choose an act if we would want every person on Earth, being in the same situation as we currently are, to act in exactly the same way.
• We should always act in a way that demonstrates respect to others and treats them as ends unto themselves rather than as means toward an end.

A swift and effective way to measure the moral degree of our maxims is to consider ourselves or a dearly loved one at the receiving end of our actions: would we still want to apply them? If not, then we should rethink them.

As with every moral theory, there are strengths and weaknesses to Universalism. A potential weakness is the fact that it can be difficult to justify our sense that our moral rules are the right ones, especially in today's diversified, global society.

Utilitarianism

Utilitarianism is a form of *consequentialism*, which entails that the end result (the "consequence") should be the most important consideration in any act implemented. The consequentialist approach, therefore, forms a stark contrast with the deontological (Universalist) approach, because Universalism focuses on intentions rather than outcomes, whereas consequentialism, and therefore Utilitarianism, focuses on outcomes rather than intentions. "Whether an act is morally right [in this theory] depends only on consequences (as opposed to the circumstances or the intrinsic nature of the act or anything that happens before the act)."[40]

In general, Utilitarianism holds the view that the action that produces the greatest well-being for the largest number is the morally right one. "On the Utilitarian view one ought to maximize the overall good—that is, consider the good of others as well as one's own good."[41] Using more economic-oriented terms, Robertson, Morris, and Walter (2007) define Utilitarianism as "a measure of the relative happiness or satisfaction of a group, usually considered in questions of the allocation of limited resources to a population."[42] Two of the most noted Utilitarian advocates, Jeremy Bentham (1748–1832), and

John Stuart Mill (1806–1873, and a follower of Bentham), felt that "the good" needed to be maximized to benefit as many stakeholders as possible. Bentham and Mill are considered the classical Utilitarians. They were major proponents of constructive reforms in the legal and social realm, which explains why they promoted the stance of "the greatest amount of good for the greatest number."[43] Bentham, for instance, was convinced that some laws were bad due to their lack of utility, which gave rise to mounting societal despondency without any compensating happiness. He felt, much to the surprise of many of his contemporaries, that the quality of any act should be measured by its outcomes. This was, of course, an instrumental-based mind-set, as it was mainly concerned with tangible results.

Due to Bentham's focus on the happiness levels of the largest group, there was a significant degree of flexibility embedded in the Utilitarian approach. After all, whatever is considered a cause for general happiness today may not be seen as such tomorrow. Tastes, perceptions, needs, and social constructs change, and "the greatest good for the greatest number" may look entirely different tomorrow than it does today.

Johnson (2012) posits that there are four steps to conduct a Utilitarian analysis of an ethical problem:[44]

1. Identifying the issue at hand.
2. Considering all groups, immediate and non-immediate, that may be affected by this issue.
3. Determining the good and bad consequences for those involved.
4. Summing the good and bad consequences and selecting the option of which the benefits outweigh the costs.

There are two types of criteria to be considered in Utilitarianism: rule-based and act-based criteria.[45] *Rule-based* Utilitarians consider general rules to measure the utility of any act, but are not fixated on the act itself. As an example, while a rule-based Utilitarian may honor the general principle of not stealing, there may be another principle under certain circumstances that serves a greater good, and thus overrides this principle. *Act-based* Utilitarians consider the value of their act, even though it may not be in line with a general code of honor. If, for instance, an act-based Utilitarian considers a chemical in his workplace harmful for a large group of people, he may decide to steal it and discard it, considering that he saved a large group of people, even though he engaged in the acts of stealing and destroying company property.

There are multiple strengths and weaknesses to Utilitarianism, and one of the understandable ones, just as with Universalism, is justification: how can we justify our claims that the consequences we envision as being important are actually the correct ones?

The Golden Rule

Sometimes classified as a deontological moral theory, due to its rule-based approach, the Golden Rule is one of the oldest-known moral theories, usually articulated as, "Do unto others as you would have others do unto you."[46] Students of philosophy have encountered the Golden Rule in recorded teachings of Zoroaster, Buddha, Confucius, Aristotle, Rabbi Hillel, Jesus of Nazareth, Thomas Hobbes, John Locke, John Stuart Mill, and Charles Darwin, as well as in Hinduism, Islam, and Taoism, among other religions and philosophies.[47] The concept of the Golden Rule seems to have arisen in several places, such as China, Greece, and Israel, around the same time, which was around 600 B.C.E. Researchers have found that Jesus of Nazareth used the Golden Rule as a positive call to following God's example in loving others. As Christianity spread in subsequent centuries, the rule made tremendous headway into Western philosophy. Analysts of the rule have established that it should be seen as a moral principle, but not as a fully developed, formal ethical system.[48] Whether considered as a broader moral concept or as a behavioral guide in interactions with others, the Golden Rule calls for its practitioners to reflect on their own preferences, and refrain from treating others in ways they would not want to be treated.

The fact that the Golden Rule was formulated so long ago may explain why it is prone to some firm criticism today. In early days, communities were close-knit, with a common culture and little diversity. Thus, one could easily assume that there were many common perspectives, common likes and dislikes. Today, humanity is exposed to immense degrees of diversity due to heavily increased global traveling trends. It is, therefore, not so self-explanatory anymore that others may want us to do unto them as we would like them to do unto us, because they may have completely different perspectives, wants, and needs. Shaw (1903) put it this way, "Do not do unto others as you expect they should do unto you. Their tastes may not be the same."[49] Particularly in leadership settings, it would be a blunder to assume that others would want the same, and therefore make decisions for them on the basis of one's personal preferences.

Placing ourselves in others' shoes is commonly a noble idea, but there should be some consideration in this act when it comes to the Golden Rule: should, for instance, a parent refrain from punishing a child for breaking a rule, just because this parent realizes that he or she would not have wanted to be punished if he or she were in the child's place?[50] And what should be said in regard to people with warped desires? A person with masochistic tendencies may want to be punished, but his or her desires should not be projected onto others.[51] The above examples may demonstrate the need for a healthy degree of caution in implementing the Golden Rule.

Virtue Ethics

Virtue Ethics finds its roots in early history, particularly Chinese and Greek philosophy, with the names of Plato and Aristotle frequently mentioned as critical founding fathers of this theory. Virtue Ethics focuses on virtues, or moral character, in contrast to duties or rules (deontology, e.g., Universalism) or the consequences of actions (consequentialism, e.g., Utilitarianism).[52] While a Utilitarian, a deontologist, and a Virtue Ethicist may decide upon the same action, their moral considerations will be different. To illustrate the difference: a Utilitarian would help someone in need because he may think that the consequences of this act will maximize well-being; a Universalist may help because he perceives the act to be in accordance with a moral rule (seeing others as an end onto themselves); and a Virtue Ethicist will help because he or she feels that helping the person in need is the charitable or benevolent thing to do.[53]

It is exactly because of the above-mentioned discrepancies in reasoning that Virtue Ethics, while ancient, found its way back into the modern annals of ethical reasoning. With their strong focus on duties and outcomes, neither of the more recent moral theories (Utilitarianism and Universalism) considered the conscious context of virtues, motives, moral character, moral education, moral wisdom or discernment, relationships, the concept of happiness, the role of emotions in moral life, and the foundational questions of what sort of person one should be.[54] This resulted in discontentment from Western philosophers, who used the re-emergence of Virtue Ethics to incorporate its conscious elements into deontology and consequentialism, as well.

It is important to emphasize that a virtue is a character trait, which means that it cannot be distinguished from one single action alone. It is consistent behavior. It is not a habit, but more of a deep-rooted sense of being, which gets translated in feelings, perceptions, decisions, and actions. Our virtues are the foundations of our personality. A virtue could actually not even be distinguished from multiple actions that create a certain impression. For instance, a person who is honest may not really hold the virtue of honesty, but may only practice honesty out of fear of being caught. The virtue of honesty means that a person will not lie, simply because he or she considers it in contradiction with his or her nature of always being truthful, regardless of others' perceptions, or of anticipated outcomes. Being a truly virtuous person can be difficult, because life presents us many challenges that create or increase the temptation to decide against virtuous acts. An extremely poor person, in dire need to feed her children, may have a hard time returning a lost wallet full of money. Yet, returning the wallet despite her own hardship and without knowing whether there would be any reward involved would be virtuous, and would most apparently indicate a deep-rooted character trait of honesty.[55]

Another important point of caution is that a cluster of great characteristics is not necessarily a guarantee of being a virtuous person. For example, a person who is generous, courageous, and compassionate—all great virtues—might engage in an unvirtuous act (for instance, tell a lie) to protect others who are in trouble. This could indicate that this person, despite his or her great virtues, might not be a morally good and admirable person.[56]

Similar to Universalism and Utilitarianism, Virtue Ethics also struggles with the justification problem: one may wonder which character traits are true virtues, and which are not.

Ethical Pluralism

The above-listed moral theories, as well as many others not listed in this chapter, include moral considerations that make sense under multiple circumstances. While we may not always agree with the outcomes of some of these theories, there is definitely some sense in their stances, if not all of the time, then at least some of the time. It is exactly for this reason that some people feel attracted to the idea of ethical pluralism. *Pluralism* implies that there can be multiple versions of the issue at hand, whether these are viewpoints, concepts, discourses, or moral theories. Therefore, there can also be multiple correct answers to the queries under review. This doesn't mean that all available options are acceptable to the pluralist, but at least he or she can see the merit in multiple considerations.

Ethical or moral pluralism is not about different value systems or viewpoints, but about different values. The ethical pluralist understands that those who reason differently may not be wrong, because they may adhere to different values, such as happiness, liberty, friendship, and so on.[57] As a result, an ethical pluralist maintains that there can be several equally correct answers to each ethical question.[58] A pluralist approach may not work under all circumstances. Those of us who have gone through many years of education understand that there is such a thing as *objectivism*, whereby one specific viewpoint is considered the correct one and all others are considered wrong. However, in the case of ethical considerations, pluralism can definitely hold, because ethics are personal, and oftentimes our considerations of what is ethical and what is not are shaped by our upbringing, education, religion, culture, and numerous other shaping factors. A pluralist approach also holds in matters of taste: whether we prefer bananas over strawberries, hot chocolate over coffee, winter over summer, or beaches over mountains depends on our personal taste, and it would be incorrect to consider those who don't share our tastes wrong, simply because they hold different opinions.

In regard to ethics, there are always multiple factors to consider in determining whether we believe an action to be right or wrong, such as pleasure and suffering, well-being and autonomy, rights and obligations, and the position of the decision-maker. The magnitude of factors to consider, and the circumstantial aspects involved, may make it complicated to blindly lean toward any single theory. While consequentialism (Utilitarianism) is solely concerned about outcomes, deontology (Universalism) about the mind, and Virtue Ethics about character, there are many situations in which it is difficult, and may even feel insufficient, to consider any of these factors in isolation. Many of us, therefore, weigh multiple factors when making an ethical choice: we look at possible outcomes, we consider our mental stance, and we consider our character, and we may find that there are multiple acceptable moral options.[59] This, then, is ethical pluralism in action.

A Behavioral Foundation Toward Corporate Social Responsibility

Ethical considerations are not only crucial in intrapersonal or interpersonal interactions and decision-making processes. They ultimately influence behavior in the larger scheme, as well. While some scholars of ethics disagree with the link between ethical values and environmental performance, we maintain in this book that ethical values influence behavior at multiple performance levels. Since we are considering the business environment in this book, we also maintain that corporate responsibility and environmental sustainability tie into moral considerations. Hence, following is a brief overview of the Value Belief Norm theory, which links individual moral values with environmental behavior.

Value Belief Norm Theory

At the dawn of the 21st century, Paul Stern published an article about an environmentalism behavior-based theory, the Value Belief Norm (VBN) theory.[60] Prior to explaining VBN, Stern warned that it is rather complicated to distinguish the motives and actions behind environmentally responsible behavior. Some actions and decisions that have no direct link to the environment can have a greater impact on it than do those that are directly geared toward environmental well-being or depletion. He listed several environmentally significant behaviors, such as:

- Environmental activism, whereby a person actively participates in the social movement
- Non-activist behaviors in the publishing sphere, whereby a person supports the social movements through contributions, petition signings, or becoming a member of one or more environmental organizations
- Private-sphere environmentalism, whereby a person makes environmentally responsible decisions in his or her private environment, such as saving on energy at home, driving an automobile that uses less fuel, saving on water usage, and other forms of green consumerism
- Other environmentally significant behaviors, such as developing products or services that may positively influence environmentally responsible behavior.

Stern is of the opinion that people's moral behavioral drivers influence their level of environmental sensitivity. Those who gravitate toward altruism usually hold a selfless mind-set about the environment as well, and will fully embrace pro-environmental behavior, while those adhering to highly individualistic and egoistic mind-sets will be prone to lower degrees of pro-environmental behavior. The VBN theory of environmentalism offers a good explanatory account of a variety of behavioral indicators of non-activist environmentalism.[61] VBN presents a causal chain, consisting of five behavior-driving variables:

1. Personal moral values: altruism is an especially powerful element here, for reasons explained above
2. The New Environmental Paradigm (NEP): the view that humanity represents only one among many species on Earth, that human activities are determined by the environment as well as by social and cultural factors, and that humans are strongly dependent on the environment and its resources
3. Awareness of Adverse Consequences (AC)
4. Ascription of Responsibility to self (AR)
5. Personal norms for pro-environmental action[62]

Bringing it together, the Value Belief Norm theory holds that altruistic behavior (especially in regards to the environment) emerges from personal moral norms that exist in people who believe that particular conditions are harmful to others (AC) and that actions they might initiate could avert those consequences (AR).[63] "Thus, people who value other species highly will be concerned about environmental conditions that threaten those valued objects, just as altruists who care about other people will be concerned about environmental conditions that threaten the other people's health or well-being. VBN theory links the NEP to norm-activation theory with the argument that the NEP is a sort of 'folk' ecological theory from which beliefs about the adverse consequences of environmental changes can be deduced."[64]

Case 2.1 Fidel Castro: A Moral Analysis

November 25, 2016, marked the end of an era, which meant different things to different people: former Cuban president Fidel Castro passed away. Born in 1926, Fidel Alejandro Castro Ruz grew up to become a strong and intelligent young man. He studied law and adopted a social justice-driven, anti-imperialist philosophy that would lead him down some radical paths. At age 33, Castro and his guerilla troop of revolutionaries—among whom were his brother, Raúl Castro, and the legendary Argentinian military radical, Ernesto Che Guevara— overthrew the nation's US-supported dictator, Fulgencio Batista, and took over reign of the island. Batista fled to Portugal and spent the rest of his life there in relative affluence until he died of a heart attack in 1973.

With his socialist ideas, Castro was not a popular figure from the US viewpoint, especially not since he resolutely seized military and political power, and declared himself Cuba's prime minister from 1959 to 1976, and subsequently its president from 1976 to 2006. In the decades after Castro's taking over the reins in Cuba, the US invested much time and attention trying to remove Castro. One particularly infamous attempt is now known as the Bay of Pigs Invasion, an unsuccessful effort from a CIA-sponsored paramilitary group in 1961 to overthrow Castro's regime. The US did not stop at assassination attempts, but also tried to weaken Castro's influence through economic blockades and counter-revolution. As a counteract against the US initiatives, Castro established an alliance with the Soviet Union, allowing this country to place nuclear weapons in Cuba. This did not make him any more favored by his powerful neighbor, but Castro steadily led his socialist state into a central-planning mode.

While he managed to build a strong foundation for advanced and freely available healthcare and education, he also alienated thousands of Cubans, who felt that their human rights were abused, and who massively fled to the United States. The country's economy became impoverished in the turbulent internal and external climate of Castro's ruling, making him a controversial figure who was revered by some and reviled by others. He has received more than 80 high honorary international awards from countries such as Indonesia, the Soviet Union, Romania, Hungary, Poland, Germany, Czechoslovakia, Chile, Vietnam, Libya, Somalia, Ethiopia, Jamaica, Bulgaria, Belize, North Korea, Spain, Angola, Mexico, Mali, the Dominican Republic, Ukraine, South Africa, Ghana, Haiti, Yemen, Qatar, Malaysia, Algeria, and more. Those who admire Castro praise him for his bravery in standing up for so long against a global giant as the US, and for the free education and advanced health-care system he established in his country. Those who despise him consider him a brutal human-rights abuser, who caused many middle- and upper-class Cubans to flee the country in fear of retaliations. They also blame him for Cuba's weak economy.

Questions

1. Do you believe Fidel Castro was a morally responsible leader? Please explain your answer.
2. Upon reading this case, what do you consider Castro's greatest strengths and weaknesses as a leader?
3. Considering the moral theories reviewed in this chapter, do you feel Castro, as a leader, was more driven by (a) utilitarian, (b) universal, or (c) virtuous ethical motives? Please explain your answer in detail.

Summary

- The 21st century started with a sequence of national and global economic upheavals, prompted by corporations that were led by self-centered leaders, who were corrupted by a mind-set of personal and shareholder focus and a blatant disregard of stakeholder well-being.
- It was particularly the collapse of Lehman Brothers that influenced the infamous financial meltdown in 2008[65], an episode that entered the annals of history as the worst recession in 80 years, and required immense taxpayer-financed bailouts to restore some balance in the financial environment.
- It seems as if humanity is slowly becoming aware of the fragility and exhaustion of planet Earth. Continuous expansion of our population is impossible with finite resources. The consideration of unlimited growth, which propelled so many corporations and their leaders forward in their decision-making processes, has come under rigid scrutiny.
- Today, progress is increasingly perceived as growth with consideration of the well-being of stakeholders: immediate and distant, human and non-human. Awareness about carbon footprints, environmental responsibility, and spiritual behavior, as advancement strategies, is rapidly winning ground in the aftermath of a turbulent first decade of the 21st century.
- Considering the unique circumstances of today's world of work, the following behavioral skills currently matter:
  - *Connection*: The will and insight to connect with people and other beings outside of our comfort zone, so that we can learn to understand, respect, and appreciate them, and elevate our readiness to work toward a collaborative coexistence.
  - *Communication*: The ability to find ways to learn from and share with others, so that broader awareness arises. Communication does not only happen in verbal ways, but very often even more in non-verbal ways, through which deeper understanding and acceptance can be attained.
  - *Consideration*: The will to internalize and interpret the communication from fellow beings. In more spiritual terms it might be phrased as "opening our hearts," so that we may understand what we see, hear, and feel.
  - *Cooperation* and *Collaboration*: The stage where we find ways—based on our connection, communication, and consideration—to undertake constructive action toward betterment for all. It must be emphasized here that actions don't always lead to success, and that they might sometimes need to be undertaken at a small level for quite some time before others will decide to follow.
  - *Courage*: Undertaking action, especially when others don't follow or understand immediately, requires courage. Doing the right things definitely does. Being morally responsible, and making strides toward doing the right thing is not always a popular task.

- *Confidence*: A phenomenon that grows with experience. It also grows when you engage in courageous acts. The great thing with confidence is that it is contagious, not only toward others, but first and foremost toward yourself.
- *Creativity*: Once you have set a goal, you will encounter the need for a large and unexpected dose of creativity to successfully reach it. Moving toward a set goal enhances confidence, which, in turn, can have a positive effect on coming up with creative solutions to unexpected issues. Yet, goals have increasingly become moving targets in our world of rapid changes, continuous surprises, and disruptive trends.
- *Candidness*: The ability to be open and frank in sharing one's viewpoints. Candidness is sometimes unjustly considered to be the gateway to saying hurtful things and damaging relationships. Yet, when people who work together have developed a relationship of trust and constructive interaction, candidness can be a major leap toward progress without barriers.
- *Compassion*: The ability to place oneself in others' shoes. Compassion remains an ambiguous topic in relationship to leadership. Some feel that compassion should be kept outside organizational doors, because it creates weakness and too much surrendering to employees' needs. Others feel that compassionate leaders get more done, due to their ability to relate.
- *Caution*: Caution, from a leadership stance, has to do with responsible decision-making. When leaders perform in a cautious way, they consider all their stakeholders, and keep in mind that decisions are always made with incomplete information at hand. They therefore ensure that the follow-up to every decision is well monitored, in order to apply adjustments where needed.
- *Care*: One of the highest and most frequent desires of employees is care from their leader. Caring leaders are valued, even though some sources feel that, like compassion, care should not have a significant place in work environments. Nonetheless, a caring leader can count on his or her employees in challenging times. This should not be underestimated as a convincing, albeit not the main, reason to care about those we work with.
- *Consciousness*: Consciousness is often equated with awareness. It is frequently described as the ability to subjectively experience wakefulness. Yet, when considered within the realm of a leader's performance, consciousness reaches beyond a mere awareness of "being there." Rather, it has to do with the leader's ability to observe, digest these observations through the lens of experience, stakeholder consideration, and moral reflection, thus arriving at a mode of action that seems the most acceptable given the circumstances.

- Ethics is as broad and divergent a concept as leadership, success, or happiness. There is no single perception about ethical behavior that holds the entire truth. Moral standards are very personal. People can only learn about moral concepts, but they will ultimately make up their own mind, influenced by what they have formally learned, along with a plethora of explicit factors such as their upbringing, culture, religious convictions, living circumstances, and character.
  - *Universalism*: The categorical imperative holds that every act we commit should be based on our personal principles or rules. Kant refers to these principles or rules as *maxims*. Maxims are the *why* behind our actions. Even if we are not always aware of our maxims, they are there to serve the goals we aim to achieve. In order to ensure that our maxims are morally sound, we should always ask ourselves whether we would want them to be universal laws.
  - *Utilitarianism*: This is a form of consequentialism, which entails that the end result (the "consequence") should be the most important consideration in any act implemented. The consequentialist approach, therefore, forms a stark contrast with the deontological (Universalist) approach. Utilitarianism focuses on outcomes rather than intentions.
  - *The Golden Rule*: "Do unto others as you would have others do unto you." Analysts of the rule have established that it should be seen as a moral principle, but not as a fully developed, formal ethical system. Whether considered as a broader moral concept or as a behavioral guide in interactions with others, the Golden Rule calls for its practitioners to reflect on their own preferences, and to refrain from treating others in ways they would not want to be treated.
  - *Virtue Ethics*: This concept focuses on virtues, or moral character, in contrast to duties or rules (deontology, e.g., Universalism) or the consequences of actions (consequentialism, e.g., Utilitarianism). While a Utilitarian, a deontologist, and a Virtue Ethicist may decide upon the same action, their moral considerations will be different.
  - *Ethical Pluralism*: Pluralism implies that there can be multiple versions of the issue at hand, whether these are viewpoints, concepts, discourses, or moral theories. The ethical pluralist understands that those who reason differently may not be wrong, because they may adhere to different values, such as happiness, liberty, friendship, and so on. As a result, an ethical pluralist maintains that there can be several equally correct answers to each ethical question.
- While some scholars of ethics disagree with the link between ethical values and environmental performance, we maintain in this book that ethical values influence behavior at multiple performance levels.
  - *Value Belief Norm Theory*: People's moral behavioral drivers influence their level of environmental sensitivity. Those who gravitate toward

altruism usually hold a selfless mind-set about the environment as well, and will fully embrace pro-environmental behavior, while those adhering to highly individualistic and egoistic mind-sets will be prone to lower degrees of pro-environmental behavior.

Reflective Questions

1. In the introductory part of the chapter, several cases of unethical leadership were mentioned. Select one, read up on it, and explain what happened with the leaders responsible for that company's fraudulent acts.
2. In the chapter, several companies are mentioned that have acknowledged our problems of water shortages, scare resources, climate change, and even social issues—such as child labor and inequity in health and education access—but their actions have remained minimal. Why would you think this is the case?
3. Consider the 12 Cs (under "What Matters Today"). Select three of these behavioral skills, and apply these to yourself. How are you faring and behaving in regard to these three skills?
4. Which of the four ethical theories appeals most to you? Why?
5. Do you feel that ethics and corporate social responsibility are related? If so, why? If not, why not?

Notes

1 The 10 worst corporate accounting scandals of all time. Infographic November 6, 2016, www.accounting-degree.org/scandals.
2 The origins of the financial crisis – crash course (September 17, 2013). *The Economist*. com. www.economist.com/news/schoolsbrief/21584534-effects-financial-crisis-are-still-being-felt-five-years-article.
3 Scott, M. (October 21, 2016). We've been treating the planet as if its resources were infinite—But they're not. *Forbes: Investing*. www.forbes.com/sites/mikescott/2016/10/21/weve-been-treating-the-planet-as-if-its-resources-were-infinite-but-theyre-not/print.
4 Ibid.
5 Green, H. (March 6, 2012). Redefining excellence for today's world. *Forbes*. www.forbes.com/sites/work-in-progress/2012/03/06/redefining-excellence-for-todays-world/#216d1ea22d85.
6 Ibid.
7 Pillay, S. (March 31, 2016). The science behind how leaders connect with their teams. *Harvard Business Review*. https://hbr.org/2016/03/the-science-behind-how-leaders-connect-with-their-teams.
8 Ibid.
9 Everse, G. (August 22, 2011). Eight ways to communicate your strategy more effectively. *Harvard Business Review*. https://hbr.org/2011/08/eight-ways-to-energize-your-te.
10 Ibid.
11 Ibid.

12 Zacher, H., Pearce, L., Rooney, D., & McKenna, B. (2014). Leaders' personal wisdom and leader-member exchange quality: The role of individualized consideration. *Journal of Business Ethics 121*(2), 171–187.

13 Ibid.

14 Carlson, D. S., & Perrewe, P. L. (1995). Institutionalization of organizational ethics through transformational leadership. *Journal of Business Ethics 14*(10), 829–838.

15 Zacher et al., 171–187.

16 Ashkenas, R. (April 20, 2015). There's a difference between cooperation and collaboration. *Harvard Business Review.* https://hbr.org/2015/04/theres-a-difference-between-cooperation-and-collaboration.

17 Ibid.

18 Pfeffer, J. (September 27, 2011). CEOs need courage. *Harvard Business Review.* https://hbr.org/2011/09/ceos-need-courage.

19 Ibid.

20 Moss Kanter, R. (January 03, 2014). Overcome the eight barriers to confidence. *Harvard Business Review.* https://hbr.org/2014/01/overcome-the-eight-barriers-to-confidence.

21 Ibid.

22 Brown, T. (November 2, 2016). Leaders can turn creativity into a competitive advantage. *Harvard Business Review.* https://hbr.org/2016/11/leaders-can-turn-creativity-into-a-competitive-advantage.

23 Ibid.

24 Ibid.

25 Seppala, E., & Cameron, K. (May 31, 2016). Happy workplaces can also be candid workplaces. *Harvard Business Review.* https://hbr.org/2016/05/happy-workplaces-can-also-be-candid-workplaces.

26 Ibid.

27 Ibid.

28 Cramm, S. (January 11, 2010). Five ways to lead with more compassion. https://hbr.org/2010/01/break-free-from-ugly-little-bo.

29 Ibid.

30 Sturt, D., & Nordstrom, T. (September 29, 2016). 6 pieces of advice leaders wish they could tell their younger selves. *Forbes.* www.forbes.com/sites/davidsturt/2016/09/29/6-pieces-of-advice-leaders-wish-they-could-tell-their-younger-selves/#31fd3ac03172.

31 Ibid.

32 Wager, M. (2011). Inspire your team. *New Zealand Management 58*(10), 64.

33 Vithoulkas, G., & Muresanu, D. F. (2014). Conscience and consciousness: A definition. *Journal of Medicine & Life* 7(1), p. 104.

34 *Conscious Leadership* (ND). November 23, 2016, www.consciouscapitalism.org/leadership.

35 Weiss, J. W. (2009). *Business Ethics: A Stakeholder & Issues Management Approach.* Mason, OH: South-Western Cengage Learning.

36 Rolf, M. (Fall 2010). *Immanuel Kant. The Stanford Encyclopedia of Philosophy.* Edward N. Zalta (ed.). http://plato.stanford.edu/entries/kant.

37 Ibid.

38 Johnson, C. (2012). *Meeting the Ethical Challenges of Leadership: Casting Light or Shadow* (4th ed.). Thousand Oaks, CA: Sage Publications, 159.

39 Weiss, *Business Ethics: A Stakeholder & Issues Management Approach.*

40 Sinnott-Armstrong, W. (Winter 2012). Consequentialism. *The Stanford Encyclopedia of Philosophy.* Edward N. Zalta (ed.), http://plato.stanford.edu/archives/win2012/entries/consequentialism/.

41 Driver, J. (Summer, 2009). The history of Utilitarianism. *The Stanford Encyclopedia of Philosophy.* Edward N. Zalta (ed.). http://plato.stanford.edu/archives/sum2009/entries/Utilitarianism-history/.

42 Robertson, M., Morris, K., & Walter, G. (2007). Overview of psychiatric ethics V: Utilitarianism and the ethics of duty. *Australasian Psychiatry 15*(5), 403.

43 Driver, J. (Summer, 2009). The history of Utilitarianism. *The Stanford Encyclopedia of Philosophy*. Edward N. Zalta (ed.). http://plato.stanford.edu/archives/sum2009/entries/Utilitarianism-history/.

44 Johnson, *Meeting the Ethical Challenges of Leadership: Casting Light or Shadow*.

45 Weiss, *Business Ethics: A Stakeholder & Issues Management Approach*.

46 Burton, B. K., & Goldsby, M. (2005). The golden rule and business ethics: An examination. *Journal of Business Ethics 56*(4), 371–383.

47 Gensler, H. J. (1998). *Ethics: A Contemporary Introduction*. New York: Routledge.

48 Burton & Goldsby, The golden rule and business ethics, 371–383.

49 Shaw, G. B. (1903). *Man and Superman: A Comedy and a Philosophy*. Westminster, UK: Archibald Constable.

50 Burton & Goldsby, The golden rule and business ethics, 371–383.

51 Ibid.

52 (July 18, 2003, rev. March 8, 2012). Virtue Ethics. *Stanford Encyclopedia of Philosophy*. ttp://seop.illc.uva.nl/entries/ethics-virtue.

53 Ibid.

54 Ibid.

55 Ibid.

56 Ibid.

57 (June 20, 2006; rev. July 29, 2011). Value Pluralism. *Stanford Encyclopedia of Philosophy*. November 27 2016, http://plato.stanford.edu/entries/value-pluralism.

58 Lengbeyer, L. A. (2004). Ethical pluralism. *Teaching Ethics 5*(1), 23–29.

59 Ibid.

60 Stern, P.C. (2000). Towards a coherent theory of environmentally significant behavior. *Journal of Social Issues 56*, 407–424.

61 Ibid.

62 Ibid.

63 Ibid.

64 Ibid, p. 413.

65 Investopedia Staff (February 16, 2017). Case Study: The Collapse of Lehman Brothers. www.investopedia.com/articles/economics/09/lehman-brothers-collapse.asp#ixzz4nuSXH3br.

3

SELF-LEADERSHIP AND PROGRESS

Abstract

Leadership continues to evolve over time. It is one of those powerful, flexible concepts that adapt to the spirit of time. While some sources claim that leadership is a relationship with others, we believe that leadership is, first and foremost, a relationship with the self. This chapter will first discuss some important elements of self-leadership, after which it will present some of the leadership styles that have been emerging in recent decades as a result of the growing awareness of compassionate progress and sustainability of human dignity as well as environmental wellbeing. The global context and cross-cultural issues will be observed within the discussion.

Self-Leadership: Why It Matters

Leadership is a popular term with an ever-changing content. Many people aspire to be leaders, even if in a small work environment. Many books define leadership as an *external* relationship: a behavior in which a leader, followers, and a situation are involved. These sources claim that leadership can only be exerted once those parameters are in place. Yet, we believe that leadership starts long before the triangular relationship of leader, follower, and situation. Leadership starts as a relationship to the self, an *internal* relationship. It is impossible to lead others if you cannot lead yourself in the first place. Unfortunately, *self-leadership* is not as abundantly described as is *relational leadership*. During self-leadership, a process of self-influence is ignited, in which a person leads, motivates, and controls his or her behavior in order to reach self-formulated goals.[1] It is easy to become skeptical about self-leadership. Some critics even claim that the bailouts of commercial banks and large corporations, as we have witnessed them during and after the 2008 economic recession, reveal to us that lack of self-leadership gets rewarded! After all, the government used responsible taxpayers' money to help out a lot of irresponsibly managed corporations, thus basically condoning their irresponsible performance or lack of self-leadership.[2] Yet, it is precisely the manifestation of numerous irresponsible leadership acts in recent decades that convinces us of the importance of self-leadership. Self-leadership is about the way we lead ourselves, from the goals we choose and the ways we decide to motivate ourselves toward achieving those goals, the degree of effort we invest, the values we adopt to add meaning and purpose, and all other ways of personal self-influence we apply.[3] In practicing self-leadership, we improve our performance by applying the management practice of self-regulation through self-guidance in reasoning, motivation, and behavior.[4] Self-leadership requires a frequent observation of your behavior, and an equally frequent reflection on the effectiveness of your performance. You could, for instance, ask yourself, "Do my actions make sense?" "Are my actions leading me, and those who rely on me, to improvement?" "Does this improvement harm others?" "How can I prevent harm to others from happening?" Such reflective questions can help us to restrain negative or destructive behaviors.

Self-leadership is not only useful to personal leadership, but it also works well in improvement of team performance, entrepreneurial performance, quality of work delivered, employee effectiveness, and performance appraisal outcomes.[5] Moreover, practicing self-leadership can boost our moral behavior, because it makes us stricter and more rigorous in setting our own goals, critically analyzing our performance, responding to cues, acting proactively, and engaging in positive self-talk.[6] People who engage in self-leadership sharpen their own awareness and reflect internally when they seek guidance. They see experiences, even painful ones, as important opportunities for growth. They also become more caring over their body, mind, and spirit; become more focused on improvement; and are more perseverant.[7] Described along similar lines, self-leadership enhances our behavior, gives us an internal sense of appreciation for the things we do, and makes us more positive in our thinking patterns.[8] Through self-leadership, we can also reach levels of greater caring for others. "Higher Self-Leadership"[9] consists of three segments: (1) authenticity, in which we reflect on why we do what we do; (2) responsibility, in which we take concern in more than our personal advancement (a "stakeholder" approach); and (3) expanded capacity, which focuses on enhancement of self-leadership behaviors toward elevating the entire performance process.

Let us briefly examine three interconnected pillars of self-leadership: self-regulation, self-control, and self-management.

Self-Regulation

People with high self-leadership skills are usually also good self-regulators.[10] Self-regulation, in turn, is a powerful quality in team performance.[11] A person who engages in self-regulation has the flexibility to adjust his or her behavior when gaps arise between performance and goals, the way a thermostat does.[12] Self-leaders always try to move upward in life, so their performance will increase as they get used to a higher level, and they will continue to adjust gaps between goals and performance through their self-regulation skills.[13] Leaders who own the skill of self-regulation will increase their efforts when challenges surface, so that they can enlarge their chances of still achieving their goals. This trend is known as the *promotion focus*. However, they also remain sensible enough to understand when it is time to cease their efforts and focus on different outcomes. This trend is known as *prevention focus*. Knowing how to self-regulate and to apply promotion and prevention focus when appropriate, therefore, enlarges a leader's confidence.[14]

Self-Control

Self-control, unlike control over others, is an internal practice through which we screen, reflect on, and adjust our own behavior. Our sense of self-control helps us to set our own goals, evaluate our performance, and decide whether we deserve a reward or punishment.[15] Self-leaders are aware that the path to increasing their self-control is to increase their personal development and personal growth.[16] Engaging in self-control also means taking responsibility for your actions, as opposed to always seeking fault with others when things don't work out as planned. Through self-control, self-leaders develop a self-regulator, which is always scanning their behavior. This is how they increase or decrease their performance, depending on the circumstances. Leaders with self-control are eager to accomplish their target, and therefore take initiative to make this happen, while they also prevent others from discouraging their efforts.[17] Self-controllers have a marvelous ability to cope with setbacks and convert them into useful lessons and opportunities for future development.

Self-Management

In order to be a good leader, one must also have good managerial skills. So, you might wonder what the difference is between leadership and management. *Leadership* is the ability to formulate a goal and monitor the process of achieving it. *Management* is the process toward achieving that goal. Management pertains to ensuring that all details are implemented properly and in a timely manner. Self-management, then, has to do with fulfilling tasks that are usually set by others.[18] Since there will always be aspects in our performance that must be fulfilled for others, the quality of self-management fits well in the pattern of self-leadership, as self-leaders understand that not all their goals are self-formulated, and not all their actions are self-monitored. Self-management is considered more externally driven, while self-leadership is more internal motivation.[19] Stewart et al. (2011) claim that self-management is externally prompted and, therefore, also motivated extrinsically. The incentives that apply to self-management are extrinsic in nature, so they are expressed in monetary and other external rewards, as opposed to self-leadership, which is more internally driven, and thrives on internal as well as external motivations. Within the context of self-management, there are a number of qualities that we also identified in self-regulation and self-control (sections above): self-observation, personal goal-setting, outlining strategies, self-encouragement, self-punishment, and preparation.[20] Self-management can, therefore, be considered a middle path between external control and self-leadership.

The relationship between self-regulation, self-control, and self-management as self-leadership pillars could be summarized as follows:

1. Self-control is the internal ability to reduce or eliminate undesirable or unacceptable behavior.
2. Self-regulation is the internal adjustment capacity to shift from undesirable to desirable or acceptable behavior.
3. Self-management is the circumstantial adaptation that drives self-regulation and self-control: it entails the ability to distinguish between and select the proper *internal* and *external* prompts to *internally* apply self-regulation and maintain self-control.

Figure 3.1 shows that self-management can prompt a number of stimuli (such as self-observation, goal-setting, outlining strategies, self-encouragement, self-punishment, and preparation) to provoke self-regulation and self-control (both internal capacities) in order to enhance performance and reach envisioned goals.

Some Challenges to Consider

As explained, it is important to develop and nurture our self-leadership skills and, therefore, also our self-management, self-regulation, and self-control abilities, because they will be critical for our performance at work and in life, and they will influence the way we feel about our self. Yet, as in everything, there are some challenges to consider when we try to develop and maintain self-leadership. Some of these challenges are:

Change. Change is an inevitable part of life. Our surrounding is constantly changing, and so are we. This can be proven if we just consider our body: every day, about 50 to 70 billion cells die in the average human adult, due to *apoptosis*,[21] which is the process of programmed cell death. With this constant process of dying and newly created cells, we are experiencing constant physical renewal, even though we may not be aware of it. We also change mentally: through thoughts, people, processes, readings, impressions, and experiences daily, all ensuring that the persons we were in the morning are not the same ones who go to bed at night. Of course, not all the changes are pleasant. Some

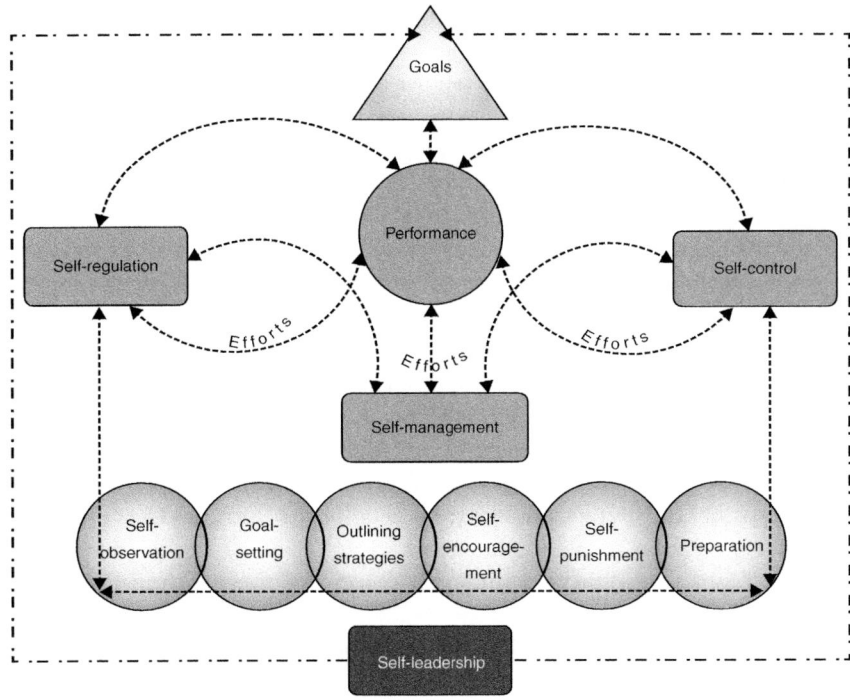

FIGURE 3.1   Self-Regulation, Self-Control, and Self-Management as Elements of Self-Leadership.

can be really stressful, such as illness, death, or rejection. Our self-leadership skills are instrumental in converting challenging situations to opportunities for growth. We can refer to this trend as "stress–related growth."[22]

Increased pace of life. Today, we increasingly find ourselves acting, thinking, and deciding in Internet–time (rapid-paced) rather than in real time. We experience the pressure of life's increased pace on a daily basis. When we receive emails, for instance, it is generally expected that we will respond rapidly. People feel compelled to respond to their emails, even when they are at home, out on vacation, or hospitalized.

Businesses, industries, and individuals are communicating at an entirely different speed today, thanks to the World Wide Web, and not merely at the local level, but with counterparts in the furthest corners of the world, as well. Information can be shared instantaneously, so advances spread more easily. New technologies are also expanding at a higher pace, making competition a more challenging endeavor than ever before, but also increasing opportunities immensely. It is, therefore, not strange that many people maintain a love–hate relationship with the increased pace of life. On one hand, pace can be a stress factor, and on the other hand, it can be a major competitive advantage.

Unexpected turns. We all know that our lives will end someday. Yet, most of us have no idea about the duration, success level, or experiences that lie in store. The same goes for segments of our lives: neither in our private nor in our professional life do we know for sure that all will remain well, and, if so, for how long. The one thing we know for sure is that many things will not go as planned. Unexpected turns have always been the spice of life. Therefore, they are a critical element in self-leadership. Many of today's work-based experiences resemble life in general: they are unpredictable, and have a tendency to change when you least expect them.

Self-leadership is helpful in converting the unexpected turns of life into positive outcomes. Keep three action steps in mind here:

1. Accept changes in the plans you made, and accept that this change will turn out to be for the better. This is how you invest trust and confidence in yourself and in a good outcome.
2. Listen. Solutions to problems don't always come from the expected corner. Sometimes the best ideas come from people who don't hold leadership positions, but have great insights nonetheless. Listening to their suggestions may result in exploring a direction that was not considered before, but turns out to be a golden one.
3. Give ownership to those who also invest their time and heart into the project. Giving those around you a sense of ownership makes them want to go an extra mile in guaranteeing success for the common project.[23]

Paradigm shifts. Many of the challenges on the self-leadership path are interrelated, and the notion of paradigm shifts is no exception. A paradigm shift is a fundamental change in approach or in assumptions, evoking a new outlook on things. As we encounter more changes and an increasing variety of unexpected turns in our professional and private circumstances, we find that we must adjust the way we look at reality, as well. We will often find that what we used to consider reality is not so anymore.

Paradigm shifts can be stressful, because they may require sacrificing mindsets we feel comfortable with and are therefore reluctant to let go of. Yet, once new trends have manifested themselves, it is impossible to hold on to outdated paradigms. And new trends seem unstoppable. Since 1990, the technological and scientific progress on Earth has grown more than in the previous 100 years combined.[24] A simple example of paradigm shifts is the way we think about business today. A few decades ago, few people were worried about ecological sustainability and corporate responsibility, and even fewer thought of valuing the businesses they patronized that way. Today, we find ourselves in need of reevaluating businesses on the basis of the reputation they build themselves through their profit and stakeholder foci. Recent confrontations with undeniable ecological threats have erected the need to reconsider how we view ourselves and the entities we want to support. Our values are due to be reconfigured, and a trend of blended value models has emerged, which indicates a clear paradigm shift.[25]

While there still are ruthless business leaders who claim that it is not their task to be responsible for problems that may escalate in the far future, a majority of these leaders has started taking more ownership of humanity's predatory occupation and exploitation of Earth's resources, in the understanding that we cannot live with a self-centered mentality anymore. We have not inherited the Earth from our fathers, but have it in loan from our children.[26] Therefore, it is our moral duty to leave for them a better world than the one we encountered.

Obsolescence of old habits, mind-sets and theories. Today's human being has little room to build up habitual patterns for an extended period of time, because they soon turn out to become outdated. Just as we develop one mind-set and its consequential behavior, it seems as if we have to release it again for new insights. Indeed, impermanence has never been as brief as it is today. While this can be frustrating at times, it could also be seen as a major relief, because there is no chance of getting bored, since even the most unpleasant events pass by rapidly. Of course, this also counts for good things. The balancing thought we could consider in the midst of all of this is that this swift impermanence compels us to stay down to earth. Coming to terms with impermanence can be useful in helping us to cope with excessive attachment, especially in workplaces where it is good to realize that not titles or positions, honors, or even unpleasant circumstances endure.[27] We can no longer afford to go through life mindlessly.

Yet, even though things change rapidly and constantly, there are many people who have a hard time accepting the obsolescence of their mind-sets, habits, and theories. It seems as if these people, a large majority unfortunately, are sleepwalking, which, in this case, should be interpreted as going through motions without questioning their merit.[28] For instance, so many people are involved in jobs that once seemed like a great fit to them, but failed to question whether they still enjoy working those jobs today. Many people adopted beliefs and theories many years ago, and refuse to assess them on their effectiveness to-day (linking to the earlier discussed challenge of paradigm shifts). Many people hold on to old theories, strategies, and behavioral patterns because it feels easier to do so. Feelings of ease can be deceptive, however, because reality continues, and old theories, strategies, and behavioral patterns will not suffice for long. As a result, these people soon find themselves facing an immense backlog in trying to catch up with reality, which will be extremely difficult.

The need for lifelong learning. Many people lose track of the fact that there are always new developments on the horizon, and that they cannot continue to grow if they don't continue to learn. Once they have finished their formal education, they often fall into a habitual pattern of doing the same old job, and engaging in the same old daily motions, year in, year out. Yet, if the pattern turns out to be tedious and unfulfilling, this is a true waste of time, energy, and opportunity, because learning has never been so easily accessible, inexpensive, and diverse as it is today.

Learning does not have to continue formally. In fact, most of our learn-ing happens informally: we surf the Internet and read things that enlarge our knowledge base in many regards. Through the relationships we develop in the many social media vehicles now, we get exposed to and learn many things we did not know before, and much of that can be put to good use. We travel more than we did before, because hopping on an airplane is no longer limited to the very wealthy. Books have become an inexpensive and easy acquisition these days with the instant download options we have for a lower price than the hard-copy.

Lifelong learning could be regarded as the cornerstone of leadership, whether this pertains to a professional or private setting, and whether others are involved in the process or not. Even though there are hundreds, or maybe thousands, of leadership theories, the best leaders end up doing different things and applying different strategies at different times to succeed. What works today may not work tomorrow, because circumstances, people involved, the means to work with, and the goals may have changed. Leaders, therefore, never cease learning.[29]

Toward a Model for Intuitive Self-Leadership

While we may not always be able to foresee or even successfully withstand the tribulations of life, we can make sure that we prepare ourselves mentally, emotionally, and skill-wise in order to lead ourselves under almost any circumstance. Reflecting on the literature review and the findings presented above, and considering the strengths needed to weather the challenges brought about by continuous change, fueled by an increased pace of life, complicated by unexpected turns, requiring frequent paradigm shifts along with awareness of the obsolescence of old habits, mind-sets and theories, and the need for lifelong learning, we are now presenting a roadmap for practicing spiritually sound, intuitive self-leadership, consisting of nine Ps:

1. *Purpose:* Having a sense of purpose in what we do is critical in ensuring that we will succeed. Purpose in this regard should be considered more in the sense of a moral compass: knowing the "why" of our actions. With a purposeful goal in mind, even if it does not coincide with others' goals, we are more likely to elevate ourselves over the setbacks that will undoubtedly arise, and develop creative ways to regain our balance when we stumble.
2. *Perceptivity:* Keeping an open mind, reflecting deeply on things that happen, and keeping our physical and mental alertness intact are all elements of perceptivity in this regard. Opportunities don't always knock loudly. Sometimes they have gloves on. Becoming a critical, creative, and conscious thinker requires being observant and eager, in order to see opportunities that others miss, and evaluate their value in light of our purpose.
3. *Pragmatism:* Much of this aspect was discussed in the section "Entrepreneurial Spirit." The quickest way to get bored with any venture is to approach it from an overly theoretical angle. There should be enough practical elements present to keep it understandable. It is essential to keep the bigger picture in mind whenever the details become too tedious, and refrain from

giving in to the urge to blame others when hurdles arise. Hurdles are valuable lessons and they help strengthen our backbone.

4. *Partnerships:* Developing mutually rewarding partnerships along the way is a strong motivator to overcome unexpected hurdles. Whether our venture is a learning program, a business project, or a social program, finding kindred spirits who will support our actions, and whom we can support in return, creates a synergistic bond that will enable performance beyond measure.

5. *Progressiveness:* While this aspect is closely aligned to perceptivity, it is used here to underscore our capacity to think critically, and refrain from accepting everything mindlessly. Even if something was successfully done the same way for 30 years, there is no guarantee that it is the right way today. In fact, if it has been done in a certain way for 30 years, it is almost sure that there is a better way to get more done today. We have to challenge our self, reflect on our values and habits, and reflect on where they came from. Do they still matter? What should be changed in order to ensure greater progress without jeopardizing our innermost virtues?

6. *Performance:* Working hard seems a self-explanatory factor, but too many people fall prey to procrastination and last-minute rush. This is often the result of poor planning: prioritizing the wrong actions at the wrong time, and leaving important matters until they become urgent. Some people deliberately procrastinate because they think that they work better under pressure, but they may find that the quality of their work increases if they allow themselves more proper planning before performing.

7. *Participation:* There are multiple ways in which we can participate. Some people are more outspoken by nature, while others may be hard workers but are rather quiet in groups. Yet, even if one is an introvert, one should share his or her views when it is critical to do so. We live in a highly assertive world, where communication fulfills an important role in conveying opinions. Ensuring that we are heard will help others to remember us.

8. *Planning:* It is not possible to plan everything, but where we have the opportunity to do so, we should. When engaging in planning, we can be better prepared for unforeseen factors, and contemplate a second or even third option in case the first one falls through. Preparedness is recognized by those who are in the habit of preparing, and they appreciate the effort, because it speaks of respect for our audience. Making plans can also help us to be calmer and more eloquent, because we have no reason to be nervous about unexpected obstacles.

9. *Promptness:* Seasoned leaders emphasize this aspect multiple times: show respect by being on time. We should not let others wait for us. Develop the habit of always being on time, even if the meeting is not of a professional nature. Once we have made promptness part of our fabric, our inner clock will guide us to our appointments in sufficient time to ensure a composed and splendid performance (Figure 3.2).

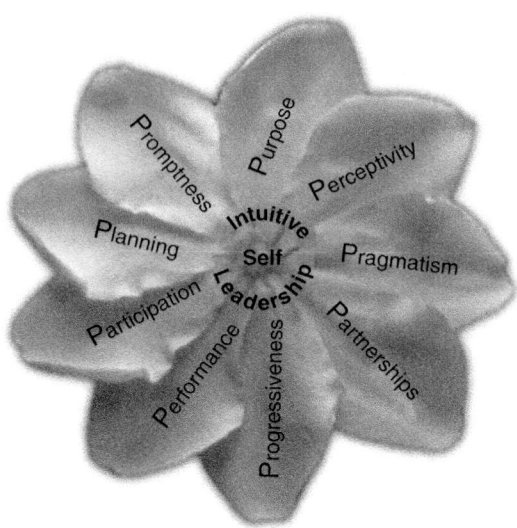

FIGURE 3.2 Model for Intuitive Self-Leadership.

Emerging Leadership Styles in the 21st Century

Today's leaders are expected to excel in different ways than did their predecessors from the past century. There are multiple aspects at the foundation of the changed views, among them:

1. Shifts in societal values—Originated by changes in the work landscape, these shifts have led to greater employee awareness and a subsequent greater need for involvement as a satisfaction tool.[30] Leaders should regularly consider the bigger picture of their performance; increase their tolerance levels for diverse environments; remain focused on their core principles rather than just following every new trend; surround themselves with people who have complementary skills; and expand their horizons, in order to remain abreast of developments and continue excelling.[31]

2. Shifts in investor focus—In contrast to the obsession with revenues and shareholder returns in the 20th century, investors are now more interested in the quality and depth of an organization's leader.[32] Corporate reputation has emerged into a discipline of its own, against the backdrop of the numerous ethical scandals and the growing mistrust in leaders' moral standards during the first years of this century.[33] It is clearer than ever that investor trust must be restored, and that this needs time and a consistent, attentive exercise of ethics by corporate leaders.[34]

3. Ability to lead organizational change—It has been proven that more than 70 percent of organizations have problems adapting to change.[35] Yet,

today's leaders have dramatically been likened to "generals leading troops across a rugged, unmapped, quake-prone battlefield, against many different armies in a struggle to the death that never ends."[36] Therefore, rather than being leery of and inhibited toward change, they must thrive on it. The concept of stability has changed from remaining the same for a long time into flexibly and undauntedly riding the tides of today's corporate sea. In order to perform well, today's leaders must react quickly; anticipate change, so that they can act proactively; be visionaries and strategists, so that they can be trendsetters rather than followers; perform as role models and set clear goals; promote and reward agility; hone team performance; and be consistent in their feedback, to minimize confusion.[37] Therefore, the focus has shifted to leadership that will be able to implement change successfully and recurrently.[38]

4. The influence of excessive stress on employees—With the elevated demands on organizational performance, the understanding has increased that employees will perform better and be more committed if they have a leader whom they trust and have a good relationship with.[39] Workforce members are impacted when stress accumulates. Cumulative stress is a consequence of recurring, unsettled stressful situations, which require an increasing level of personal resilience to manage. Given the many turns in the contemporary performance landscape, stress accumulations are a real factor to consider. Leaders have the ability to support their employees by responding to stressful situations with openness, support, and compassion.

Leadership Qualities: An Overview

In addition to all of the above, 21st-century leaders must be critical and creative thinkers, because they are practically reinventing the entire concept of leadership in a different performance setting. Most of what has been learned about leadership in past eras was based on hierarchic and bureaucratic structures.[40] That type of leadership worked when organizational environments were stable and evolved slowly. In those 20th-century work environments, decisions were usually based on recurring issues, and could be made by a central source of power and influence. As a result, this structure of leading caused delays in decision-making and, thus, slow responses to market challenges.[41] All of that is history now. The pace of performance, change, and problem-solving has picked up enormously. Instead of the proverbial "great man" or "great woman" traits, which were customary in the past century, this era calls for leadership as a process, consisting of collaboration and novel thinking to address problems with little or no familiar structure.[42]

Given the above and other developmental factors, 21st-century work environments are looking for leaders who are not only visionaries, but who are also sensitive to the needs of stakeholders at large.[43] Twenty-first-century leaders work with their followers. They ensure compatibility between these follow-ers' values and the organization's needs, as well as ensuring opportunities for followers' growth. They do this because they care, and because they know that support for creativity and individuality will lead to greater performance.[44] Contemporary leaders are aware that their strategies should include effective ways to produce cooperation, high efficiency, and participative roles to em-power employees.[45]

Today's followers are, on average, more educated, and more independent in their thinking than their predecessors. They expect more input, and get demoralized when they are summoned to follow their leaders mindlessly. Twenty-first-century leaders are, therefore, expected to have some psycho-logical foundations that can assist them in critical areas, such as humanism, moral awareness, and a communal approach. The need for these psychological foundations becomes even more apparent when considering the major financial and ethical business crises the US and other nations on the globe experienced in the first decade of this century, leading to an enhanced call for more sustain-able business models, and increased focus on a triple bottom line, with people, planet, and profit as equally important parts.[46] Leadership and management theorists and practitioners are still digesting the transition that is happening in this area, as many workplaces, especially those in the for-profit arena, as well as business school programs, are still struggling with the notion that leaders are no longer per se Type A personalities with a major sense of urgency and a carrot-and-stick approach, or Type X, to reward or punish followers. (Management theorist Douglas McGregor identified Type X and Type Y managers. Theory X stresses the importance of strict supervision, external rewards, and penalties, while Theory Y focuses on job satisfaction and encourages workers to approach tasks without direct supervision.)

Type X and Type Y management styles were named as such in the 1960s by Douglas McGregor in a process of fine-tuning an earlier management based finding by Tannenbaum and Schmidt.[47] The general message in Theory X and Y is that some leaders (Type X) prefer to be directive, solve problems, and issue orders, with little or no involvement of their employees other than to follow those orders, whereas other leaders (Type Y) work better in a team setting, and share responsibilities and functions with followers.

The competitive advantage of the typical 20th-century leader no longer works as such. It seems, actually, that leaders today focus on exactly the oppo-site.[48] Twenty-first-century leaders are not infatuated by the traditional win–lose approach, and don't necessarily have to be aggressive and narcissistic, as seemed to be promoted in previous century leaders.[49] They adhere more to a Type Y style, in which they involve and collaborate with others as their strat-egy toward achieving a competitive advantage. Behaviors such as openness, sharing of viewpoints, and shared governance, a voice for minority members, emotional intelligence, and mindfulness are leading concepts in this approach.

While individual performance is important, these leaders strive toward as much inclusion as possible. And even though this style of leading usually takes longer to get to decisions, the outcomes are better considered, and work morale is higher.[50]

Leadership Styles That Work Today

Considered within the realm of leadership styles, today's leaders must be flexible enough to tap from a multitude of these: old, proven, newly formulated, and some that are yet to be structured. Below, we briefly explain nine of the most germane styles in 21st-century leadership practices. As the more-seasoned styles, we will review transactional, transformational, team, servant, and situational leadership, and as the more-recent styles, we will discuss authentic, empathetic, awakened, and resonant leadership.

1. *Transactional leadership:* This is an exchange-based relationship and, only on basis of that, it will continue to exist in processes where people use each other's products or services. In a transactional relationship, the leader often uses rewards or punishments to instigate performance or task completions from followers. "A transactional leader is more concerned with the routine maintenance activities of allocating resources, monitoring, and directing followers to achieve task and organizational goals."[51] While it may be effective in getting results, transactional leadership usually does not lead to commitment or long-term relationships.[52] Within the transactional leadership theory, there are various dimensions. For example, a leader could choose to explain the requirements, and provide material and rewards to the extent in which followers perform. In addition, a leader can also choose whether he or she wants to be actively or passively involved in the transaction, which will determine his or her intensity in steering the project.[53]

    The transactional leadership style is useful in today's leadership landscape because it has the potential of contributing to effectiveness, which is a factor we cannot overlook when it comes to the very existence of organizations. Because the transactional leadership style primarily focuses on performance, it can drive leaders to develop clear strategies and structures in laying out their expectations from employees. Once these strategies and structures are in place, the daily management processes will be much easier to assess and, where needed, adjust.[54]

2. *Transformational leadership:* As the name of this style already indicates, a transformational leader typically establishes a deeper relationship with his or her followers. The transformational leadership model was developed from charismatic leadership, which first evolved into transactional leadership, and subsequently progressed into the deeper, caring-based branch

of transformational leadership.[55] In general, a transformational leader uses influence strategies and techniques that empower followers, elevate their performance, and change their values, norms, and attitudes to become more aligned with the leader's vision.[56] Thus, a transformational leader develops actual relationships with followers, often entailing significant levels of trust, loyalty, and mutual respect. Because of the depth of transformational relationships, followers are far more dedicated to their tasks, because the leader shares with them a vision, a set of common values, and a sense of meaning.

The transformational leadership style is useful in today's leadership landscape because it enables leaders to successfully cope with the only constant in contemporary performance and organizational change, while adhering to a three-tier focus: understanding the need for change, creating a vision that enables the change, and implementing the change.[57] In addition, transformational leaders perform as role models in the process, clarify goals, collaborate, and provide individualized support as well as intellectual stimuli.[58] It is particularly the intellectual stimulation that inspires today's employees to be more creative and innovative and challenge their own expectations.[59]

3. *Team leadership:* Within this context, the "team" consists of the people with whom the leader works toward a common goal. In the broadest sense, this would be an entire organization, even though leaders usually have a more direct team with which they interact on a more frequent basis. One of the pillars in the relationship between a leader and his or her direct-report team is trust.[60] Equally instrumental in an effective team is clear and frequent communication, to ensure information sharing and effective decision-making. A team leader ensures that processes run well, without making all the decisions single-handedly. A team leader is more of a facilitator, who warrants that resources are used effectively and that team members have a voice, are inspired, and receive training and attention when needed, with the aim of allowing them to grow.[61]

The team leadership style is useful in today's leadership landscape because the immense competitive and technological challenges that organizations face today have driven them toward more reliance on team-based work structures in order to remain productive and competitive.[62] Team leadership requires understanding of interpersonal differences and the ability to successfully resolve issues that arise due to opposing characters in a team. Leading teams also requires the understanding that different types of teams call for different structures. For instance, teams that focus on radical innovation should perform independently from the existing organization,[63] while others, such as project teams or task forces, should be more integrated.

4. *Servant leadership:* According to Robert Greenleaf,[64] the servant-leader is first and foremost a servant, giving in to the natural feeling of wanting to

serve. The act of leading, hence, comes forth from the desire to serve in order to ensure that others' needs are being met.[65] A servant-leader, therefore, focuses primarily on serving followers. There is no requirement to engage in such a serving attitude. It happens at the leader's discretion, and is therefore oftentimes linked to authenticity, morality, and spirituality. Servant leadership is a deviation from other leadership styles, because in this style, the leader is not concerned with personal advancement, but acts primarily for the well-being and needs, advancement, and autonomy of others. Because servant leadership enables followers to grow, they often get inspired by this style and emerge into servant-leaders, as well.[66]

The servant leadership style is useful in today's leadership landscape because it instills a sense of humility in the leader who practices it. Given the many instances of self-centered and narcissistic leadership in recent years, this style may be an outstanding guide toward adjustment of our perspectives. In leading from a servant perspective, the leader serves those who need guidance, and places special emphasis on serving those with the greatest need.[67] Servant leadership holds a spiritual foundation of mutual caring, trust, and a sense of community, which can enable great things to happen.[68]

5. *Situational leadership:* This leadership style is popular among practitioners and coaches, but not so in academic circles, simply because it is rather difficult to measure. Yet, if we consider that leadership is an organic process that changes all the time, and can therefore not be structured too rigidly, then we can understand why actual leaders gravitate so enthusiastically to this style. Situational leadership entails four leadership styles (S1–S4) that represent different combinations of directive and supportive behaviors. Directive behavior is defined by structure, control, and supervision, whereas supportive behavior is related to praise, listening, and facilitation.[69] In other words, situational leadership suggests the use of different approaches toward different types of followers, determined by their individual degree of preparedness and understanding of the task at hand. Leaders can select one of the following approaches toward followers:

   - Directing (S1, which recommends high direction and low support)
   - Coaching (S2, which recommends high direction and high support)
   - Supporting (S3, which recommends low direction and high support)
   - Delegating (S4, which recommends low direction and low support).

In reviewing this series of options, it may become clear that the leader has to make an assessment of each follower's need in order to engage the right approach.[70]

The situational leadership style is useful in today's leadership landscape because it validates both a task and a relationship focus in a leader,[71] which entails that the work gets done, while relationships are nurtured in a rewarding manner. Leaders must be in tune with the diverse maturity levels of their employees in order to ensure gratifying outcomes in both regards. They must develop or sharpen their skills and competency in task as well as relational orientation.[72] The fact that it works has been proven in several studies, among which a recent investigation among 150 leaders and 300 employees in China, which yielded that when the situational style matches employee readiness, employees' organizational citizen behavior increases.[73]

6. *Authentic leadership:* This leadership style has everything to do with refraining from being anything else than what one is. "Authentic leaders use behaviors of idealized influence, inspirational motivation, intellectual stimulation, and individualized consideration in an ethical manner and influence the perception of follower."[74] A leader who engages in authentic leadership will, therefore, be spontaneous and genuine. Today's followers are on average better educated, and consequently more critical in their demands and expectations than their predecessors, and can quickly assess whether their leaders are honest and truthful. If this is the case, then a relationship of trust and reciprocity develops. Authentic leaders remain true to their passion and purpose, and include their hearts as well as their heads in the process of leading. They learn from their life story, know their authentic self, balance their extrinsic and intrinsic motivation, build a support team, stay grounded, and empower others to lead. The relationships they establish are meaningful and long term.[75]

   The authentic leadership style is useful in today's leadership landscape because it speaks to the imagination and desires of today's workforce members, who are looking for role models with high moral standards and integrity to look up to.[76] Several researchers[77] agree that authentic leaders, by the virtue of their moralistic and honest behavior, instill high moral values in their followers, thereby elevating their social identification as well. Studies also confirmed that authentic leaders, through their open communication lines, increase employees' perceptions of inclusion, thus giving them a sense of importance, value, and trustworthiness, and advancing their organization citizen behavior.[78]

7. *Empathetic leadership:* Empathy is still a frequently disputed term when it comes to leadership. Particularly, business schools have been rather slow and reluctant to acknowledge empathy as a serious aspect of leadership. Business students seem to have a tendency to rate empathy rather low on their perceived list of important leadership qualities.[79] This may be seen as an after-effect of the firm, decisive 20th-century Type X leader, who had little or no concern for the opinions or feelings of followers. Yet, as has become clear in the discussion of 21st-century leadership, increasing awareness emerges about the value of empathy in leading, especially because the entire concept of leading is changing, and so, too, are the values and approaches that are needed in its implementation.

The empathetic leadership style is useful in today's leadership landscape because today's employees prefer a closer relationship with their leaders. While not formally molded into a theory, behaviors of empathetic leaders have convinced observers that this style is exactly the opposite of what it used to be considered. While many feared that empathy would make for a weak, easily overpowered leader, it has come to light that empathetic leaders are highly appreciated and, therefore, more respected. One great example is the CEO of WestJet, Gregg Saretsky, who uses his travel time to work as a flight attendant alongside his crew, and is highly appreciated for sharing his employees' experiences. Due to Saretsky's engagement with his employees, and direct communication with customers (passengers), he is not just well liked, but the company is also doing very well.[80]

8. *Awakened leadership:* Awakened leadership (AL) is a meta–leadership style that encompasses multiple styles and traits, in observance of the fact that no single leadership style or trait will work at all times. "Awakened leaders . . . lead from the heart and soul. They are the corporate, community, and household leaders, official or unofficial, who refuse to put on different hats when it comes to their personality. They . . . practice a holistic and authentic approach in every environment and at every time."[81]

Given the numerous rapid changes that leaders face in today's performance environment, AL predominantly rests on the foundations of flexibility and creativity. Awakened leadership honors concepts of, among others, servant, situational, self, laissez-faire, authentic, authoritative, team, and transformational leadership, underscoring that there is a time and place for each style to be appropriate, given the needs that arise from the participants and the situation. Engaging in AL requires the consciousness of a spiritual being connected with other living beings, and mindfulness of the circumstances in which situations occur. Awakened leadership, thus, involves, (1) the leader's awareness to incorporate the proper approach, given the needs of followers and situation; (2) the leader's desire to continue developing himself or herself in an effort to guide the self, followers, and the organization to advancement; and (3) the leader's ability to remain emotionally attuned to self, stakeholders, and environment, while remaining authentic.[82]

The awakened leadership style is useful in today's leadership landscape because it harbors multiple leadership styles, transcending the boundaries of one particular approach. This reflects the capriciousness of contemporary performance demands, and lifts AL to a way of *being* rather than a leadership style.[83] When discussing AL, authors stress the importance of addressing contemporary needs through mindfulness, which will help leaders determine a proper approach in the ever-changing leadership landscape.[84] These authors address topics that have high appeal in today's educated workforce, such as mutual growth[85] and a deviation from narrow-minded, rigid approaches.[86] All of these factors resonate well in our current performance climate, where nothing is predictable and everything relies on sensitivity, connectivity, and creativity.

9. *Resonant leadership:* This leadership style has a number of common elements with authentic, empathetic, and awakened leadership: it is highly intuition driven, and relies on the leader's emotional intelligence. Resonant leaders are making it their mission to inspire the people in their organizations. They convert challenges into opportunities, and find a glimmer of hope when there is despair all around. They are passionate, have a high sense of purpose, and understand the sacrifices that come along with being a leader. They care deeply for others, but also ensure taking care of themselves and engaging in renewal. There is also a transformational element in resonant leadership, because these leaders inspire their people to achieve goals that were considered unachievable before.[87]

The resonant leadership style is useful in today's leadership landscape because—just like situational, authentic, and awakened leadership—it does not adhere to one rigid style. Congruent with today's ever-changing demands, resonant leadership promotes a blend of approaches, depending on the situation at hand. "Resonant leadership styles include visionary, coaching, affinitive, and democratic approaches."[88] The resonant leadership approach is relational oriented, because it focuses strongly on emotions. Resonant leaders keep themselves immersed in their surroundings, and this deep engagement results in great appreciation from those who work with them.[89]

Common Threads between the Leadership Styles

As explained in the closing paragraph of each of the nine reviewed styles, these styles resonate with the demands of today's work environments. Each of the styles harbors elements of motivation and collective excellence, even though not all styles correspond fully with one another. For instance, the transactional style, with its primary focus on task achievement, may coincide in some instances with the transformational, situational, and team leadership styles, but may come across as calculative when compared to the servant, authentic, awakened, and resonant leadership styles.

Some critical common factors within the more recent styles (authentic, empathetic, awakened, and resonant leadership) are reflectiveness and relationship orientation. In these contemporary styles, leaders don't perceive themselves as supreme beings that stand far above the common workers, but are open and collaborative in their performance. Leaders practicing these styles maintain open lines of communication with their employees, and are not disturbed by the stigma of being considered "weak," only because they listen to and share information with employees. On the contrary, these leaders realize the increased influence they have on their co-workers by reflecting, connecting, relating, and communicating.

Table 3.1 depicts the discussed leadership styles, some of their main characteristics, and their contemporary usefulness.

TABLE 3.1 Discussed Leadership Styles and Their Key Points

		Main Characteristics	Contemporary Usefulness
Seasoned Styles	Transactional	Exchanged based. Task oriented. Directive	Performance. Effectiveness.
	Transformational	Relationship based. Influence. Support.	Performance. Empowerment.
	Team	Relationship based. Facilitative. Trust-based.	Performance. Effectiveness. Flexibility.
	Servant	Relationship based. Facilitative. Inspiring.	Performance. Community. Caring.
	Situational	Relationship based. Task oriented. Facilitative. Flexible.	Performance. Effectiveness. Flexibility.
Recent Styles	Authentic	Relationship based. Inspiring. Truthful.	Performance. Moralistic. Trust.
	Empathetic	Realtionship based. Caring. Values Centered.	Performance. Community. Caring.
	Awakened	Realtionship based. Reflective. Values Centered.	Performance. Creativity. Flexibility.
	Resonant	Realtionship based. Influence. Inspiring.	Performance. Empowerment. Flexibility.

Case 3.1 Groundbreaking Leadership in an Unpredictable World

Ranking number 62 on *Forbes's* list of "most powerful people" in 2016, and number 5 in the category "most powerful women," Mary Barra has already established a legacy. It doesn't happen every day that a woman makes it to the position of CEO at one of the most notorious "old boys club" companies, GM, also known as one of the Big Three. Yet, she did it, in all the conventional and unconventional ways imaginable. Armed with degrees in electrical engineering and business administration, 33 years of experience in the company, and a plethora of insights, Barra climbed the career ladder at GM with patience and perseverance from the 1980s on. She inherited an ailing company, troubled by the 20th-century mind-set of prioritizing short-term profits at all costs, which most recently manifested itself in a decade of automobile sales with faulty ignitions leading to several deaths. It seems that several people in the company were aware of the problem. Yet, no one did anything about the problem. So, once in power, Barra stood up to the problem, took responsibility, and approached it with frankness and honesty. She did not pass the blame on her predecessors, but started with an apology on behalf of herself and the entire company, after which she courageously took all the actions to resolve the problem once and for all, starting with the appointment of a new safety manager at GM.[90]

As one of only 23 women currently heading Fortune 500 companies, and the first to head a major automaker, it can safely be stated that Mary Barra possesses some decent leadership skills and values. Her perseverance became apparent when she stuck to her belief that the company would overcome its 2008 bankruptcy. At that time, Barra was Vice President of Global Manufacturing Engineering. In her current position as CEO, Barra has nurtured a team spirit, which she displays through her hall meetings, aimed to garner as broad an input in decision-making processes as possible. At the same time, however, she is known to be decisive enough to make a bold decision when the circumstances require. Barra is also appreciated by her workforce for treating them as adults: she did away with the dress code, explaining that people who are responsible enough to make decisions worth tens of thousands of dollars should also be responsible enough to determine their own appropriate ideas of appearance.[91]

True to the needs of our times, Mary Barra has profiled herself as an inclusive leader. She has held many positions at GM, from executive assistant to communications and human resources, to Executive Vice President in Global Product Development and Global Purchasing & Supply Chain, and now CEO. Barra has seen much in the course of her multi-decade career at GM, molding her into a leader who listens and collaborates well and maintains a high degree of approachability, while also keeping clear focus on keeping the company profitable. She has increased innovation and efficiency by creating more vehicles that use the same parts, and aligning critical departments in their collaboration activities. Barra also stays alert in regard to the market: she keeps herself aware of what stakeholders want, and responsibly embraces new trends and technologies.[92]

Barra's humble approach stands in stark contrast with the flamboyant style of 20th-century "star" CEOs, who used to make all decisions as if they were alone in the world. Barra's humble and collaborative approach, with a desire to share credit with those who deserve it, is a refreshing wind in the leadership climate. Yet, her desire to provide others the chance to give input doesn't mean that she lacks confidence. As a leader, Barra does not underestimate the strength of managerial skills: as soon as she took control, she capably started creating order from the former production chaos. She also understands the importance of continuous education, and regularly exposes herself to learning environments in order to upgrade her knowledge in various useful areas.[93]

Mary Barra is still proving herself as a leader, but so far, she has done a great job demonstrating what matters. Her openness in the recent GM ignition switch scandal reveals a powerful nature and a great understanding of current needs from internal and external stakeholders. As a result of the ignition scandal, more than 29 million vehicles were pulled from the market, and Barra set out to change the culture at GM. Unlike what other leaders might have wanted, she told her workforce that she refused to put the ignition scandal behind her, as she wanted to engrave the painful memory into the collective mind-set moving forward, so that it would never happen again. She stepped up internal employee screening, sharpening the feedback system in order to encourage optimal performance across the board. She also has no problem with shared leadership. It took two years from her instatement as CEO before she was also granted the position of Chairperson of the Board. This never held her back in making the proper decisions. Barra, as mentioned before, is a good listener who asks for input, but who doesn't hesitate to make decisions on her own when needed.[94]

Questions

1. Based on the leadership styles discussed in this chapter, which one(s) do you feel Mary Barra adheres to, and why?
2. Having read the case, which leadership qualities do you consider most useful for Mary Barra, given the type of company she leads?
3. Do you envision Mary Barra becoming a successful leader in her industry? Please explain your answer.

Summary

1. Self-leadership matters because leadership starts as a relationship to the self, an internal relationship. It is impossible to lead others if you cannot lead yourself in the first place. During self-leadership, a process of self-influence is ignited, in which a person leads, motivates, and controls his or her behavior in order to reach self-formulated goals.

   - Self-leadership is not only useful to personal leadership, but also works well in improvement of team performance, entrepreneurial performance, quality of work delivered, employee effectiveness, and performance appraisal outcomes.
   - Practicing self-leadership can boost our moral behavior, because it makes us stricter and more rigorous in setting our own goals, critically analyzing our performance, responding to cues, acting proactively, and engaging in positive self-talk.
   - Three interconnected pillars of self-leadership are:
     - Self-Regulation, a powerful quality in team performance. A person who engages in self-regulation has the flexibility to adjust his or her behavior when gaps arise between performance and goals, the way a thermostat does.

- Self-Control, an internal practice through which we screen, reflect on, and adjust our own behavior. Our sense of self-control helps us to set our own goals, evaluate our performance, and decide whether we deserve a reward or punishment.
- Self-Management, has to do with fulfilling tasks that are usually set by others. Since there will always be aspects in our performance that must be fulfilled for others, the quality of self-management fits well in the pattern of self-leadership, as self-leaders understand that not all their goals are self-formulated, and not all their actions are self-monitored.
- Some challenges to consider when we try to develop and maintain self-leadership are:
  - *Change.* Our surrounding is constantly changing, and so are we. We also change mentally: through thoughts, people, processes, readings, impressions, and experiences daily, all ensuring that the person we were in the morning is not the same one who goes to bed at night.
  - *Increased pace of life.* Businesses, industries, and individuals are communicating at an entirely different speed today thanks to the World Wide Web, and not merely at the local level, but with counterparts in the furthest corners of the world as well.
  - *Unexpected turns.* The one thing we know for sure is that many things will not go as planned. Unexpected turns have always been the spice of life. Therefore, they are a critical element in self-leadership.
  - *Paradigm shifts.* As we encounter more changes and an increasing variety of unexpected turns in our professional and private circumstances, we find that we have to adjust the way we look at reality, as well. Paradigm shifts can be stressful, because they may require sacrificing mind-sets we feel comfortable with and are, therefore, reluctant to let go of.
  - *Obsolescence of old habits, mind-sets, and theories.* Just as we develop one mind-set, it seems as if we have to release it for new insights. While this can be frustrating at times, it could also be seen as a major relief, because there is no chance of getting bored, since even the most unpleasant events pass by rapidly.
  - *The need for lifelong learning.* Learning does not have to continue formally. In fact, most of our learning happens informally: we surf the Internet and read things that enlarge our knowledge base in many regards.

2. The roadmap for practicing spiritually sound, intuitive self-leadership consists of nine Ps:

- *Purpose*: With a purposeful goal in mind we are more likely to elevate ourselves over the setbacks that will undoubtedly arise, and develop creative ways to regain our balance when we stumble.

- *Perceptivity*: Becoming a critical, creative, and conscious thinker requires being observant and eager, in order to see opportunities that others miss, and evaluate their value in light of our purpose.
- *Pragmatism*: It is essential to keep the bigger picture in mind whenever the details become too tedious, and refrain from giving in to the urge to blame others when hurdles arise. Hurdles are valuable lessons and they help to strengthen our backbone.
- *Partnerships*: Whether our venture is a learning program, a business project, or a social program, finding kindred spirits who will support our actions, and whom we can support in return, creates a synergistic bond that will enable performance beyond measure.
- *Progressiveness*: We have to challenge our self, reflect on our values and habits, and reflect on where they came from. Do they still matter? What should be changed in order to ensure greater progress without jeopardizing our innermost virtues?
- *Performance*: Some people deliberately procrastinate because they think that they work better under pressure, but they may find that the quality of their work increases if they allow themselves more proper planning before performing.
- *Participation*: We live in a highly assertive world, where communication fulfills an important role in conveying opinions. Ensuring that we are heard will help others remember us.
- *Planning*: Preparedness is recognized by those who are in the habit of preparing, and they appreciate the effort, because it speaks of respect for our audience.
- *Promptness*: Once we have made promptness part of our fabric, our inner clock will guide us to our appointments in sufficient time to ensure a composed and splendid performance.

3. Twenty-first-century work environments are looking for leaders who are not only visionaries, but who are also sensitive to the needs of stakeholders at large. Twenty-first-century leaders work with their followers. Today's followers are, on average, more educated, and more independent in their thinking. They expect more input, and get demoralized when they are summoned to follow their leaders mindlessly.

4. Leadership Styles that Work Today

- Seasoned styles:
  - *Transactional leadership*: A transactional leader is more concerned with the routine maintenance activities of allocating resources, monitoring, and directing followers to achieve task and organizational goals.
  - *Transformational leadership*: A transformational leader develops actual relationships with followers, often entailing significant levels of trust, loyalty, and mutual respect.

- *Team leadership*: A team leader is more of a facilitator, who warrants that resources are used effectively, and that team members have a voice, are inspired, and receive training and attention when needed, with the aim of allowing them to grow.
- *Servant leadership*: A servant leader focuses primarily on serving followers. There is no requirement to engage in a serving attitude. It happens at the leader's discretion, and is, therefore, oftentimes linked to authenticity, morality, and spirituality.
- *Situational leadership*: Situational leadership entails four leadership styles that represent different combinations of directive and supportive behaviors.
- Recent styles:
  - *Authentic leadership*: This leadership style has everything to do with refraining from being anything other than what one is.
  - *Empathetic leadership*: Empathy is still a frequently disputed term when it comes to leadership. Yet, increasing awareness emerges about the value of empathy in leading, especially because the entire concept of leading is changing, and so, too, are the values and approaches that are needed in its implementation.
  - *Awakened leadership*: Awakened leadership is a meta-leadership style that encompasses multiple styles and traits, in observance of the fact that no single leadership style or trait will work at all times.
  - *Resonant leadership*: This leadership style has a number of common elements with authentic, empathetic, and awakened leadership: it is highly intuition driven, and relies on the leader's emotional intelligence.

Reflective Questions

1. Self-leadership is discussed as an internal relationship. Do you consider yourself a self-leader? Why or why not?
2. What are some of the advantages to self-leadership? Which one do you consider most important, and why?
3. This chapter presents a number of challenges to self-leadership. Discuss two that you consider most challenging to yourself, and explain your choice through reflection.
4. Reflect on the nine Ps discussed in this chapter as a roadmap toward intuitive self-leadership. Which of these nine Ps do you consider most challenging to yourself? Why?
5. Review and reflect on the various leadership styles discussed in this chapter: which one(s) appeals most to you, and why?

Notes

1 Steinbauer, R., Renn, R. W., Taylor, R. R., & Njoroge, P. K. (2014). Ethical leadership and followers' moral judgment: The role of followers' perceived accountability and self-leadership. *Journal of Business Ethics 120*(3), 381–392.

2 Manz, C. C. (2015). Taking the self-leadership high road: Smooth surface or potholes ahead? *Academy of Management Perspectives 29*(1), 132–151.

3 Ibid.

4 Marques-Quinteiro, P., & Curral, L. A. (2012). Goal orientation and work role performance: Predicting adaptive and proactive work role performance through self-leadership strategies. *Journal of Psychology 146*(6), 559–577.

5 Steinbauer et al., Ethical leadership and followers' moral judgment, 381–392.

6 Ibid.

7 Fadla, A. (2014). Self-leadership. *Leadership Excellence 31*(8), 10–11.

8 Furtner, M. R., Rauthmann, J. F., & Sachse, P. (2010). The socioemotionally intelligent self-leader: Examining relations between self-leadership and socioemotional intelligence. *Social Behavior & Personality: An International Journal, 38*(9), 1191–1196.

9 Manz, Taking the self-leadership high road, 132–151.

10 Furtner et al., The socioemotionally intelligent self-leader, 1191–1196.

11 Antoni, C., & Hertel, G. (2009). Team processes, their antecedents and consequences: Implications for different types of teamwork. *European Journal of Work and Organizational Psychology 18*(3), 253–266.

12 Neck, C. P., & Houghton, J. D. (2006). Two decades of self-leadership theory and research. *Journal of Managerial Psychology 21*(4), 270–295.

13 Ibid.

14 Ibid.

15 Manz, C. C. (1986). Self-leadership: Toward an expanded theory of self-influence processes in organizations. *Academy of Management Review 11*(3), 585–600.

16 Ross, S. (2014). A conceptual model for understanding the process of self-leadership development and action-steps to promote personal leadership development. *The Journal of Management Development 33*(4), 299–323.

17 Williams, J. C. (1997). Self-control. *Baylor Business Review 15*(2), 9.

18 Stewart, G. L., Courtright, S. H., & Manz, C. C. (2011). Self-leadership: A multilevel review. *Journal of Management 37*(1), 185–222.

19 Ibid.

20 Manz, Self-leadership, 585–600.

21 Ameisen, J. (2002). On the origin, evolution, and nature of programmed cell death: A timeline of four billion years. *Cell Death & Differentiation 9*(4), 367.

22 Dolbier, C. L., Jaggars, S. S., & Steinhardt, M. A. (2010). Stress-related growth: Pre-intervention correlates and change following a resilience intervention. *Stress & Health: Journal of the International Society for the Investigation of Stress 26*(2), 135–147.

23 "*When life serves you lemons, make a lemon-berry slush.*" (2010). *Baylor Business Review 29*(1), 22–25.

24 Taylor, J. S., & Machado-Taylor, M. L. (2010). Leading strategic change in higher education: The need for a paradigm shift toward visionary leadership. *At the Interface/Probing the Boundaries 72*, 167–194.

25 Pirson, M. A., & Lawrence, P. R. (2010). Humanism in business—toward a paradigm shift? *Journal of Business Ethics 93*(4), 553–565.

26 Berry, W. (1971). *The Unforeseen Wilderness: An Essay on Kentucky's Red River Gorge.* Lexington, KY: University Press of Kentucky.

27 Marques, J. (2012). Consciousness at work: A review of some important values, discussed from a Buddhist perspective. *Journal of Business Ethics 105*(1), 27–40.

28 Marques, J. (2014). *Leadership and Mindful Behavior: Action, Wakefulness, and Business.* New York: Palgrave-MacMillan.
29 Bell, S. B. (2012). A year of learning for your lifelong leadership journey. *College & Research Libraries News 73*(8), 458–459.
30 Higgs, M. (2003). How can we make sense of leadership in the 21st century? *Leadership & Organization Development Journal 24*(5), 273–284.
31 Marques, J. (2010). Inside-out insight: Considerations for 21st century leaders. *Journal of Global Business Issues, 4*(1), 73–81.
32 Higgs, How can we make sense of leadership? 273–284.
33 Resnick, J. T. (2004). Corporate reputation: Managing corporate reputation—applying rigorous measures to a key asset. *The Journal of Business Strategy 25*(6), 30–38.
34 Jennings, M. M. (2005). Ethics and investment management: True reform. *Financial Analysts Journal 61*(3), 45–58.
35 Higgs, How can we make sense of leadership? 273–284.
36 Developing agile leaders for the 21st century. (2010). *People and Strategy 33*(4), 12–13.
37 Ibid.
38 Higgs, How can we make sense of leadership in the 21st century? 273–284.
39 Ibid.
40 Novelli, L., & Taylor, S. (1993). The context for leadership in 21st-century organizations: A role for critical thinking. *The American Behavioral Scientist (1986–1994) 37*(1), 139–147.
41 Ibid.
42 Ibid.
43 Williams, J. C. (1986). Managerial leadership for the 21st century. *Baylor Business Review 4*(3), 22–25.
44 Ibid.
45 Kennedy, J. W. (2010). Empowering future organizational leaders for the 21st century. *The International Business & Economics Research Journal, 9*(4), 145–148.
46 Kelly, L., & Finkelman, J. M. (2011). The psychologist manager: Uniquely qualified to address 21st-century leadership challenges? *The Psychologist Manager Journal 14*(3), 196–210.
47 Russ, T. L. (2011). Theory X/Y assumptions as predictors of managers' propensity for participative decision making. *Management Decision 49*(5), 823–836.
48 Kelly & Finkelman, The psychologist manager, 196–210.
49 Ibid.
50 Ibid.
51 Kanungo, R. N. (2001). Ethical values of transactional and transformational leaders. *Canadian Journal of Administrative Sciences 18*(4), p. 257.
52 Zagorsek, H., Dimovski, V., & Skerlavaj, M. (2009). Transactional and transformational leadership impacts on organizational learning. *Journal for East European Management Studies 14*(2), 144–165.
53 Ibid.
54 Waldman, D. A., Ramirez, G. G., House, R. J., & Puranam, P. (2001). Does leadership matter? CEO leadership attributes and profitability under conditions of perceived environmental uncertainty. *Academy of Management Journal 44*(1), 134–143.
55 Bottomley, K., Burgess, S., & Fox, M. (2014). Are the behaviors of transformational leaders impacting organizations? A study of transformational leadership. *International Management Review 10*(1), 5–9, 66.
56 Kanungo, Ethical values of transactional and transformational leaders, 257.
57 Kim, S., & Yoon, G. (2015). An innovation-driven culture in local Government: Do senior manager's transformational leadership and the climate for creativity matter? *Public Personnel Management 44*(2), 147–168.

58 Podsakoff, P. M., MacKenzie, S. B., Moorman, R. H., & Fetter, R. (1990). Transformational leader behaviors and their effects on followers' trust in leader, satisfaction and organizational citizenship behaviors. *Leadership Quarterly 1*(2), 107–142.

59 Kim & Yoon, An innovation-driven culture in local Government, 147–168.

60 McHale, N. (2012). Great leaders lead great teams. *Human Resource Management International Digest 20*(4), 3–5.

61 Wu, C., Wang, P., & Tsai, L. (2010). The effect of organizational culture on team interaction and team effectiveness: Team leadership as a medium. *Journal of International Management Studies 5*(2), 190–198.

62 Aronson, Z. H., Dominick, P. G., & Mo, W. (2014). Exhibiting leadership and facilitation behaviors in NPD project-based work: Does team personal style composition matter? *Engineering Management Journal 26*(3), 25–35.

63 Ibid.

64 Greenleaf, R. K. (1991). *The Servant as Leader.* Westfield, IN: The Robert K. Greenleaf Center.

65 Murari, K., & Kripa, S. G. (2012). Impact of servant leadership on employee empowerment. *Journal of Strategic Human Resource Management 1*(1), 28–37.

66 Senjaya, S., & Pekerti, A. (2010). Servant leadership as antecedent of trust in organizations. *Leadership & Organization Development Journal 31*(7), 643–663.

67 Johnson, K. A., Grazulis, J., & White, J. K. (2014). Sleep out on the Quad: An opportunity for experiential education and servant based leadership. *Critical Questions in Education 5*(3), 232–241.

68 Ibid.

69 Blanchard, K. (2008). Situational leadership. *Leadership Excellence 25*(5), p. 19.

70 Avery, G. C., & Ryan, J. (2002). Applying situational leadership in Australia. *The Journal of Management Development 21*(3), 242–262.

71 McCleskey, J. A. (2014). Situational, transformational, and transactional leadership and leadership *development. Journal of Business Studies Quarterly 5*(4), 117–130.

72 Ibid.

73 Luo, H., & Liu, S. (2014). Effect of situational leadership and employee readiness match on organizational citizenship behavior in China. *Social Behavior and Personality 42*(10), 1725–1732.

74 Nichols, T. W., & Erakovich, R. (2013). Authentic leadership and implicit theory: A normative form of leadership? *Leadership & Organization Development Journal 34*(2), 182–195 (p. 183).

75 George, B., Sims, P., McLean, A. N., & Mayer, D. (2007). Discovering your authentic leadership. *Harvard Business Review 85*(2), 129–138.

76 Avolio, B.J., Zhu, W., Koh, W., and Bhatia, P. (2004). Transformational leadership and organizational commitment: mediating role of psychological empowerment and moderating role of structural distance. *Journal of Organizational Behavior 25*(8), 951–968.

77 Ibid. Also, Joo, B., & Nimon, K. (2014). Two of a kind? A canonical correlational study of transformational leadership and authentic leadership. *European Journal of Training & Development 38*(6), 570–587.

78 Cottrill, K., Lopez, P. D., & Hoffman, C. C. (2014). How authentic leadership and inclusion benefit organizations. *Equality, Diversity & Inclusion 33*(3), 275–292.

79 Holt, S., & Marques, J. (2012). Empathy in leadership: Appropriate or misplaced? An empirical study on a topic that is asking for attention. *Journal of Business Ethics 105*(1), 95–105.

80 Empathetic leadership won't make you a pushover—It'll give you more power (Dec. 28, 2014). *Inspired HR.CA*, http://inspiredhr.ca/empathetic-leadership-wont-make-you-a-pushover-itll-give-you-more-power

81 Marques, J. F. (2010). Awakened leaders: Born or made? *Leadership & Organization Development Journal 31*(4), 307–323 (p. 308).

82 Marques, J. (2008). Awakened leadership in action: A comparison of three exceptional business leaders. *The Journal of Management Development 27*(8), 812–823.
83 Ibid.
84 Marques, J. (2006). Issues & observations: Awakened leadership in today's organizations. *Leadership in Action 26*(2), 23–24.
85 Ryan, P. (November 8, 2012), *Awakened Leadership. Awakened Wisdom Experiences.* http://awakenedwisdom.com/awakened-leadership
86 Marques, Awakened leadership in action, 812–823.
87 Boyatzis, R., & McKee, A. (2006). Inspiring others through resonant leadership. *Business Strategy Review 17*(2), 15–19.
88 Laschinger, H. S., Wong, C. A., Cummings, G. G., & Grau, A. L. (2014). Resonant leadership and workplace empowerment: The value of positive organizational cultures in reducing workplace incivility. *Nursing Economics 32*(1), 7.
89 Ibid., 5–44.
90 Loftus, G. (March 19, 2014). Mary Barra's leadership legacy. *Forbes.* www.forbes.com/sites/geoffloftus/2014/03/19/mary-barras-leadership-legacy/#79f1ce893c7a
91 Mary Barra's leadership (2016). *Center for WorkLife.* December 18, 2016, www.centerforworklife.com/mary-barras-leadership
92 Engelmeier, S. (January 22, 2014). Did Mary Barra's inclusive leadership style propel her to the top? *IndustryWeek.* www.industryweek.com/companies-amp-executives/did-mary-barra-s-inclusive-leadership-style-propel-her-top?page=2
93 Snyder, S. (January 15, 2014). Five leadership lessons from General Motors CEO, Mary Barra. *Snyder Leadership Group.* http://snyderleadership.com/2014/01/15/five-leadership-lessons-from-general-motors-ceo-mary-barra
94 Fairchild, C., & Colvin, G. (October 5, 2014). 5 things you probably don't know about Mary Barra. *Fortune.* http://fortune.com/2014/09/19/5-things-you-probably-dont-know-about-mary-barra

PART II

Toward a Moral Compass

4

THE RIGHT THING IN PRE-MILLENNIAL CONTEXT

Abstract

The scope of what used to be the right thing was rather narrow in past centuries: if shareholders received their dividends and saw their investments growing, and if the organization expanded, then the "right thing" was achieved. Moreover, the right thing was also achieved if competitors were eliminated, regardless of what it took. Examples of leaders praised for doing the "right thing" in these past times will serve as illustration. The term *sleepwalking* will be discussed as a delineation of mindless performance.

The Corporation of the 20th Century

Corporations, as they were established and as they performed in the 20th century, were very much tailored to the late-19th-century model, built on the industrial revolution model: many of the reporting lines were top-down; decisions were made in a centralized way, by top management in headquarters; employees were considered easily expendable; and processes as well as product lines were used for a long time, as there was little or no disruption. This was particularly the case during the first half of the 20th century. Because entering a market was not something that could be accomplished easily, corporations could expand undeterred, and their leaders could remain in their position, unconcerned about too much competition, let alone market disruption. Many of these leaders were not leader material at all, but gained control either because of family ties, or as handpicked successors of previous leaders. This often led to corporate kingpins with very little consideration for either internal or external stakeholders. Since concern for fellow humans was already low on their list of priorities, it is not hard to imagine their complete lack of empathy toward other living beings, such as animals, trees, and the environment.

The way work was perceived was entirely different from how it is conceived today: employees would work for the same employer during most of, if not their entire, professional career, which would usually span a timeframe of 40–50 years. Large corporations were powerhouses that were shielded from great minds with little means, as there was no way for these gifted minds to get a foot in the door.[1] In other words: if you were bright and had great ideas but were not part of the in-group of such a top corporate echelon, you might as well forget ever getting your ideas heard, let alone implemented.

Yet, in its own way, the 20th century brought a large number of developmental waves, and with that, insights into the nature of business and its leadership requirements:

> In their article "Zeitgeist Leadership," Mayo and Nohria (2005) reveal some fascinating findings from a study of 1,000 20th-century business leaders. They explain the importance of understanding the spirit and focus of any given time in history in order to take a corporation to the next level. Sheer intelligence and great ideas may not always work, as any era brings its own challenges and demands. Those corporations that managed to thrive in the 20th century, as well as those that will in the 21st, are the ones that were led by individuals who understood and played into the critical moves required to attain and safeguard expansion. There are times when connections and suave negotiation skills are crucial, times that trend disruption and inventive skills are vital, times when inward focus and development make more sense than external grandeur, and times when radicalism takes you further than incrementalism. They refer to this skill as "a notion of zeitgeist" or "contextual intelligence,"[2] and repeatedly underscore its importance for successful business performance. With two world wars, a Great Depression, and a number of other time-related physiognomies, the American corporate and leadership history over the 20th century paints a colorful and versatile picture. Leaders with entrepreneurial skills may be excellent corporate up-starters, but may not be cut out for weathering the developmental ups and downs, just like ship builders may not necessarily be good captains. Conversely, those with great negotiation or engineering skills may not be the most prudent strategists. Historical icons such as Alfred Sloan (General Motors) and Juan Trippe (Pan American World Airways) are just some of the many examples they offer to illustrate this point. In Sloan's case, the big picture skills were present, but the will to deal with organized labor was absent. In Trippe's case, the talent to shape an airline into a major leader was there, but the skills to work with employees were minimal. In both cases, these leaders had to be replaced in order to ensure continued growth of the corporation.[3]

One common lack of contextual intelligence throughout most of the 20th century was the one pertaining to corporate social responsibility and environmental

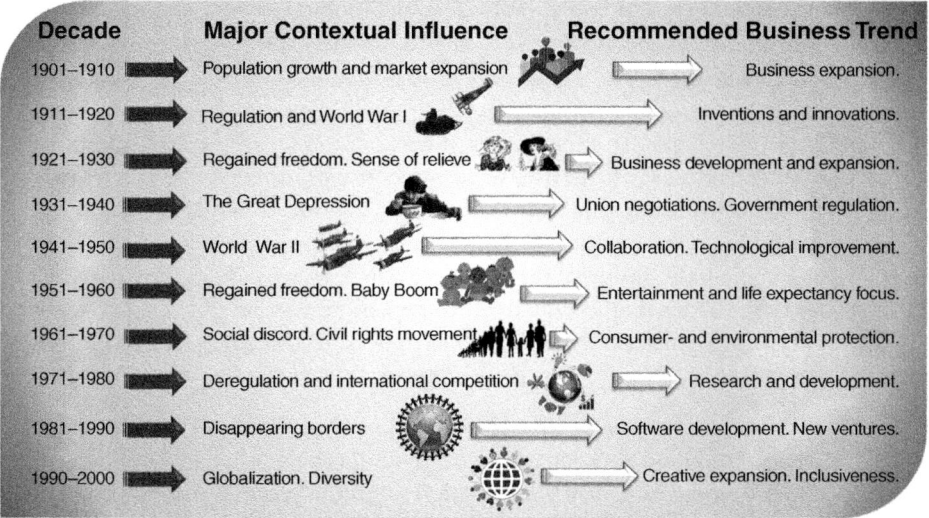

Decade	Major Contextual Influence	Recommended Business Trend
1901–1910	Population growth and market expansion	Business expansion.
1911–1920	Regulation and World War I	Inventions and innovations.
1921–1930	Regained freedom. Sense of relieve	Business development and expansion.
1931–1940	The Great Depression	Union negotiations. Government regulation.
1941–1950	World War II	Collaboration. Technological improvement.
1951–1960	Regained freedom. Baby Boom	Entertainment and life expectancy focus.
1961–1970	Social discord. Civil rights movement	Consumer- and environmental protection.
1971–1980	Deregulation and international competition	Research and development.
1981–1990	Disappearing borders	Software development. New ventures.
1990–2000	Globalization. Diversity	Creative expansion. Inclusiveness.

FIGURE 4.1 Decade–Based Influences in the 20th Century.
Source: This figure was developed based on data provided in the article from Mayo and Nohria (2005), as cited above.

sustainability: it seems as if the majority of leaders in that century were indifferent to the reality that resources were finite, and that expansion of their corporate practices should, therefore, be finite as well. Throughout the past century, numerous circumstances were factored into corporate decision-making, but notions about the environment only entered the corporate radars near the end of that era. Contextual aspects that famously influenced the 20th century are represented in Figure 4.1.

Moral Considerations

Morality, as will be repeatedly stated in this book, is not a concept with a unified definition. Moral perspectives differ as widely as perspectives on leadership, happiness, and success do. Morality becomes even trickier to pinpoint when it is brought in the context of corporations. Over the years, there have been numerous arguments about the moral responsibility of corporations. Some sources consider corporations to be hollow entities that are steered by human beings, which means that corporations could not be held responsible for moral actions. Others insist that, since corporations have acquired the status of legal persons, they should be held responsible for their actions, which also include their moral behavior:

> Michael Phillips has presented an interesting deliberation on corporate moral personhood.[4] Emphasizing the complexity around the question whether or not corporations hold moral responsibilities, he described three dominant 20th-century conceptions of the corporation: the concession, aggregate, and real entity theories. Phillips lays the groundwork

for his deliberation by explaining that corporate actions can sometimes, but not always, be attributed to the individuals running them. It would have been easy if every corporate action could simply be pinned on a group of individuals in charge of the entity, but reality is not always that straightforward. Sometimes, a corporation's misbehavior cannot be attributed to just one person or just one group of people. Rather, it may be a long-running sequence of individual actions, of which each was relatively innocent, but of which the whole became an atrocity. A sequence of bureaucratic failures, for instance, can lead to a disastrous outcome with no particular individual left to be held responsible.[5]

In his discussion of the three conceptions of the corporation, Phillips posits that:

1. The *concession theory*, developed and used in the late-19th century, is based on the concept that a corporation is established by law, and that it is, therefore, an artificial entity, subject to legal regulations, but not capable or eligible of holding moral obligations. Based on this perspective, corporations are artificial persons without a conscience, thus also without intentions or awareness of the consequences of their actions.[6]

2. The *aggregate theory*, developed closer to the 20th century, was based on the simplification of creating corporations, reducing state involvement in their instatement, and becoming more of a mechanical process. Having now become the product of free private agreement, corporations were seen as clusters of people, holding contractual relationships with each other. So, within this context, corporations were a cluster of people and contracts, a symbolic entity, and could not be separately held morally responsible.[7]

3. The *real entity* theory, emerging at the dawn of the 20th century, came forth from the argument from legal scholars that corporations are real entities and are not mere accumulations of their human components or artificial creations of state law. Many corporations own properties beyond the wealth and power of those running them. By considering corporations as real entities, they should also be considered having moral personhood.[8]

Phillips concludes that the concession theory is invalid because it has little descriptive value; that the aggregate theory is too convoluted to maintain as a corporate identity, and that the real entity theory holds most validity as it considers corporations capable of actions, possessions, and thus also moral responsibilities.[9]

The Employee of the 20th Century

The employee of the 20th century, definitely in the US, was much better off at the end of the era than at the beginning.[10] Over this 100-year period, the workforce grew to six times its original size, while workers' rights, wages, and working circumstances improved significantly. Child labor, which was still rampant in the early decades of the 20th century, practically disappeared by the end of the century. While 10 years was an accepted age for a working person in the early 1900s, this age had increased to 16 around the 2000s.

Another shift that happened for workers in the 20th century was the very nature of their work: in the early years, manufacturing and agricultural labor were prevalent, but as the century progressed these activities were entrusted to the more-populated nations of the world, while the US workforce increasingly shifted its focus to technology and service.[11] The percentages speak for themselves: farm work decreased from nearly 40 percent of labor practices at the beginning of the century to less than 3 percent at the end; physical factory labor, such as mining, manufacturing, and construction, dropped from 31 to 19 percent. Over that same time period, the service industry increased from 31 to 78 percent.[12]

Yet another area in which the 20th century brought workforce change was in the structure: more women entered the workplace than in the centuries before, displaying a leap from 19 percent at the beginning of the era to 60 percent at the end. Within this structural change, there was also a shifting dimension: women and minorities gradually started taking on more prominent positions, due to their increased opportunities to obtain higher education.[13]

Salaries and wages also saw an increase, even though we should also consider that the value of the dollar steadily devaluated throughout the century, which implies that consumerism had to be kept intact by ensuring that workers could continue to meet required living standards. In addition, the length of a work-week dropped from 50-plus to 40-plus hours per week.[14]

The drivers behind all these changes can be found in a wide range of developments: technology, demographic changes, with populations moving from rural to urban areas, immigration, education, and government involvement are just some of these factors. *Technology*, in particular, is a collective term for a plethora of groundbreaking developments that changed the ways people communicated, commuted, worked, and even thought about life in general. Numerous devices enabled more effective and efficient ways of performing, and entirely new industries (appliances and computers, for instance) saw the light of day. The many advancements in transportation modes also contributed to the shifts of the day: not only did people move more easily between cities, counties, and states, but workplaces also moved toward less expensive areas, now that the commute to and from work had become less of an issue.[15]

The Need to Release Obsolete Practices

Many of the business practices of the 20th century have blown over into the current era. Even though we pride ourselves about new ways of communicating (via social networks and numerous apps on our mobile devices), and oftentimes claim that we would not be comfortable doing things the way they were done in the past century, we are still engaging in so many practices, some of them originating even longer ago than the past century.[16] A handful of behaviors that we inherited and still apply without too much consideration for change are:

1. Hierarchical organizational structures, many of which still run top–down, even though the work landscape has entirely changed. One big leader is still in charge over some smaller ones, who in turn are in charge over yet smaller ones, who then oversee the field workers.[17] This industrial revolution model, implemented when workers were still lowly educated individuals in need of close supervision, has not been changed, even though today's workers, especially in countries such as the US, are oftentimes college educated.

2. The carrot and stick approach. Employees are still rewarded and punished as a way to keep them in line, as if they were mules.[18] It has been proven time and again that this system, which used to work in highly mechanistic work environments, no longer suffices in workplaces where people don't do repetitive, mind-numbing work, but rather solve novel problems through their creative skills. Yet, bringing about a change in this system seems to be too complicated to those in charge, and so it is left as is.

3. The construct of top-level management setting policies for the entire organization, while these folks have very little experience or insight in the day-to-day operations.[19] In many organizations there is still not enough faith in the opinions of the well-educated, customer-serving frontline workers to allow them a voice in the policies that are intended to make an organization run more smoothly and satisfactorily.

4. The approach of having ideas designed at top levels, and then ordered for implementation at the bottom,[20] while, in a similar vein as the point above, most top-level folks (managers) have little or no insight in the real needs and desires of customers.

5. The hesitance to share bad news with, or speak up to, higher-ups.[21] This often leads to a phenomenon known in management as "filtering," whereby lower-level managers withhold certain information that they consider inappropriate, less important, or damaging to their superiors. Behavior like this causes a communication disconnect between top management and lower echelons, and may even lead to a breach of trust between the floor-level workers and higher management.

Ryan (2016) suggests that we finally start following up on things we already realize, such as a) sharing more information throughout our organization rather than withholding critical data but still expecting people to perform optimally.[22] The better a company's strategy is communicated with its workforce, the more unified movement toward progress can be achieved; b) respecting co-workers enough to give them some discretion and allow them to make small executive decisions, because that is what will cause them to go an extra mile, not their paycheck or even a raise; and c) ensuring the passion stays in the task, so that employees feel positively challenged to do their work with pleasure and don't get bemused, bored, or burned out.

Business Expansion in the 20th Century: The Automobile Industry

As with many consumer goods, the automobile started off as an elite product. The first automobiles were unattainable for simple working people, so only members of the elite groups could afford to purchase this piece of transportation. In the early days of the 20th century, only 1 in 9,500 Americans owned a car.[23] The price of an automobile was around $2,000 US dollars in 1900, with total sales running at about 4,100 cars. The first mass-produced auto in America was the Oldsmobile Curved Dash, which was developed and produced first in 1901.[24]

In 1903, Henry Ford entered this promising industry and founded the Ford Motor Company. While assembly lines already existed, Ford improved the concept to ensure faster and cheaper production of automobiles. His first economical car was the Model T, especially produced for the working class: a car that would soon dominate the auto market in the US. In the meantime, the competition in the industry continued to grow, especially when William C. Durant founded the General Motors Corporation (GM), first uniting three companies, Buick, Oldsmobile, and Oakland, and later expanding this corporation further by adding Cadillac to the cluster.[25]

Henry Ford turned out to be an insightful and trailblazing businessman, further evolving the assembly line production system, and offering employees double the hourly rate he paid them before. He also started granting loans to Model T customers, and auto sales skyrocketed in 1915 to almost 900,000 units. The next year, US auto production reached the 1-million mark, a milestone that would only be matched four decades later by another country, the UK.[26]

As World War I ended and the booming 1920s arrived, the nation was eager to celebrate its freedom and regained carefree lifestyle. There was still room for competitors in the automobile industry, and Walter Chrysler founded the Chrysler Corporation. By the time that the 1920s came to a close, automobile manufacturing had become America's largest industry. Then, when the Great Depression hit, employees in the largest industry understood the importance of uniting in order to stand up for their rights, and the United Auto Workers (UAW) was created in Detroit. Through an organized strike, UAW workers obtained a contract agreement with GM, thus confirming the strength of the union movement. During World War II, automobile production was halted, but right after the war's end, production and sales of automobiles surged to a degree that had not been achieved before. In 1948, almost 5 million cars were sold in the US.[27]

In the years thereafter, import cars were brought to the US as well, such as the Volkswagen Beetle, while luxury features, such as air conditioners, were installed in newer auto models. At the end of the fifties, the first interstate roads (freeways) were built, enabling more-convenient and rapid car travels throughout the nation. Right before 1960, the first Japanese cars made their way into the US. In that same timeframe, safety features increased, bringing in and mandating safety belts. Then, as the number of cars on the road grew into multiple millions on a continuous basis, air pollution and control acts were passed on instate rules for automobile owners, followed by even more safety measures, such as collapsible steering columns and safety windshields.[28]

Yet, every industry has a lifecycle, usually divided into four stages: infancy, growth, maturity, and decline. Even though automobiles will remain a hard item to eradicate or replace, the US auto industry reached its decline stage in the 1970s, when a shift in circumstantial factors took place: foreign cars, especially from Japan, rose in prestige and purchasing attraction as the American automobiles acquired the reputation of being overrated and underperforming. The seventies were also turbulent in regards to oil purchasing, as they were marked by an oil embargo from Arab nations. An increasing number of Japanese cars, specifically Toyota and Nissan, found their way to the hearts and garages of American consumers. Toyota had established sales headquarters in the US since 1957, in Hollywood, California. After some trial and error, the company found the Corona to be highly successful with the American buyers, and focused mainly on the production of this brand. In 1967, Toyota had grown out to be the third best-selling car brand in America.[29] Yet, it was not until 1986 that the company established its first auto factory in the US as a joint venture with GM.[30] Six years prior to that, in 1980, Japan had formally taken over global leadership of automobile production.[31] The auto industry in America was going through a tough time, with four major firms manufacturing commercial vehicles: GM, Ford, Chrysler, and AMC.[32]

Chrysler, in particular, was seeing grim times. But then, Ford's star executive, Lee Iacocca, took over the reins at Chrysler, and reorganized its production and financial operations toward greater profitability.[33]

The end of the 20th century presented an entirely different picture than the beginning: the auto industry had emerged, grown, and re-formatted itself; leadership in automobile production had shifted away from the US, to a point where Japanese and German factories became top producers of automobiles in the world, and US auto makers were producing fewer than two-thirds of the cars on American roads. Electric vehicle production returned to the frontlines of attention, even though it would still take a few more years before they would become big news. Daimler-Benz merged with the Chrysler corporation in 1998, and a year later, Ford acquired the Swedish corporation Volvo.

The Daimler–Chrysler marriage lasted less than a decade. It had been pursued and closed as a way to respond to the advancing globalization trend. Soon, new model series in cars, busses and trucks started rolling out of the factories. Yet, as leadership at Daimler changed in 2005, so did visions, and it wasn't too long after that, that the company sold its stakes in other major auto corporations, among which were Chrysler, Mitsubishi, and Hyundai. By 2009, Daimler had sold all shares in these external entities, and changed its name again from DaimlerChrysler to Daimler.[34]

A similar sentiment, bracing for the globalization trend, drove Ford to acquire Volvo in 1999. It cost Ford $6.45 billion to finalize this purchase, but the stakes were high enough: Ford's CEO, Jac Nasser, saw synergistic opportunities in market coverage for both brands in Europe as well as the US. Besides, Volvo had a good reputation, and a high appeal to affluent Baby Boomers, which made the takeover even more attractive to Ford. Ten years prior to this acquisition, Ford had acquired Jaguar, and managed to streamline production of both Jaguars and Lincolns on the same basic platform. With this new purchase, Ford was now responsible for the production of seven well-known brands: Ford, Lincoln, Mercury, Jaguar, Mazda, Aston Martin, and Volvo.[35]

The above overview of the automobile industry in the 20th century entailed a number of important business practices:

1. *Expansion strategies:* these became apparent not only in the early years, when Henry Ford expanded production of Ford automobiles by improving the assembly line production system and offering employees higher hourly rates than competitors, but also through the Daimler–Chrysler merger and the Ford–Volvo acquisition discussed near the end. Driven by the need to compete, and the unremitting confrontation with relentless new market entrants, corporations in the auto industry were often placed before challenges, which demanded creative thinking and diehard negotiating, but also "contextual intelligence"[36] in order to figure out which approach was most prudent at what time.

2. *Infiltration strategies:* these also became apparent in the last section of the automobile industry overview, as two globally performing automakers were preparing themselves for globalization challenges. Daimler, a European automaker, saw a merger with Chrysler as a swift and beneficial way of gaining market share in the US, while Ford, an American automaker, wanted to infiltrate the European market, but also hoped to expand its profits by acquiring Volvo.

3. *Profit maximization:* this concept could be detected throughout the review presented above, as each of the automakers were focused on this notion. Profit maximization is a core concept in business, and there is nothing wrong with maximizing profit, as long as a corporation remains ethical.

Yet, when facing diehard competition, sometimes even large corporations run into trouble, such as the Chrysler corporation in the late 1970s, having to call in the creative leadership of a seasoned, external leader to change the tide and get out of trouble.

Patrick Primeaux presents a compelling perspective on profit and profit maximization in an article that was published a few decades ago. He starts out by explaining the importance of profit for business, yet also underscores the importance of holding moral considerations in mind when defining profit. When profit is merely perceived within the scope of revenues minus costs, a numerical approach, it holds a bottom-line foundation, but not always an ethically sound approach.[37] Profit is good or bad, based on the way it is acquired. Costs and revenues should, therefore, be considered in a broader light: within the realm of how they are created. Profit, seen in this light, is a reflection of human achievement and social good, symbolizing the contribution of business to shared and personal well-being. When we consider the maximization of profit, we should be mindful of the following three factors:

1. There must be an agreed moral standard under which the costs and revenues are acquired and generated. While each member in an organization has his or her own ethical convictions, there should be a coherent ethical standard when a group of people perform for the same entity, so that there is also a common understanding and focus.
2. There must be a moral foundation to business decisions, from the allocation of resources to the input of products and the way they are produced. So, the means used to perform efficiently also must be ethically sound.
3. There must be moral sense in identifying and benefiting from "opportunity costs," whereby the well-being of stakeholders is considered.[38]

Several articles after Primeaux's supported the notion to consider profit maximization as the ultimate moral code. Keller (2007), for instance, asserts that "modern business theory . . . has established a moral code for business based on efficiency of outcome and the assumed link of efficiency to self-interested behavior. The result is markets as the arbitrators of ethical outcomes, and profit maximization as the ultimate moral code."[39] Keller warns that neoclassical economists, among them Milton Friedman, have transferred partial sections of Adam Smith's famous theory into modern capitalism, thereby making it seem that unregulated business with a sole focus on shareholders' returns should be the only purpose for corporations. Smith's notion about the well-being of society has thereby completely been ignored, which is incorrect and irresponsible,[40] as has become apparent in recent years with the depletion-related effects on our biosphere and ecology, as a result of unbridled extraction of resources without any care about replenishing what has been taken.

This point is presented here (as well as in other parts of this book) because it confronts us with the fact that much of what we experience today (and will experience in the future) is a result of our own self-centered, shortsighted approach: one that has been mindlessly adopted from neoclassical economists, with very little concern about the effects of their teachings and actions.

Case 4.1 Immoral Leadership: The Path to Destruction

One of the late 20th century's most infamous names in business performance is Albert Dunlap. "Chainsaw Al," as he became known, earned his nickname from his practices in preparing corporations for take over. Dunlap was a typical example of a leader who believed in profit maximization, but not necessarily with moral foundations. He was a remorseless cost cutter and bottom-line man.[41] Rather than being concerned about stakeholder well-being, he believed in maximizing profits for shareholders. Whoever had to suffer to achieve that end would just have to suffer. Dunlap would downsize beyond the bone to reduce overhead and create a distorted, unrealistic picture of profits. Starting in the seventies, throughout the eighties, and well into the nineties, Dunlap built a reputation for himself. Even though his callous managerial style and brazen accounting manipulations at a Niagara Falls–based paper-mill company called Nitec led to him being fired, Dunlap managed to walk away without being prosecuted, because the company had to go out of business. The main reason for Nitec to go belly up was the fact that a booked profit turned out to be a major loss, from which the company did not recover. Dunlap kept his Nitec experience a secret, and maneuvered his way into the business world, finally landing a leadership position at a Fortune 500 company, Scott Paper, one of the two companies that led to his "Chainsaw" reputation. It was the early nineties, and Scott had suffered major losses, causing internal turmoil, finger-pointing, and massive expenses in areas that were not making business any better. Internal organization and financial control was erroneous, and it had been a long time since Scott had had anything new to show to customers. The company's reputation was waning and something needed to be done.

Dunlap entered the company and immediately began his rigorous turnaround plan. He sold Scott's expensive headquarter location near Philadelphia, and moved it to a far-less-expensive location, swiftly reducing many millions in overhead expenses. As part of his turnaround plan, Dunlap dismantled Scott's strategic team, and eliminated 70 percent of its upper-management positions. He got rid of all excess jobs, sold noncore businesses, and managed to eradicate the company's

$2.5 billion debt within two years.[42] As a result of his drastic measures, Scott's stock price surged, and the company's value skyrocketed, with outstanding shares growing from $2.5 billion to $9 billion. Once this was accomplished, Dunlap sold the company to Kimberly-Clark, and earned $100 million in the process: a strategy that made many business analysts and performers wonder whether Dunlap was not the person with all the right answers. As Dunlap's strategies were reviewed, advocates praised him for cutting from the top down, thus getting rid of the overpaid and overvalued individuals that only push up the company's overhead. His opponents, however, claimed that he was not considering the lives of the company's average workers in his massive layoffs, and in his quest to increase shareholders' profits.

In 1996, Dunlap became chairman and CEO of Sunbeam, and followed exactly the same strategy as he had followed two years earlier with Scott, and many years before that with Nitec. Initially, everything seemed to go the way Dunlap envisioned it: he curtailed top management positions, slashed the workforce in half, and divested noncore production units. Sixteen of the company's 26 production units and five of its six headquarters were sold. He advertised heavily, and Sunbeam's sales soared, while its stock rose by 400 percent.[43] One year after Dunlap stepped in, Sunbeam's reported earnings had run up to $189 million, but when Dunlap tried to sell the company, he couldn't find a buyer. The Dutch electronics giant, Philips, was interested in buying Sunbeam at about $50 per share, but Dunlap wanted $70, and Philips walked away.[44] In order to keep moving, Sunbeam purchased two companies, causing its stock to increase even more. But then some disturbing facts started rolling out: non-seasonal products had been sold at huge discounts, and sales had been booked before the goods had left his warehouses. Soon enough, more accounting manipulations became apparent, and Dunlap was fired. Investigations brought to light that Dunlap had highly exaggerated Sunbeam's initial losses to make his turnaround seem greater than it really was. It also became apparent that about $60 million of the reported earnings under Dunlap's leadership were deceitful. Like Nitec, Sunbeam did not recover from Dunlap's practices, and the company went into bankruptcy in 2002.

The investigations in Sunbeam made it clear that Dunlap had also engaged in questionable practices at Scott a few years earlier. Similarly, it became clear that he had implemented the same strategy before at Lily Tulip and Consolidated Press Holdings, two of his other corporate assignments: cutting half of the staff, sending home top management, and bringing in his own support team.[45] In hindsight, Sunbeam executives explained that cutting as far as Dunlap did in the work-force actually led to additional costs, because a number of employees involved in seasonal production had flexible work schedules. Closing those plants and letting those full-time workers go, caused overhead in certain production lines to grow rather than decline. Additionally, it also became clear that Dunlap did not care about the day-to-day operations of the business and his aloof mentality was not appreciated by the workforce.[46] Interestingly, it was the strategy that Dunlap most believed in, maximizing shareholder value by cutting costs to the bone that cost him his career and his reputation as a CEO in big business. The 20th century was coming to an end, and so was the narrow-focused shareholder profit maximization focus. In 2002, Dunlap reluctantly agreed to pay $15 million to settle a class-action lawsuit brought by Sunbeam's shareholders who accused him and other former executives of manipulating the company's financial results.[47]

Questions

1. Do you consider Al Dunlap's corporate turnaround strategies morally sound? Please explain your answer.
2. Upon reading this case, what do you consider Al Dunlap's greatest strengths and weaknesses as a corporate fixer?
3. Al Dunlap was solely focused on shareholder's returns. What do you think a leader needs to focus on today to successfully run a corporation?

Leadership and Sleepwalking

There have been, and still are, many corporate leaders who engage in sleep-walking. *Sleepwalking* is mindless behavior: when we implement our work or home activities without investing too much thought in them and without wondering what the meaning of these activities is to us. Many people sleepwalk, because they don't realize that there is an alternative to the way they go through life. Leaders who go by priorities and rules set in less-enlightened times, are sleepwalking. Leaders who ignore the bigger picture of their decisions, and only focus on narrow parameters, such as only shareholder profits and not stakeholder well-being, are also sleepwalking. They go through the motions and don't engage in any reflection.

In a more general sense, human beings have a tendency to become mindless and do things either because they have done them for a long time, or because they were done this way for a long time. Mindless continuation of traditions is an often-occurring form of sleepwalking. Something was once considered the proper strategy, and nobody wonders whether it still makes sense today. In business arenas, this often goes for strategies: corporate leaders rarely consider their strategy. They will blame the workforce, the market, the community, the competitors, or even the government for their company's poor performance, but will not question whether their strategy has become obsolete.

Sleepwalking has a lot to do with focusing too much on the details and forgetting to zoom out in order to obtain a broader scope. As Dunlap's case demonstrated, sleepwalking can lead to trouble, not only for the person who sleepwalks, but also for those who get affected by this behavior. Unfortunately, sleepwalking is a widespread phenomenon because human beings, by default, are creatures of habit, hence, change averse. We love to dwell in what we consider our comfort zones: once we have developed a pattern, it is just easier to follow the same trend repeatedly, just like Dunlap did with Nitec, Scott, and Sunbeam. There is less mental energy needed to find our way through our routine. It is like performing on autopilot. But there are limits to everything: performing on autopilot for too long can derail our focus on new trends, and new trends keep emerging, whether we like it or not. Especially in professional circles, it will be self-destructive to behave like a sleepwalker.

Individuals are not the only ones who sleepwalk. Organizations can also fall prey to this behavior. This is understandable, because organizations are run by people, and if the people driving the organization are unaware of or unwilling to apply necessary changes, the organization may land in an indolent situation that will harm its competitiveness and general performance and growth. There are numerous examples of businesses that once thrived but lost their edge due to sleepwalking. To stick with the auto industry discussed earlier in this chapter, GM and Ford, once the biggest and most prestigious car companies on the globe, have been losing market share and profits due to their failure to keep up with younger generations of automakers.

The reasons why so many people sleepwalk through life are widely diverse. Here are some:

1. They confine their thinking to their current field of action, or they have learned to think within the boundaries of their daily environment.
2. They are not rewarded for creative thinking. There are still many work environments—and bosses—who can become displeased with out-of-the-box thinkers or healthy risk takers.
3. They may have erected some mental blockades, such as self-esteem issues, or fear what others may think of them, which prohibit them from wading into areas outside of their mental comfort zone.
4. They are subjected to a highly routine-based (mechanistic) environment, which does not encourage critical thinking.
5. They may come from cultures or living environments where mindfulness was punished, or where mindless following was rewarded.

The effect of sleepwalking on business entities may decline if business leaders decide to reinvent themselves and focus on trends, products, or services that can improve their position in their field.

Summary

- Corporations in the 20th century were built on the industrial revolution model: many of the reporting lines were top-down, decisions were made in a centralized way, by top management in headquarters; employees were considered easily expendable; and processes as well as product lines were used for a long time, as there was little or no disruption.
- Many 20th-century corporate leaders gained control either because of family ties, or as handpicked successors of previous leaders. This often led to corporate kingpins with very little consideration for either internal or external stakeholders.
- Employees in the 20th century would work at the same employer during most of their, or their entire, professional career, which would usually span a timeframe of 40–50 years.
- The 20th century brought a large number of developmental waves and insights into the nature of business and its leadership requirements. Leaders learned about "contextual intelligence": the importance of understanding the spirit and focus of any given time in history in order to take a corporation to the next level.
  - One common lack of contextual intelligence throughout most of the 20th century was the one pertaining to corporate social responsibility and environmental sustainability.
- Moral perspectives differ as widely as perspectives on leadership, happiness, and success do. Morality becomes even trickier when brought in the context of corporations. Over the years, there have been numerous arguments about the moral responsibility of corporations.
- The employee of the 20th century, definitely in the US, was much better off at the end of the era than at the beginning.
  - Workers' rights, wages, and working circumstances improved significantly.
  - The nature of work shifted from manufacturing and agricultural labor to technology and service.
  - More women entered the workplace than in the centuries before.
  - Women and minorities gradually started taking on more prominent positions.
  - Salaries and wages also increased.
- In contemporary workplaces, we still engage in many practices that originated longer ago than the past century. Some are:
  - Hierarchical organizational structures, many of which still run top-down, even though the work landscape has entirely changed.

- The carrot-and-stick approach. Employees are still rewarded and punished as a way to keep them in line.
- The construct of top-level management setting policies for the entire organization, while these folks have very little experience or insight in the day-to-day operations.
- The approach of having ideas designed at top levels, and then ordered for implementation at the bottom.
- The hesitance to share bad news with, or speak up to, higher-ups.
- An overview of the automobile industry in the 20th century demonstrated a number of important business practices:
  - Expansion strategies: these became apparent not only in the early years, when Henry Ford expanded production of Ford automobiles, but also through the Daimler-Chrysler merger and the Ford-Volvo acquisition near the end of the century.
  - Infiltration strategies: these also became apparent in the last section of the automobile industry overview, as globally performing automakers engaged in mergers and acquisitions outside their countries.
  - Profit maximization: there is nothing wrong with maximizing profit, as long as a corporation remains ethical. Yet, when facing diehard competition, sometimes even large corporations run into trouble.
- When profit is merely perceived within the scope of revenues minus costs, a numerical approach, it holds a bottom-line foundation, but not always an ethically sound approach. When we consider the maximization of profit, we should be mindful of the following three factors:

  1. There must be an agreed moral standard under which the costs and revenues are acquired are generated.
  2. There must be a moral foundation to business decisions, from the allocation of resources to the input of products and the way they are produced.
  3. There must be moral sense in identifying and benefiting from "opportunity costs," whereby the well-being of stakeholders is considered.

- Sleepwalking is mindless behavior: when we implement our work or home activities without investing too much thought in them and without wondering what the meaning of these activities is to us.
  - Sleepwalking has a lot to do with focusing too much on the details and forgetting to zoom out in order to obtain a broader scope.
  - Sleepwalking is a widespread phenomenon because human beings, by default, are creatures of habit, hence, change averse.
  - Organizations can also fall prey to sleepwalking. There are numerous examples of businesses that once thrived but lost their edge due to sleepwalking.

Reflective Questions

1. In the first part of the chapter, the term *contextual intelligence* is used in regard to leadership. Explain in your own words what contextual intelligence means and why it is important for leaders.
2. Consider Phillips's three concepts of corporations. Which of these concepts do you consider most sensible to today's corporations, and why?
3. The chapter discusses a number of the work-related changes that workforce members experienced throughout the 20th century: select one of these change areas, and do some additional research on the topic as it unfolded or progressed in the 20th century. Share your findings in about 200–300 words.
4. Five obsolete practices that are still widely applied in workplaces are discussed in this chapter. Which of these five practices (you may select more than one) do you consider most destructive to today's work environments, and why?
5. Profit maximization is brought within the scope of moral performance, based on Primeaux's perspective. Do you agree that there should be a moral component to profit maximization? Please explain your answer.

Notes

1 Griffin, M. (June 10, 2015). Disruption, innovation and reinventing business: The death of the 20th-century corporation. CIO. www.cio.com/article/2933413/it-strategy/the-death-of-the-20th-century-corporation.html
2 Mayo, A. J., & Nohria, N. (2005). Zeitgeist leadership. *Harvard Business Review* *83*(10), 45–60.
3 Ibid.
4 Phillips, M. J. (1992). Corporate moral personhood and three conceptions of the corporation. *Business Ethics Quarterly 2*(4), 435–459.
5 Ibid.
6 Ibid.
7 Ibid.
8 Ibid.
9 Ibid.
10 Fisk, D. M. (2001). American labor in the 20th century. *Bureau of Labor Statistics-Compensation and Working Conditions.* https://stats.bls.gov/opub/mlr/cwc/american-labor-in-the-20th-century.pdf
11 Ibid.
12 Ibid.
13 Ibid.
14 Ibid.
15 Ibid.
16 Ryan, L. (January 4, 2016). Three 19th-century management ideas to ditch in 2016. *Forbes.* www.forbes.com/sites/lizryan/2016/01/04/three-19th-century-management-ideas-to-ditch-in-2016/print.
17 Ibid.
18 Ibid.

19 Ibid.
20 Ibid.
21 Ibid.
22 Ibid.
23 Evolution of the U.S. Auto Industry. (2009). *Congressional Digest 88*(2), 34–35.
24 Ibid.
25 Ibid.
26 Ibid.
27 Ibid.
28 Ibid.
29 Toyota Company History. *Toyota Corporation.* Retrieved on December 24, 2016, from http://corporatenews.pressroom.toyota.com/corporate/company+history.
30 Ibid.
31 Evolution of the U.S. Auto Industry. *Congressional Digest,* 34–35.
32 Binder, A. K. & Bell Rae, J. (March 7, 2012). Automotive industry. *Encyclopædia Britannica.* www.britannica.com/topic/automotive-industry.
33 Evolution of the U.S. Auto Industry, *Congressional Digest,* 34–35.
34 *Company History: "World Corp." vision: The merger between Daimler and Chrysler (1995–2007).* December 24, 2016, www.daimler.com/company/tradition/company-history/1995-2007.html.
35 Ford swallows Volvo. *The Economist* (January 30, 1999), 58.
36 Mayo & Nohria, Zeitgeist leadership, 45–60.
37 Primeaux, P. (1997). Business ethics in theory and practice: Diagnostic notes B. "A prescription for profit maximization." *Journal of Business Ethics 16*(3), 315–322.
38 Ibid.
39 Keller, A. C. (2007). Smith versus Friedman: Markets and ethics. *Critical Perspectives on Accounting 18*(2), 159–188, (159).
40 Ibid.
41 Sellers, P. (1998). Exit for Chainsaw? *Fortune 137*(11), 30–31.
42 Miniter, R. (1996). Al Dunlap and the shareholder revolution. *American Enterprise 7*(6), 82.
43 Sellers, P. (1998). Can Chainsaw Al really be a builder? *Fortune 137*(1), 118–120.
44 Sellers, Exit for Chainsaw? 30–31.
45 Bing, S. (1998). Hail and farewell, Chainsaw Al! *Fortune 138*(2), 43–44.
46 Byrne, J. (October 17, 1999). Chainsaw Al, Pt II. www.bloomberg.com/news/articles/1999-10-17/chainsaw-al-part-2.
47 (January 15, 2002). Chainsaw Al Dunlap agrees to settle suit. Ex-Sunbeam chief to pay $15 million to shareholders. *KNIGHT RIDDER/TRIBUNE.* http://articles.baltimoresun.com/2002-01-15/business/0201150314_1_sunbeam-arthur-andersen-chainsaw-al.

5

THE RIGHT THING IN CURRENT CONTEXT

Abstract

Thanks to the increased exposure to global developments through multiple factors—such as the Internet, less-expensive traveling, and social media—awareness has emerged that humanity holds the responsibility now, more than ever before, to ensure that life and its quality are sustained, even if it means sacrificing some profits. Money is shifting from being a driving motive to being a consequence of doing the right thing. The global context and cross-cultural issues will be observed within the discussion.

An Era of Expanded Horizons

The growing connectivity among people around the world has served as a tremendous and massive eye-opener. Since the Internet became a widespread commodity, the human race has grown more aware of developments, challenges, victories, and disasters in other parts of the world. What used to be far from our world, and therefore insignificant in our lives, has now become part of our daily concerns. Our circle of concern has expanded, and so has our circle of influence.[1] Management expert Stephen Covey alluded to these phenomena, explaining that we should understand that our *circle of concern* will always be larger than our circle of influence, but that our primary focus should be our *circle of influence.*[2] In other words, we should concentrate on changing those things that are within our control, and not frustrate or distract ourselves with things we cannot change. This is very much in line with Reinhold Niebuhr's Serenity Prayer, which also tells us, "Grant me the serenity to accept the things I cannot change, courage to change the things I can, and wisdom to know the difference."

While the above consideration about keeping our focus to our circle of influence and maintaining our serenity by accepting the things we cannot change makes good common sense, it also calls for some caution: It is easy to throw our hands in the air and say that we are powerless toward whatever is outside of our circle of influence. People do it all the time. When they find it more convenient to look the other way, they can produce hundreds of reasons to explain why working toward any solution would be beyond their scope. By keeping our circle of influence small, we can reject any additional responsibility, and continue to dwell in what we consider our safe comfort zone. This is the point of caution. Deliberately reducing our circle of influence is not only destructive to others, whom we could have helped, but also to ourselves, because we have failed to fulfill the core moral duty of reaching out and doing something constructive while we could. We should, therefore, try to expand our circle of influence, as Covey also recommends, in order for it to meet the size of our circle of concern.

One major shift in reality we experience these days is that, thanks to the many communication avenues available, we can develop better insights, establish deeper and wider connections, and undertake actions that have broader effects than in the past. Depending on our means and circumstances, we can initiate or engage in distant support programs, as people did during major disasters, such as the Indian Ocean tsunami (2004), Hurricane Katrina in the US (2005), the Haiti earthquake (2010), and the Tohoku earthquake and tsunami (2011). This global involvement has become part of our daily routine, and has sharpened our collective awareness about our responsibility, which we now understand not to be limited to ourselves and the current inhabitants of the Earth, but also to future generations. An ancient Indian proverb (also presented in an earlier chapter) puts it well:

> Treat the Earth well: it was not given to you by your parents, it was loaned to you by your children. We do not inherit the Earth from our Ancestors, we borrow it from our Children.

The entire nature of doing business has changed, as well. The 20th century as it used to be is disappearing. The way 21st century businesses run was unforeseeable and definitely incomprehensible 40 or 50 years ago. The entire platform has shifted: Uber is now one of the largest taxi companies, but doesn't own vehicles of its own; the largest global social media, Facebook, Twitter, and YouTube, thrive without delivering their own content, and Alibaba, the world's largest retailer, has no inventory of its own. The future belongs to those who dare to change the way we think, behave, and see the world. IQ has taken over where dollars used to have the last word. Those who doesn't understand that will simply perish.[3]

Never before have businesses been more involved in a stakeholder perspective than in our time. The shareholder wealth concept, as prioritized in the past century, has become obsolete, as today's business leaders have come to understand its dreadful limitations and, even more concerning, its danger for the conservation and progression of humankind as a whole.

Along with the expanded trend of virtual access to the rest of the world has come the expansion in physical access as well. People travel more today than they did before. The International Air Transport Association (IATA) released an industry traffic forecast in 2012, claiming that airlines expected to welcome some 3.6 billion passengers in 2016, which would be about 800 million more than the 2.8 billion passengers carried by airlines in 2011.[4] The 2016 estimate turned out to exceed these expectations, because the 3.6 billion figure was almost achieved in 2015.[5] At that time, the IATA adjusted its expectations to 3.8 billion airline travelers for 2016, which was almost half of the world population at that time.[6] China and the Middle East were in that year, as well as in the years before, the leaders in passenger growth numbers.

> The numbers should be interpreted with caution: travelers are counted as numbers of people boarding airplanes, which means that one person could be counted multiple times, depending on the number of airplanes he embarked on any given day. A person making five roundtrips per year with two flights each way is therefore counted as 20 passengers.[7]

Indeed: airplanes are the modern-day autobuses: they stay on the ground just long enough to let off one group of passengers, and load another group for the next trip. Thanks to the exposure we currently get to multiple countries, cultures, and ways of living, we realize and learn about ways of living and behaving different than our own, causing our horizons to enlarge, so that we can rethink our past perspectives. It makes us more grateful for the things we once used to take for granted. It familiarizes us with alternative ways of problem-solving and decision-making, based on different ways of perceiving reality. A series of important human characteristics that has been on the rise in the first decade of this century will be discussed next. The series consists of mental models, critical thinking, emotional intelligence, consciousness, and reflection.

Mental Models

Mental models are our internal pictures of how the world works.[8] Because our mental models are our own deeply ingrained ideas about the world around us, influenced by our upbringing, education, culture, ethnic background, religion, and other determining factors, they often form a major hurdle in accepting new ways of thinking and acting. If we are unaware of our mental models—and many people are—they can severely debilitate how we perceive the world. Peter Senge, who is a prominent thinker and author on mental models, explains,

> Mental models can be simple generalizations, such as "people are untrust-worthy," or they can be complex theories. But what is most important to

grasp is that mental models shape how we act. If we believe people are untrustworthy, we act differently from the way we would if we believed they were trustworthy."[9]

In striving to do the right thing, it is important to understand how mental models work and what they do: they are represented in the stories we believe and the assumptions we hold. Because we take them for granted, and assume they are the only way reality can be considered, our mental models shape—and can often distort—our interpretation of external impulses. Therefore, it may happen that two people listen to the same statement, yet one hears a compliment, while the other hears an insult. Mental models don't just differ among people from different backgrounds or cultures: sometimes people from the same family or circle of friends can have differing mental models. This is because our characters, personal experiences, and mind-sets also play a major role in the shaping of our mental models.

Once we become aware of them, we should also notice that our mental models are highly imperfect. They are limited, unbalanced, and are often irrational and miserly.[10] Yet, they evolved as a natural process: through our interactions with other people and a variety of situations. Human beings require their mental models, because they provide simplified explanations to complex situations.[11] We develop behavioral patterns on basis of our mental models. We develop beliefs about how our devices work, for instance, and take extra measures because of those beliefs. If your computer is frequently crashing, then you may develop the mental model of shutting it down in a particular way to prevent another crash. When you purchase a new computer, you may apply the same mental model to this new machine, even if unnecessary and outdated.[12] While our mental models enable us to filter the abundance of information that comes to us, and helps us determine our stance with more ease and make quicker decisions, they may be inaccurate and withhold us from new paths and possibilities that could be advantageous.[13]

In most Western nations, such as the US, people are taught that an individualistic mind-set is the natural way for human beings to perform. A focus on self-progress and selfish gain, even if at the expense of others, is therefore highly preferred. This self-focus has even grown into a societal addiction, oftentimes creating a series of ignorant behaviors in personal and professional environments. Selfish gain is generally rewarded, because accumulating wealth or profits is a sign of having understood the dominant mental model. This shows that mental models, or perceptions, are not always internally created, but very often prompted by signals from our environment. Some of the social factors that can influence our mental models are,

1. *Social contradiction:* Most human communities are full of contradictory forces. Previous generations exert mixed messages to younger ones by rewarding exactly those things that they claim should be avoided or punished.

You can even see this at both personal and professional levels. In personal regards, we are told to nurture a team spirit, but often find that individual performance is more abundantly rewarded. In professional regards, many business and government departments quickly understand that they should never try to stay under last year's budget, even if they are told to do so. Remaining under budget means that next year's budget will be reduced. Going over the limits ensures a larger budget for next year.[14]

2. *Mental inconsistencies:* Our paradigms shift as we mature. At younger ages, we usually don't care too much about others and try to achieve our goals at any cost. As we mature, we gradually start to understand that there is more to life than making money: we have then been confronted with the crucibles of life, and have learned that happiness is made up of different factors.[15]

3. *The price of moral performance:* This often manifests itself in the business world. Doing the right thing usually costs much more and requires a tremendous amount of effort compared to risking a fine. The fine is usually tens or even hundreds of times cheaper than proper behavior. The unwritten rule is, therefore: go ahead and take the chance, and we'll see what happens if we get caught.[16] A sad example of this trend is the Union Carbide Corporation, which was responsible for a major gas leak in India in 1984, whereby more than a half million people were exposed to dangerous chemicals, resulting in an immediate death toll of 2,259 souls. The company only paid $470 million instead of the initially demanded $3 billion, without an option to prosecute the responsible management team, because the US refused to extradite the guilty managers to India, where the accident had transpired.[17]

It is critical to understand that we harbor mental models, because it can help us in becoming aware of the fact that other people view things differently from the way we do. Knowing about our mental models also helps us to understand how often we are wrong due to our limited view. It can help us to cease our attempts to prove others wrong, because we become more aware of our own limitations in seeing, reasoning, and concluding. Most importantly, knowing about our mental models can encourage us to rethink them and change them in areas where they make us miserable. Below are some suggestions for proactive measures to change potentially damaging mental models:

1. *Active note-taking:* This may require some self-discipline, but walk around with a pen and notebook and actively take notes of your beliefs. When reviewing them, you will find which ones come from your upbringing, and which ones are new. Then you can decide which ones to change and which to keep.[18]

2. *Meditation:* An effective strategy toward changing mental models, there are several ways of meditating, so it is left to the meditator to decide how, when, and where to practice this exercise. Vipassana meditation is also

known as mindfulness meditation or insight meditation. While it is often associated with Buddhism, some sources maintain that it existed even before the Buddhist philosophy was developed. Vipassana is a practice of turning inward in order to gain insight into one's existence, the workings of cause and effect, and the destructive workings of mental biases.[19] Practicing Vipassana meditation awakens us to the impermanence of everything, including our own impermanence. As we become familiar with that awareness, we also become aware of the futility of entitlement, pettiness, holding grudges, and other negative emotions. Vipassana raises our awareness of the damage that both craving and aversion do to us.[20] In the next chapter, we will elaborate on this meditation technique.

3. *Practice of interbeing.* Thich Nhat Hanh, one of the world's most revered and well-known Buddhist monks, coined the term *interbeing* and explained it this way:

> "If you are a poet, you will see clearly that there is a cloud floating in this sheet of paper. Without a cloud, there will be no rain; without rain, the trees cannot grow; and without trees, we cannot make paper. The cloud is essential for the paper to exist. If the cloud is not here, the sheet of paper cannot be here either. So we can say that the cloud and the paper inter-are. 'Interbeing' is a word that is not in the dictionary yet, but if we combine the prefix 'inter-' with the verb 'to be,' we have a new verb, inter-be."[21]

Just like with Vipassana, the concept of interbeing is not intended from any religious or poetic angle, but from a pure realistic standpoint. When we take the time to think on our dependence on others, and how all we are is the collective input from so many factors, we awaken from the narrow mind-set of "I," "me," and "mine." Thanks to this realization, we no longer cling to things and end our suffering of attachment and aversion.

Critical Thinking

As indicated earlier in this chapter, our modern-day exposure to different ways of thinking and behaving in virtual and physical ways, through social networking and traveling, has tremendously elevated our collective ability to reconsider our thoughts, no longer take our current behavioral patterns for granted, and seriously consider the alternatives we encounter. Critical thinking could be defined as purposeful, self-regulatory judgment, resulting in interpreting, examining, evaluating, relating, and explaining the many considerations on which we base our judgment.[22] Critical thinking involves the quality of our thinking, and is much more than just decision-making, creative thinking, intuitive thinking, problem-solving, brainstorming, or out-of-the-box thinking.[23] It requires us to evaluate information, challenge our assumptions, consider and understand the context of a situation, analyze the arguments, and use metacognition,[24] which is the awareness and understanding of our own thought processes. Whether for our personal purposes or when related to our professional performance, critical thinking is a vital skill to nurture and improve. At the personal levels, critical thinking enhances our capacity to cope and become more flexible and creative in facing challenges and working toward solutions.[25] In workplaces, it is recommended to put together teams, consisting of members with diverging viewpoints, who can then work together toward a healthy consensus,[26] and, in the process, learn from one another. Today's work environments rely heavily on the ability of their members to engage in critical thinking in order to solve the ever-novel problems that emerge. Some have even described critical thinking as today's replacement of what technical knowledge was in the past.[27]

As can be concluded, critical thinking is crucial in our performance today. It always was, but as the pace of life has accelerated, emerging from a great quality into an absolute must. People who fail to question their current situation will never look for ways to improve their circumstances. Failure to engage in critical thinking equals failure to advance in life. Alex Pattakos, author of *Prisoners of Our Thoughts*, explains that human beings, in spite of their ability to think, are stuck with two major problems: fear and misconception. Our *fear* robs us from the courage to stray from a familiar path and embark on new avenues, especially if those are in unknown territory. Our *misconception* makes us think that we engage in critical thinking, but we actually continue to confine our thoughts to preset boundaries that have been instated by our culture or environment. Pattakos presents an example of a fly trapped in a room with closed doors and windows. Once it has found out that there is no way out here, the fly will start exploring other spaces in the house, in order to find an opening to escape. Human beings often fail to do that. We often just consider those options that fit within what we consider to be "acceptable" cultural, habitual, religious, psychological, or emotional boundaries. As a result, we may explore the "windows" in one room, but fail to try windows and doors in other rooms.[28] The diehard reality is, however, that we must step up our critical thinking skills in the fast-changing professional environment of today. Being a critical thinker is now everybody's job, not just the manager's or the CEO's. Some organizations, where critical thinking is the daily trend, have already proven their value to the world. Google, IKEA, Whole Foods, and Southwest Airlines are some examples of companies that continue to do well, regardless of the challenges of their times. That is because everyone in these companies is trained to think critically and come up with constructive ideas when needed.[29]

Wrapped into the acronym "THINK' the following activities can be used to enhance our critical thinking skills:

- *Traveling:* this was already discussed earlier in the chapter: Traveling exposes us to new environments and new ways, and challenges our existing beliefs and actions.
- *Holism:* As we advance in education, our left brain gets triggered by mathematical and other number-based challenges. This is the case, because, by

default, society places more value on jobs that require logical and analytical skills (accounting, economics, and finance, for example). By prioritizing logical and analytical skills, we neglect the equally important skills of intuition and thoughtfulness, which are the right-brain activities. Picking up a hobby that incites our right brain may, therefore, be a good idea. The arts are a great expression of right-brain activities, whether drawing, painting, sculpting, reading and writing, or dancing: the balance between left and right brain can be restored that way, and with that, the ability to think more critically.

- *Investigation:* This should be interpreted in the sense of self-inspection and reflection. A great start is to examine where our habits come from, and analyze whether they still make sense and are still useful to us today.
- *Nexus:* The need for connection has also amply been emphasized in this chapter. It is particularly due to networking events, whether online or in physical regards, and the massive access to news and other sources online, that we can learn so much more today than ever before.
- *Kindle:* This point reminds us to wake up from the sleepwalking life patterns and start shifting to mind-challenging activities. All of the four previous elements, Traveling, Holism, Investigation, and Nexus, are crucial in order to get ourselves into mental and physical action again and ignite a fire inside.

A simple, yet effective way to boost critical thinking at work is the five-why approach. This approach entails asking "why?" five times in order to get to the bottom of an issue. The five-why approach has its own flaws: asking why five times doesn't always lead to a deeper insight. Sometimes it can take us in perpetual circles. One possible way to solve this is to engage in more reflective questioning when we don't make any progress with the five-whys. The reflective questioning should consider (a) the exact issue; (b) the reasons; (c) ambiguous parts of the issue; (d) possible conflicts or assumptions, examination of the reasoning used so far to find out if there are any flaws; (e) potential rival causes that underlie the issue; (f) possible omission of critical information; and (g) possible conclusions to be drawn.[30]

Regardless of the strategy selected, enhancing our critical skills is imperative for our advancement in the world. It is also important in understanding where others come from, and developing a greater sense of understanding and empathy for ways that don't coincide with our own.

Emotional Intelligence

Emotional intelligence (EI or EQ), and spiritual intelligence (SQ) are believed to be intrinsic concepts in leadership of our times.[31] Goleman defines emotional intelligence as "the ability to rein in emotional impulses, to read another's innermost feelings and to handle relationships and conflict smoothly."[32] Mayer et al. explain it this way: "Emotional intelligence refers to an ability to recognize the meanings of emotion and their relationships, and to reason and problem-solve on the basis of them. Emotional intelligence is involved in the capacity to perceive emotions, assimilate emotion-related feelings, understand the information of those emotions, and manage them."[33] In simpler terms, EI is the ability to monitor our own and others' emotions, and use them as guides in what we say and do. EI encompasses four component abilities: the perception, use, understanding, and regulation of emotion.[34]

EI is considered to be a critical predictor for success at work.[35] When leaders fail to incorporate EI in their practices, they will have less empathy and social skills toward their employees, which can easily lead to employer–employee abuse, and end in increasing employee discontentment, with all its consequences.[36] As performance cycles accelerate in the workplace, the need for EI increases. The speedier a workplace is in its actions, the more vital it is to inspirational leadership with emotional intelligence and an empathy and understanding of the development needs of their staff.[37]

EI should also not be underestimated as a critical prompter of employees' creativity. While not all EI researchers agree that there is a relationship between EI and employee creativity, there is some merit to this notion: When EI is applied in work environments, others' opinions are encouraged and considered. Once this encouragement or consideration becomes apparent, those others will be more willing to share their insights and ideas, and feel more inspired to become more proactive and present creative options.[38] A recent study among 250 full-time employees at two public sector organizations in Bhutan supported the above assertion that EI is significantly related to employee creativity, especially when those employees have proactive personalities.[39] Another recent study among 88 Hispanic American professionals working in technical projects also showed a clear relationship between EI and project outcomes, leading to the recommendation to explore the possibilities of integrating EI in the employee development curriculum for project teams, and making it a routine part of employee development.[40] Yet another study, this time in India among 155 professionals in the information technology (IT) and manufacturing sector, found significant impact of leaders' EI on subordinates' levels of emotional attachment. The study underscored that emotionally intelligent leaders create and nurture emotional bonds between their organizations and employees.[41]

While a great quality, EI does not come naturally and spontaneously to people. Some don't have to do anything, and just have the skill to interact in an emotionally intelligent way, whereas others will need to work on the development of their EI. These are some ways that EI can be increased:

1. Reflect on your own emotions: how do you respond in multiple situations, such as when someone is sad and in despair, when someone makes

you angry, when someone offends you by saying something rude, or when someone blames you unjustly? Reflecting on your reactions may enhance your perceptiveness and your future ways of responding to such situations.[42]

2. Ask others for their impressions of your behavior. Trusted and close people will be honest about this, and their perspectives may come as an eye opener about the ways you are perceived, even though you may have had an entirely different idea of your own responses. It is important to discuss specific circumstances and specific reactions from your side, so that you can evaluate more purposefully.[43]

3. Pay attention. After completing steps 1 and 2, you will have the opportunity to be more mindful of your emotions, and engage in self-reflection. This will bring you more in sync with your feelings.[44]

4. Give yourself some time. This particularly pertains to pausing before acting. Think before blurting out something or engaging in an action that you may later regret. By taking this precaution, you can make your life far less complicated and you can free yourself from having to apologize or carrying the burden of others being mad or hurt due to your careless behavior.[45]

5. Examine the reasons. In this case, the "reasons" pertain to our habit of refraining from showing empathy and compassion, even though we are aware of their importance in a relationship. Why do we do that? It seems that we often forget the feelings associated with bad circumstances, so it's hard for us to relate, even if we have actually experienced the same thing in the past. What may help is to ask ourselves why: why does another person feel the way he/she does? What may he/she be dealing with that you are unaware of? Why do you feel differently than him/her?[46]

6. Shift your guard for a learning mind-set: Rather than feeling offended when someone criticizes you, you could wonder what lesson you should learn from the experience. Criticism, while hard to take, emerges from truth, regardless of how it is presented. We always have a choice: if being criticized, we can get angry and let our emotions drain us, or we can step over our feelings and seek the lesson to be learned.[47]

7. Practice continuously. While there is no such thing as having total control over our emotions, we can observe them and improve in areas where our behavior used to be shortsighted, rude, or cold.[48]

Consciousness

With a number of disturbingly immoral business practices coming to light in the past two decades, the call for increased consciousness has increased. With this increased interest, there seems to also be some more receptivity to alternative ways of experiencing the world and, more importantly, our current circumstances.[49] Among growing numbers of global society members, there is a mounting quest for long-term solutions to recurring problems, related to dishonesty, self-centeredness, greed, and disregard for stakeholders, including the environment. Consciousness is a highly valuable quality to have and nurture, because it can change the way we perceive the world, shift our priorities into a more proper order, and thereby enhance the quality of our lives.

David Hawkins, who wrote several books on consciousness from a Western perspective, supports some of the insights he adopted from Eastern philosophies, claiming that one of the major aspects to be conscious about is causality: everything is interconnected with everything else, so our actions and their consequences should not be seen as independent instances. One mistake we often make is to try and discover direct lines between actions and reactions, but there is so much happening at any given time that an action today can be a reaction to something that happened long ago, and in a totally different context.[50] A mind-boggling insight Hawkins shares is that our motivation to act is driven by our level of consciousness. He rates the levels of consciousness as follows: shame (20), guilt (30), apathy (50), grief (75), fear (100), desire (125), anger (150), pride (175), courage (200), neutrality (250), willingness (310), acceptance (350), reason (400), love (500), joy (540), peace (600), and enlightenment (between 700 and 1,000).[51] He refers to these as *energy levels*. As one may discover, the energy levels from 200 on are more constructive in nature than the ones under 200. This means that any of the energy levels below 200 represents a negative motivation for the person driven by that action, as well as for those in his or her surroundings. The energy levels over 200 are positive, inspiring, and beneficial to the well-being of humanity. The message is clear: we should work on getting inspired by energy levels of 200 and over, rather than the ones below 200, because the outcome will always be more constructive, not only to us, but also to all those who are affected by our actions.[52] Hawkins also explains that 700 is about the top of normal human energy levels. Performance within an energy level that lies between 700 and 1000 entails that the person undertaking the action has released a sense of self and is driven by what can be considered a divine motivation.

In one of his other books, Hawkins explains that enlightenment is not impossible to attain, but that it requires self-examination, meditation, and a deep look into our personal motives.[53] He also shares two pieces of information regarding his view on humanity: on the negative side, he states that 85 percent of the human race still calibrates below the energy level of 200. On the positive side, however, he concludes that the average level of human consciousness today balances out to approximately 207. Hawkins explains that the problem with low consciousness or low energy levels can be attributed to ego. He explains that we all have a tendency to think of the ego as a unique "me" or "my," but egos are all functioning about the same, so there is nothing unique or personal about them. All egos, invariably, hold the traits of self-service, egotism, vanity, and deception, and focus on gain of position, possession, status, wealth, renown, praise, and control.[54] We can only outgrow this, if we are willing to evolve spiritually and guide ourselves to higher levels of consciousness. If we choose not to do that, then our performance will always be driven by motivations listed as energy levels below 200: shame, guilt, apathy, grief, fear, desire, anger, and pride. Yet, as we try to overcome our ego, we should be careful not to treat it as an enemy, because we needed it to gain the insights of having to overcome it. In that regard, our ego is useful and even necessary in cases of survival. It is just something we need to overcome, once we are aware of its workings and the consequences thereof.[55]

Shifting from the Western perspective to an Eastern context, it turns out that the notions of consciousness—how to attain it, and what the role of the ego is—are largely similar to what Hawkins explained in his books. Especially in Buddhist circles, where there is not necessarily a God to be addressed, but where the focus lies on human behavior toward improvement for all, the role of the "self" is deeply examined. Eastern spiritual traditions have long understood the problem with this "self" centeredness, and the damage it can bring to others. Consciousness is a major topic in Buddhist learning. It is believed to come forth from its own, existing even before birth, and continuing after death of a person.[56] Buddhist teaching maintains that consciousness depends on matter, sensation, perception, and mental formations and that it cannot exist independently of them.[57] The famous Buddhist monk Thich Nhat Hanh brings the message home in a strong way: "Our consciousness is eating all the time, day and night, and what it consumes becomes the substance of our life. We have to be very careful which nutriments we ingest."[58] Another famous Buddhist monk, the 14th Dalai Lama, identifies consciousness as an important aspect to spiritual growth. He explains that our consciousness enables us to make mental improvements and experience high realizations of our path. The Dalai Lama also claims that consciousness has no beginning and no end.[59]

In order to expand our consciousness, meditation can be helpful. It is important to keep in mind, however, that all our experiences feed our consciousness, so we should be mindful of what we expose ourselves to.

Reflection

In the previous sections, on mental models, critical thinking, emotional intelligence, and consciousness, the concept of reflection was embedded, mostly in the sense of reflection at a personal level. However, reflection doesn't stop at personal levels. In professional settings, there is as great a need to reflect as with individuals. Yet, as the pace of life increases, there seems to be little time left to reflect in workplaces. Demands are so immense, competition is so fierce, and change so fast, that we can barely keep up the pace without having to sit calmly and evaluate. Still, reflection has been proving its merit abundantly in recent years. Today, it is more widely accepted that taking time to reflect on our work improves job performance in the long run.[60] Routinely creating some space in our agenda to reflect can make a tremendous difference in our performance. People think and learn using two distinct types of processes: 1) Learning by doing, which allows us to get better as we gain experience; and 2) Reflective learning, which is often associated with decision-making.[61] It has become apparent that these two processes should be combined in order to ensure better output in the future, so not just mindlessly doing, but also regularly reflecting on what we do. In a test whereby 202 adults were divided into groups of a) mere action takers and b) groups of action followed by reflection, it turned out that those who also reflected in between their actions (groups b) ended up being about 18 percent more effective in their output. When this test was brought to the actual workplace, it turned out that the performance of people in groups "b" was even higher: 22.8 to 25 percent more than the group "a" members.[62]

Reflection is also important at strategic levels. So many corporate boards fail to take the time to reflect on the deeper purpose of their existence, and by refraining from doing so, lose sight of their direction or whether it still makes sense. Whenever there are gatherings, the foundational question begins with "how" rather than "why." "How" just assumes that the foundations are still appropriate and that we only need some momentary directions about implementing. "Why" runs much deeper, as it reflects on the entire purpose of an entity's existence. Once the "why" question has been asked (and answered), it may be useful to ask "what," thus questioning the means in use to accomplish the "why." It should be pointed out here that asking "what" after "why" leads to much deeper outcomes, because the very level of the contemplation has deepened. Once the "what" is clarified, a "which" may be in place to select the products, services, partners, and assets needed to achieve the most effective ways to reach the goal.[63]

In sum, reflection has been moving to the forefront of our attention, as we collectively start to understand that there is more to life than unremitting, yet mindless drive, and maximized profit, yet with a revolving door of disheartened people who decide to quit. Reflection is a great habit at any level. It enhances connectivity with others, and results in better insights that can lead to a more rewarding life. Here are some questions to ask by way of getting self-reflection started:[64]

1. Am I true to my core values and personal mission? It is important to formulate and keep a set of personal rules to live by.
2. Am I being a person others can feel respect for? This is a good moment to consider your behavior and think of ways to improve your attitude toward others.
3. Am I respecting my body in a proper way? Especially when we age, this is a critical question in remaining healthy and physically fit.
4. Am I living up to the standards I have set for others? Here is where you examine whether you are fair and forthcoming to others, and don't lead them astray.
5. Am I utilizing all my talents well? This can be a great question to explore talent avenues that you have so far left untapped.

6. Am I performing at my uppermost ability? This is where you evaluate whether you are maintaining the balance that keeps you happy and functional in the most optimal way, with inclusion of proper down time.

7. Am I giving my family and friends my most and my best? The more selective you are in spending time with people, the less worrisome this reflection will be: smaller circles of friends and relatives require less balancing than do large ones.

8. Am I doing things that are worthy of being done? This is where you may look into whether you are working toward leaving the legacy you would like to leave.

9. Am I making a positive impact on the world? This ties well into the Buddhist value *ahimsa* or no-harming. Reflecting on your impact on the world may bring many important behaviors to light that you either want to augment or change.

10. Am I on the proper path to my preferred future? We have more of our future in our hands than we believe. Reflecting about it, and then working diligently toward it, is a major aspect of achieving it (Figure 5.1).[65]

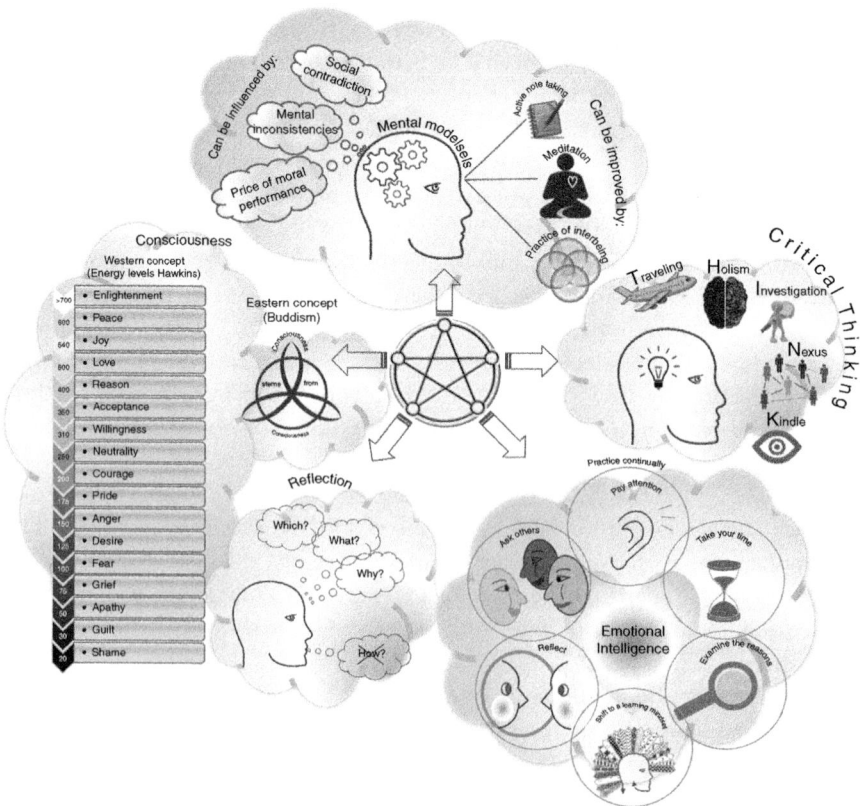

FIGURE 5.1 Doing the Right Thing—Five Critical Characteristics.

Case 5.1 Reflective Innovation: Airbnb

In 2007, two young graduates from the Rhode Island School of Design were out of jobs and facing an increase in their rent. Living in San Francisco at the time, they thought hard about a possible way to get out of their precarious situation while creating value for others. One of them, Joe Gebbia, came up with the idea of renting out airbeds in their apartment for participants in a major upcoming conference from the Industrial Design Society of America. The surrounding hotels were already booked, so their chance of succeeding with their idea was reasonable. Gebbia and his roommate, Brian Chesky, created a website called "AirBed & Breakfast," and the foundation was laid for a soon-to-become multi-billion-dollar venture: Airbnb.

The first two years were challenging: funding for the new company was not easy to find, even after Gebbia and Chesky attracted a third cofounder, Nathan Blecharczyk, in early 2008. Eventually, Gebbia met Paul Graham, a programmer, writer, investor, and the founder of Y Combinator, a startup incubator that had already successfully funded some very successful startups such as Dropbox, Stripe, and Reddit. Graham gave the young trio their first round of seed funding in 2009.[66]

As Airbnb started taking off, it turned out that the world was ready for something that used to be considered crazy and dangerous in the not-so-far past: a person-to-person home and apartment rental option. Yet, Airbnb does exactly that: its business is to connect travelers with local residents who are willing to rent extra rooms by the night. In 2014, the company closed a large new funding round, catapulting the three cofounders into billionaire status. Each of the cofounders holds a personal stake of just over 15 percent in Airbnb, and the three men prefer simple living over grandeur. As they were ranked as some of the world's youngest billionaires, Gebbia and Chesky still lived in the same modest apartment in which they started the company, while Blecharczyk sill held on to his bike as his transportation mode to and from work.[67]

By 2014, Airbnb had become a leader in the share economy, providing lodging for more than 25 million guests, [68] expanded to provide services in more than 30,000 cities across 160 countries, covering 600,000 listings used by millions of guests, with a record of 250,000 guests per night and a guest checking in somewhere on the globe every 2 seconds![69] The company has a current value of more than $25 billion. Gebbia alone is worth $3.3 billion, and he has not even hit the age of 40! The fascinating gist of this story is that it has a Cinderella sensation to it: rising from financial modesty to extreme wealth in less than a decade. What did it take for Airbnb to become such a success? It definitely took critical thinking: looking at reality from a lens that was untainted by the fog of the status quo.

Gebbia and his cofounders realized that they had to establish a paradigm shift, and that they would have to sell "trust," an intangible product that is challenging to instill in others. This means that they also had to change a shift in people's mental models of lodging and the aspect of letting strangers into their homes. Gebbia and Chesky used their design education to create a reputation system for hosts and guests. They engaged in studies to find out where the best trust synergies could be found. They discovered that people trust those who resemble them, in age, ethnicity, culture, etc., while they have a tendency to mistrust those who are different. Yet, in such cases, recommendations from others were helpful. So, they built a system of reviews: the more recommendations a person received, the higher a person's reputation became and the more this person was trusted as a host.[70]

Airbnb is a popular company: in 2016 the company received 50,000 applications for just 300 job openings! In the past years, the leaders have learned some valuable lessons, such as making sure to treat job applicants in an organized and respectful manner. In the early years, Airbnb was troubled by a rather messy HR process, leading to applicants often turning down the opportunity when they finally received a job offer. Gebbia took on the design of this important reputational factor, reintroducing concepts of timeliness, clarity, and courtesy, leading the company to a tremendous improvement in that regard.[71]

Today, nine-year-old Airbnb manages more than two million properties in 191 nations, is financially stable, and is a target of tax investigations because the smart cofounders are making sure that they take advantage of any tax break they can get worldwide.[72] Meanwhile, however, the owners have moved into philanthropy, and joined the pledge that was established in 2010 by Bill and Melinda Gates, to give away more than 50 percent of their wealth, either during their lifetime, or after their passing. The Airbnb founders have focused on the areas where they want to donate: children, transformative ideas, and young entrepreneurial initiatives, so that more great ideas can come to fruition.[73]

Questions

1. In what ways is Airbnb different from 20th-century companies?
2. Earlier in the chapter, we discussed mental models, critical thinking, emotional intelligence, consciousness, and reflection. Try to explain how Airbnb's leaders exert these characteristics.
3. In order to make the concept of Airbnb successful, the founders had to work on a paradigm shift. Explain this.
4. Do you think the leaders of Airbnb are doing the right thing? Please explain your reasoning.

Summary

- Since the Internet became a widespread commodity, the human race has grown more aware of developments, challenges, victories, and disasters in other parts of the world. Our circle of concern has expanded, and so has our circle of influence.
- The way 21st-century businesses run was unforeseeable and definitely incomprehensible 40 or 50 years ago. The entire platform has shifted. The future belongs to those who dare to change the way we think, behave, and see the world. IQ has taken over where dollars used to have the last word.
- People travel more today than they did before. About 3.8 billion airline travelers were registered for 2016—almost half of the world population at that time.
- Some important human characteristics that have been on the rise in the first decade of this century are:
  - *Mental models:* These are our internal pictures of how the world works. In striving to do the right thing, it is important to understand how mental models work and what they do: they are represented in the stories we believe and the assumptions we hold. Some of the social factors that can shape our mental models are:
    - Social Contradiction: Most human communities are full of contradictory forces.
    - Mental Inconsistencies: Our paradigms shift as we mature.
    - The Price of Moral Performance: This often manifests itself in the business world. Doing the right thing usually costs much more and requires a tremendous amount of effort, compared to risking a fine.

      Some suggestions for proactive measures to change damaging mental models are:
    - Active Note-Taking: This requires actively taking notes of your beliefs.
    - Meditation: Vipassana meditation is a practice of turning inward in order to gain insight into one's existence, the workings of cause and effect, and the destructive workings of mental biases.
    - Practice of Interbeing. When we take the time to think of our dependence on others, and how all we are is the collective input from so many factors, we awaken from the narrow mind-set of "I," "me," and "mine."
  - *Critical thinking:* This requires us to evaluate information, challenge our assumptions, consider and understand the context of a situation, analyze the arguments, and use metacognition, which is the awareness and understanding of our own thought processes. Critical thinking is crucial in our performance today. The following activities ("THINK") can be used to enhance our critical thinking skills:
    - Traveling: exposes us to new environments and new ways, and challenges our existing beliefs and actions.
    - Holism: restores the balance between our two mental hemispheres.

- Investigation: should be interpreted in the sense of self-inspection and reflection.
- Nexus: is particularly due to networking events, whether online or in physical regards.
- Kindle: reminds us to wake up from the sleepwalking life patterns and start shifting to mind-challenging activities.
- *Emotional intelligence:* EI is the ability to recognize the meanings of emotion and their relationships, and to reason and problem-solve on the basis of them. EI is considered to be a critical predictor for success at work. When leaders fail to incorporate EI in their practices, they will have less empathy and social skills toward their employees. EI is also a critical prompter of employees' creativity. These are some ways that EI can be increased:
  - Reflect on your own emotions: how do you respond in multiple situations?
  - Ask others for their impressions of your behavior. Trusted and close people will be honest about this.
  - Pay attention. Be more mindful of your emotions, and engage in self-reflection.
  - Give yourself some time. Think before blurting out something or engaging in an action that you may later regret.
  - Examine the reasons. Why do we refrain from showing empathy and compassion, even though we are aware of their importance in a relationship?
  - Shift your guard for a learning mind-set. Try to learn a lesson from criticism rather than to get offended.
  - Practice continuously.
- *Consciousness:* Among growing numbers of global society members, there is a mounting quest for long-term solutions to recurring problems related to dishonesty, self-centeredness, greed, and disregard for stake-holders, including the environment. Consciousness is a highly valuable quality to have and nurture, because it can change the way we perceive the world, shift our priorities into a more proper order, and thereby enhance the quality of our lives. Our motivation to act is driven by our level of consciousness. According to David Hawkins:
  - Consciousness or energy levels can be rated as follows: shame (20), guilt (30), apathy (50), grief (75), fear (100), desire (125), anger (150), pride (175), courage (200), neutrality (250), willingness (310), acceptance (350), reason (400), love (500), joy (540), peace (600), and enlightenment (between 700 and 1,000).
  - 85 Percent of the human race still calibrates below the energy level of 200.
  - The average level of human consciousness today balances out to approximately 207.

Eastern spiritual traditions have long understood the problem with this "self" centeredness, and the damage it can bring to others. Consciousness is a major topic in Buddhist learning. It is believed to come forth from its own, existing even before birth, and continuing after death of a person.

In order to expand our consciousness, meditation can be helpful. It is important to keep in mind, however, that all our experiences feed our consciousness, so we should be mindful of what we expose ourselves to.

- *Reflection:* Reflection happens at the personal and professional level. In professional settings, there is just as much of a need to reflect as with individuals. Studies have proven that working groups who also reflected in between their actions ended up being about 18 percent more effective in their output than those who worked without reflection.

Reflective Questions

1. The chapter suggests that we should try to expand our circle of influence to meet our circle of concerns. What are some ways in which you could do that?
2. Consider a mental model that you have been carrying for a long time, but would like to change. Share this mental model, as well as the ways you plan to go about changing it.
3. Consider one of your less constructive habits. Now, apply the "five whys" approach to it. Share your answers and your conclusion.
4. How do you think EI can be helpful in leadership situations?
5. Review Hawkins's energy levels: which energy levels motivate you mostly into action? How do you feel about Hawkins's classification of this energy level?

Notes

1 Covey, S. (2013). *The 7 Habits of Highly Effective People: Powerful Lessons in Personal Change.* New York: Simon & Schuster.
2 Ibid.
3 Griffin, M. (June 10, 2015). Disruption, innovation and reinventing business: The death of the 20th-century corporation. CIO. www.cio.com/article/2933413/it-strategy/the-death-of-the-20th-century-corporation.html
4 *Airlines to Welcome 3.6 Billion Passengers in 2016* (December 6, 2012). IATA. www.iata.org/pressroom/pr/Pages/2012-12-06-01.aspx
5 Air Transport Action Group: Facts and figures. (December 31, 2016). ATAG. www.atag.org/facts-and-figures.html
6 Negroni, C. (January 6, 2016). How much of the world's population has flown in an airplane? Some numbers, and some guesses. *Air Space Magazine.* www.airspacemag.com/daily-planet/how-much-worlds-population-has-flown-airplane-180957719
7 Ibid.
8 Senge, P. M. (1992). Mental models. *Planning Review 20*(2), 4.

9 Ibid.
10 Norman, D. (1983). *Some observations on mental models.* In Gentner, D. & Stevens, A. L. (eds), *Mental Models (Cognitive Science Series).* Hillsdale, NJ: Lawrence Erlbaum Associates.
11 Ward, K. (2012). Mental models: The key to reality-based decisions. King of Prussia, PA: *HRDQ.*
12 Marques, J. (2014). Leadership and mindful behavior: Action, wakefulness and business. New York: Palgrave-MacMillan.
13 Ward, Mental models: The key to reality-based decisions.
14 Marques, J. (2013). From caterpillar to butterfly: Shifting gears from selfish gain to shared growth. *Interbeing* 6(1), 7–14, 47.
15 Ibid.
16 Ibid.
17 Ibid.
18 Spodek, J. (November 2013). *ReModel: Create Mental Models to Improve Your Life and Lead Simply and Effectively.* New York: Saturday Morning Hudson River Press.
19 Snelling, J. (1991). *The Buddhist Handbook: The Complete Guide to Buddhist Schools, Teaching, Practice, and History.* Rochester, Vermont: Inner Traditions International.
20 Marques, Leadership and mindful behavior: Action, wakefulness and business.
21 Thich Nhat Hanh (August 2005). *The Heart of Understanding: Commentaries on the Prajnaparamita Heart Sutra.* Berkeley, CA: Parallax Press, 3.
22 Hobaugh, C. F. (2010). Critical thinking skills: Do we have any? Critical thinking skills of faculty teaching medical subjects in a military environment. *U.S. Army Medical Department Journal,* (10/12), 48–62.
23 Ibid.
24 Cotter, E. M., & Tally, C. (2009). Do critical thinking exercises improve critical thinking skills? *Educational Research Quarterly* 33(2), 3–14.
25 Sawin, G. (2004). General semantics as critical thinking: A personal view. *et cetera* 61(2), 238–242.
26 Natale, S. & Ricci, F. (2006). Critical thinking in organizations. *Team Performance Management* 12(7/8), 272–277.
27 Schott Karr, S. (2009). Critical thinking: A critical strategy for financial executives. *Financial Executive* 25(10), 58–61.
28 Pattakos, A. (December 29, 2010). The wisdom of futility: Are you trying to break through a closed window? *The Huffington Post.* www.huffingtonpost.com/alex-pattakos/the-fly-and-the-window_b_801414.html.
29 Marques, J. (2012). Moving from trance to think: Why we need to polish our critical thinking skills. *International Journal of Leadership Studies* 7(1), 87–95.
30 Ayad, A. (2010). Critical thinking and business process improvement. *Journal of Management Development,* 29(6), 556–564.
31 Kubicek, M. (2005). Meaningful management. *Training Magazine,* (7), 10–11.
32 Goleman, D. (1998). The emotionally competent leader. *The Healthcare Forum Journal* 42(2), 36.
33 Mayer, J. D., Caruso, D. R. and Salovey, P. (1999). Emotional intelligence meets traditional standards for an intelligence. *Intelligence* 27(4), 267.
34 Mayer, J. D., & Salovey, P. (1997). What is emotional intelligence? In Salovey, P., & Sluyter, D. J. (Hrsg.) (Eds), *Emotional Development and Emotional Intelligence* (pp. 3–31). New York: Basic Books.
35 Goleman, D. (1995). *Emotional Intelligence.* New York: Bantam Books.
36 Karnes, R. (2009). A change in business ethics: The impact on employer–employee relations. *Journal of Business Ethics* 87(2), 189–197.
37 Mill Chalmers, W. (2010). Training to survive the workplace of today. *Industrial and Commercial Training* 42(5), 270–273.

38 Caruso, D. R., & Salovey, P. (2004). The Emotionally Intelligent Manager: *How to Develop and Use the Four Key Emotional Skills of Leadership.* San Francisco, CA: Jossey-Bass.

39 Jafri, M. H., Dem, C., & Choden, S. (2016). Emotional intelligence and employee creativity: Moderating role of proactive personality and organizational climate. *Business Perspectives & Research 4*(1), 54–66.

40 Trejo, A. (2016). Project outcomes improved by emotional intelligence. *Business Perspectives & Research 4*(1), 67–76.

41 Bhalerao, H., & Kumar, S. (2016). Role of emotional intelligence in leaders on the commitment level of employees: A study in information technology and manufacturing sector in India. *Business Perspectives & Research 4*(1), 41–53.

42 Bariso, J. (April 11, 2016). How to increase your emotional intelligence: A short guide to start making emotions work for you, instead of against you. *INC.com.* www.inc.com/justin-bariso/how-to-increase-your-emotional-intelligence.html.

43 Ibid.

44 Ibid.

45 Ibid.

46 Ibid.

47 Ibid.

48 Ibid.

49 Marques, J. J. (2012). Consciousness at work: A review of some important values, discussed from a Buddhist perspective. *Journal of Business Ethics 105*(1), 27–40.

50 Hawkins, D. R. (1995). *Power vs. force: The hidden determinants of human behavior.* Carlsbad, CA: Hayhouse, Inc.

51 Ibid.

52 Ibid.

53 Hawkins, D. R. (2003). *I: Reality and Subjectivity.* West Sedona, AZ: Veritas Publishing.

54 Hawkins, D. R. (2001). *The Eye of the I: From Which Nothing Is Hidden.* West Sedona, AZ: Veritas Publishing.

55 Hawkins, D. R. (2006). *Transcending the Levels of Consciousness.* West Sedona, AZ: Veritas Publishing.

56 Wallace, B. A. (2001). *Buddhism with an Attitude: The Tibetan Seven-Point Mind Training.* Ithaca, NY: Snow Lion Publications.

57 Rahula, W. (1959). *What the Buddha Taught.* New York: Grove Press.

58 Thich Nhat Hanh (1998). *The Heart of the Buddha's Teaching: Transforming Suffering into Peace, Joy, and Liberation.* New York: Broadway Books, 36.

59 The Dalai Lama. (1995). *The World of Tibetan Buddhism.* Boston: Wisdom Publications.

60 Nobel, C. (May 5, 2014). Reflecting on work improves job performance. *Working Knowledge—Harvard Business School.* http://hbswk.hbs.edu/item/reflecting-on-work-improves-job-performance.

61 Ibid.

62 Ibid.

63 Haque, U. (November 24, 2010). Making room for reflection is a strategic imperative. *Harvard Business Review.* https://hbr.org/2010/11/reflection-items-not-action-it.

64 Daum, K. (November 21, 2014). The power of self reflection. Sometimes, you need to just stop and ponder. Here are some insights to get you started. *INC.com.* www.inc.com/kevin-daum/the-power-of-self-reflection.html.

65 Ibid.

66 Joe Gebbia, Airbnb. *Business Insider.* January 3, 2017, www.businessinsider.com/23-americans-who-are-changing-the-world-2016-3/#james-song-faircap-partners-8.

67 Konrad, A., & Mac, R. (March 20, 2014). The little black book of billionaire secrets: Airbnb cofounders to become first sharing economy billionaires as company nears

$10 billion valuation. Forbes. www.forbes.com/sites/alexkonrad/2014/03/20/airbnb-cofounders-are-billionaires/#da7d23e41ab2.

68 Anders, G. (May 6, 2015). Tired of recruiting's broken image, Airbnb rewrites the playbook. *Forbes*. www.forbes.com/sites/georgeanders/2015/05/06/airbnbs-5-star-recruiting-twist-the-competitive-power-of-nice/#28665947d07e.

69 Konrad, A., & Mac, R.

70 Helft, M. (February 16, 2016). The little black book of billionaire secrets: How Airbnb used design to break through its biggest challenge. *Forbes*. www.forbes.com/sites/miguelhelft/2016/02/16/how-airbnb-used-design-to-break-through-its-biggest-challenge/#52830b372886.

71 Anders, G.

72 Cave, A. (December 31, 2016). The little black book of billionaire secrets: Airbnb comes of age and causes a tax investigation. *Forbes*. www.forbes.com/sites/andrewcave/2016/12/31/airbnb-comes-of-age-and-causes-a-tax-investigation/#54b8e57f725c.

73 Gallagher, L. (June 1, 2016). Airbnb cofounders join Buffett and Gates's 'Giving Pledge.' *Fortune*. http://fortune.com/2016/06/01/airbnb-cofounders-join-buffett-and-gates-giving-pledge/?iid=sr-link2.

6

DEFINING AND POLISHING OUR MORAL COMPASS

Abstract

This chapter will present an overview of various theories and practices that can enhance reflection and, subsequently, consciousness as a means toward developing and polishing our moral compass. Mindfulness meditation and several additional positive psychology-based practices will be discussed. The global context and cross-cultural issues will be observed within the discussion.

A Plethora of Moral Considerations

Formulating a moral compass is not an easy task if you plan to evaluate and choose from existing moral theories. First and foremost, there is such an abundance of moral theories, and secondly, the more you review them, the less chance there is that you will end with a solid view on your own moral stance. In Chapter 2 we reviewed some of the most frequently taught moral theories of our times: Universalism, Utilitarianism, the Golden Rule, virtue ethics, and the concept of ethical pluralism. In this introductory part to Chapter 6, we will review some different classifications of moral theories, in order to place it all into a broader scope.

Inasmuch as some moral scholars are telling us that we should adhere to one particular moral framework, real life teaches us something different. Life is a mosaic of circumstances and contexts, making it practically impossible to draw one hard line in every situation. Let us first try to demonstrate that by partially summarizing a dated, yet still adequate, and broadly overarching overview of moral theories of the 20th century by John Hospers.[1]

- *Meta-ethics* explores the status, foundations, and scope of moral values, properties, and words. Rather than examining acts that are moral or immoral, meta-ethics focuses on the concept of morality itself. In other words, rather than questioning whether doing this is right or whether that is, meta-ethics question what "right" should look like, because this is the foundational concept behind further judgment.

- *Ethical non-naturalism* is a meta-ethical view that presumes that ethical statements express propositions. Some of these propositions are true. The way these propositions are made true is by objective features of the world, independent of human opinion. As an example, "goodness" is a typical nonnatural property, because it cannot be described through other terms or through shapes.[2]

- *Ethical naturalism* is a meta-ethical view that also presumes that ethical statements express propositions. Some such propositions are true. However, those propositions are made true by objective features of the world, independent of human opinion. Ethical naturalism holds that the meanings of these ethical sentences can be expressed as natural properties without the use of ethical terms.[3]

- *Ethical emotivism* is a meta-ethical view that presumes that ethical statements do not express propositions but emotional attitudes. In other words, ethical emotivism is a view that people use ethical terms not to refer to their ostensible objects (people and actions), but rather to express certain attitudes toward them and to attempt to evoke those attitudes in others.[4] On basis of that, it is sometimes also referred to as the *hurrah/boo theory.*

Normative ethics, on the other hand, considers ethical action, which explains why it is also referred to as *theories of conduct.* It focuses on whether or not something is right, just, or responsible, thus assuming that there is a common understanding of what "right," "just," or "responsible" look and feel like.

- *Ethical egoism* is a normative ethical stance that presumes that each person should act in such a way as to promote his or her own self-interest (usually long-term self-interest).[5] It is considered a *consequentialist theory.* It differs from psychological egoism, which claims that people can only act in their self-interest. As a moral viewpoint, ethical egoism has a long history. Unlike what some people think, ethical egoism should not be confused with blatant selfishness, as it does not promote the mind-set of harming the interests and well-being of others when making moral decisions. Ethical egoism also doesn't specifically mean that a person should always do what she or he wants to do, because in the long run our desires can be detrimental to ourselves, and this should be seriously considered in making moral decisions within this stance. Arguably the most important guideline to take away from ethical egoism may be that a person should never, under any circumstances, act contrary to one's own self-interest.

- *Utilitarianism* (also considered a *consequentialist theory,* and earlier discussed in Chapter 2) in its simplest form is explained as John Stuart Mill's "the greatest happiness for the greatest number." Other sources have explained

Utilitarianism as acting to maximize intrinsic good, thus omitting happiness as the only form of "good" to strive for. *Rule Utilitarianism*, as opposed to "Act Utilitarianism, prescribes that we should act in accordance with the *rule of conduct* (and not the act) that delivers the most desirable consequences. Rule Utilitarianism emerged in the second part of the 20th century, and has received criticism from those who feel that, when it comes to implementation, it still boils down to Act Utilitarianism.[6] Utilitarianism has also been criticized on several foundations, such as the two below:

1. The foundation of what makes a group of people happy. If, for instance, killing someone would make the greatest number of people happy, would that then be a morally responsible act? According to the utilitarian view it would.
2. Continuous adherence to the utilitarian approach would make for a very unsatisfying life, because every person would continuously have to engage in actions that would create the greatest good for the greatest number, which means, that we would all have to forego our personal pleasures.[7]

- *Deontological theories* (of which *Universalism* was earlier discussed in Chapter 2) differ from consequentialist theories in that they don't base the rightness of an action on its consequences, but rather on its face value. Universalism, Immanuel Kant's theory, presumes that we should act in such a way that the maxim of our action could become a universal law. In other words, what is right should always be considered right, and what is wrong should always be considered wrong, without exceptions. Since lying is considered an immoral act, we should therefore never lie, regardless of the consequences of telling the truth. Kant further dictated that we should treat everyone as an end onto themselves and not as a means toward any end. In other words, we should respect people for themselves and not for what they can do for us. Universalism has also been criticized on several foundations, such as the two below:

1. Moral judgments may not always be universalizable, which means that what is wrong in one society may not be considered wrong in another.
2. Moral behavior is not necessarily based on general rules or reason, but on human nature and his/her judgment within the realm of the moment.[8]

- *Rights* is not necessarily an ethics theory, but can be critical in ensuring that moral decisions are made. The very implementation of some ethical theories may open potential doors for rights violation. We have all heard of techniques (such as wiretapping or torture strategies) that could help solve heinous crimes, but that are not allowed in court because they violate human rights. A telling example can be found within the Utilitarian theory: if an innocent person is incarcerated to send a strong message and stop a crime wave, then the aim might be achieved, and many people might be happy, but this person's rights have been desecrated.[9] Considering the aspect of rights is, therefore, an important support aspect in "mindful" moral behavior. The fact that there are so many rights classifications (e.g., legal, moral, specific, and general rights) underscores the need to observe them within the scope of every moral theory.[10]

- *Justice* is yet another concept that can critically support or complement the interpretation of ethical theories. In a case of one person's death, which would benefit many others, the concept of justice can be a determinant in ensuring that "the greatest good for the greatest number" gets implemented in a conscious and fair way. Justice distinguishes itself from rights, because there are many unfair actions that do not violate anyone's rights, such as leaving all assets to one of your children, while completely excluding another.
- *Individual justice* pertains to the treatment of an individual.
- *Comparative justice* is the application of justice in relation or comparison to others. If, for instance, a person is receiving a deserved penalty for an offense, while two others who have committed the same offense are unpunished, then there may be individual justice, but there is no comparative justice.[11]

It is important to realize that the concise overview of ethical theories and their classification is incomplete. However, it provides an idea to the reader how diverse and complex ethical theories, and more specifically, developing a personal moral compass on basis of these theories, can be.

Positive Psychology

Positive Psychology studies the strengths that enable us to thrive, whether as individuals or in communities. Positive Psychology presumes that people have a foundational desire to lead meaningful and fulfilling lives, to cultivate what is best within themselves, and to enhance their experiences of love, work, and play.[12] To put it in the simplest possible way: Positive Psychology explores what makes life worth living.[13] As a study, Positive Psychology seeks to establish scientific evidence focused on optimizing well-being so that people can move beyond mere functioning to thrive, prosper, and flourish in life.[14]

Seph Fontane Pennock compared seven definitions and found that the following elements appear most often throughout the terms used to describe Positive Psychology: flourishing, meaning, strengths, optimal functioning, and other people (or relationships). Pennock's own take on this concept is, "Positive Psychology studies what is going right with the human mind and behavior and how to foster these types of well-being on both the macro-, group- and individual-level."

In describing the origins of Positive Psychology, Pennock explains that, for the longest time, studies have been focusing on all the things that were wrong with people, resulting in the discovery and treatment of a wide range of problems. Finally, as the 21st century set in, a team of psychology enthusiasts decided to focus on the entire opposite of studies done till then, and try to define what is right with humanity. By focusing on that, a number of human strengths started surfacing, and strategies were developed to increase people's wellbeing.[15]

The reason why we include positive psychology in this book, then, is because it pertains to a movement of finding our inner best, improving our own performance and experience, and in doing so, becoming more satisfied, contented human beings. It is generally established that happy people have a greater preference to help enhance happiness in others than unhappy people. So, in a sense, Positive Psychology and its effects can be instrumental in spreading a positive vibe among humanity, thus positively influencing our individual and collective acts, toward greater happiness of all life on earth.

Positive Psychology aims to augment our strengths and improve our weaknesses. While it is not intended to disregard problem-focused psychology, it does aim to complement and extend this line of study. Positive Psychology acknowledges good and bad in life as genuine, equal entities; it doesn't consider good to be the absence of bad, so good life should not be perceived as the absence of disorders, but embraced as a genuine possibility.[16]

Through the study of Positive Psychology, a number of ancient, yet long repressed, facts resurfaced. Christopher Peterson, one of the prominent scholars of Positive Psychology, lists the following:

- Happiness comes forth from good things in life, and has an upward spiral effect: happy, satisfied people find life more fulfilling and, in turn, encounter more fulfillment as well in their activities. They are also generally healthier and live longer lives.
- Most people are happy and resilient. If we nurture our happiness and build our character strength, as well as good relationships, then we will be better able to weather setbacks and disappointments.
- Crisis situations reveal our character.
- In most human lives, other people, religious views, and engaging work are important contributors to meaning in life.
- Money is not a great contributor to well-being and can only bring happiness when it is spent on other people.
- There is more life satisfaction to be gained from human flourishing than from self-indulgence.
- The emergence of Positive Psychology also underscored the fact that we should consider the heart even more than the head, which implies that it is important to care, and not only to engage in critical thinking.
- A great sense of satisfaction is gained by maintaining a decent balance between autonomy (being self-sufficient), competency, and feeling connected to others. Most importantly, living a good life is a virtue that can be taught. This is important, as it implies that we don't necessarily have to win the genetic lottery to be a happy person.
- People can be happy under different life circumstances if they choose to be.[17]

The trend of good things triggering other good things can be found in the fact that Positive Psychology has so far led to some interesting paradigm shifts in some important business fields. Just as Positive Psychology advocates are calling to shift the mind-set from studying the human psyche from a negative angle into looking at it from a positive side, so are financial planning advocates now describing an evolution from the traditional way of meeting needs to get by financially and avoid getting in trouble, to maintaining financial stability so that not just financial security can be achieved, but even financial flourishing.[18]

Martin Seligman, another pioneer of Positive Psychology, engaged in longitudinal studies to find out what makes happy people happy.[19] Without underestimating or ignoring stark realities, Seligman chose to focus more on the positive side of living and performing. Seligman's particular focus in Positive Psychology is to help people acquire the skills to be able to deal with the stuff of life in ever fuller, deeper ways. He found that most satisfied, upbeat people are the ones that have identified their unique combination of "signature strengths." Seligman concluded that happiness has three dimensions to be cultivated:

1. *The Pleasant Life.*[20] We can attain a pleasant life by savoring basic life pleasures, such as companionship, the natural environment, and our physical needs. Seligman's strategy to help people attain a sense of "pleasance" in their lives is to invite them to (a) think constructively about the past, (b) gain optimism and hope for the future, and, as a result, (c) gain greater happiness in the present.

   (a) In working up a constructive mind about the past, Seligman suggests gratitude and forgiveness as the driving emotions. Rather than ventilating and being upset with our past, which jolts up unpleasant emotions, he leans toward East Asian traditions of calmly dealing with difficulties. By refraining from expressing negative emotions, people can learn to cope better with their stress and feel happier, in general.
   (b) Regarding the outlook on the future, Seligman suggests an outlook of hope and optimism.
   (c) In order to establish happiness in the present, Seligman relies on the constructive attitudes toward past and future, and subsequently recommends mindfulness as a happiness source in the present.

   As Peterson stated as well, people with positive emotions encounter more fortunate circumstances, such as longer life, better health, and a larger social network.

2. *The Good Life.*[21] We can achieve this by discovering our unique virtues and strengths, and utilizing them creatively to enhance our lives. This also enhances our self-esteem, because through identifying our unique virtues and strengths, we discover value internally. Seligman engaged in a cross-cultural study to create a measurement system for the human strengths.

Along with Christopher Peterson (cited earlier), he found six virtues that were valued in almost every culture: wisdom & knowledge, courage, love & humanity, justice, temperance, and spirituality & transcendence.

People who manage to exercise and cultivate their signature strengths and virtues on a daily basis are engaging in the good life, as they most likely experience gratification and happiness. Once this level is achieved, Seligman encourages moving upward to the next level.

3. *The Meaningful Life.*[22] We acquire this when we manage to employ our unique strengths to a purpose greater than ourselves. This gives the highest sense of meaning, and thus, fulfillment. To probe a bit deeper on this: we attain a meaningful life when we have identified and mastered our signature strengths, applied them well toward our own gratification, and now implement them to the betterment of others, in the process of which we forget our own personal gratification and get more fulfilled and gratified by the achievements of others. There is a sense of altruism in this level, because we surpass the personal stage of feeling rewarded, and rise to greater meaning by servicing others with our strengths.

    A nice example of a meaningful life can be found in the movie *Finding Forrester*, where a successful author (played by Sean Connery) lives a secluded life, even though his book is one of the most reserved ones in the local libraries, and his portrait adorns his school's library as one of the most revered authors of his era. When a young student from a challenged living environment happens to cross his path, Forrester takes the young man under his wing and teaches him the art of writing by helping him to find the passion within. The young man moves on to earn a writing scholarship, but the reward is mutual, because Forrester has also recaptured meaning in his own life through the sheer act of helping another: he spends his final years traveling, and, when he passes, leaves his belongings to his once-youthful protégé, who is now a successful man in his own right.

Buddhist Psychology

Buddhist psychology offers an understanding of a mental process that has developed over the past 2,500 years. It offers the West an important new perspective on human interaction and mental processes.[23] Within this stance, Buddhism should not be perceived as a religion, but as a way of living or a (constructive) psychological outlook on life. Buddhist teaching focuses on peace, drawing a mental bridge from internal peace with peace in the world: when a person feels peaceful inside, she or he will also strive for peace in the external world. Similar to Positive Psychology, Buddhist psychology focuses on happiness and constructive living, and on enhancing awareness that individual advancement should not happen at the expense of the community.[24]

Buddhist psychology teaches that our mind is the product of past impressions. These past impressions impacted our views, and shaped the way we perceive the world today (our mental models, see Chapter 5). This explains why some people are so driven by fear or are obsessed with certain outcomes that entirely consume their behavior. The conclusion that we, human beings, are a product of our exposures to past impressions, is not unique to Buddhist psychology. In fact, it is rather similar to the Western psychological view. But this is also where the similarity ends, because from that point onward, the Western approach teaches its followers to shift out of the negative self-impression and build up one's self-esteem, while the Buddhist approach suggests releasing the entire "self" structure, and becoming liberated from the ego deception. Becoming a balanced person, then, means being focused on the well-being of the world. This viewpoint may be of critical value, especially when we consider what the over-inflated sense of self has brought us in the late 20th century: so-called leaders who were so narcissistic and self-indulgent that they couldn't care less about the well-being of their workforce members or other stakeholders, and disastrous economic outcomes as a result of that.[25] Some have referred to Buddhist psychology as liberation psychology, because it aims to free its practitioners from a self-centered outlook on life, and focus more on a compassionate and respectful engagement with others. Buddhist psychology is not concerned with accumulating pleasant feelings, but with living more wholesome and creative lives to the benefit of the entire community. Buddhist psychology also instills awareness of karma, teaching us that we become what we do: rather than waiting for the right moment to do anything, we should start doing the right thing now, in order to enjoy a better life afterward.[26]

Two strategies often practiced in Buddhist circles to nurture a calmer, more constructive mind are Vipassana (see Chapter 5, and more below), and the Seven-Point Mind Training.

Vipassana

Vipassana is often associated with Buddhism, because it was the meditation in which Siddhartha Gautama (the Buddha) engaged when he attained enlightenment. Yet, many sources claim that this meditation practice was already in existence long before Gautama lived. The Buddha is therefore credited as one of the best-known ambassadors and role models of Vipassana meditation and its cleansing effects.[27] Vipassana is a mindfulness technique, aimed at gaining awareness of the emptiness or nonexistence of a self.[28] It is practiced by focusing on our breathing, and engaging in a body scanning practice in order to observe without judgment. This practice is sometimes explained as an "analytical examination of the nature of things that leads to insight into the true nature of the world—emptiness."[29]

Vipassana meditation is practiced individually and in special meditation centers throughout the world. It consists of four progressive steps:

1. *Slow scan:* At this stage, the meditator moves her attention slowly from the top of her head to the tip of her toe and back, part by part, piece by piece. As her mind moves from one body part to another, she merely observes, and abstains from senses of affection or aversion.
2. *Free flow sweep:* At this stage, the meditator sweeps her attention freely *en masse* (as a whole) upward and downward, where subtle sensations are experienced. Some special attention can be given to areas that delivered coarse sensations or areas that were initially not attentively explored.
3. *Spot check:* This is a brief exercise in which the meditator quickly takes her attention to any spot (as if touched by a finger), moving back and forth. It is recommended to try just four or five spots, and then resume the scan and sweep.
4. *Penetrating and piercing:* The above steps mainly involve scanning the external part of the body (skin area). The attention during these three steps is the kind of moving vertically, up and down. At the fourth stage, the meditator penetrates or pierces the body, which is an internal scanning process, in which she moves her attention inside her body, moving from left to right, right to left, front to back, and back to front. This is a highly advanced technique, mainly implemented by advanced practitioners who work under the close guidance of an experienced teacher.[30]

The idea is that, during the practice of the techniques above, the meditator remembers and gains greater awareness of the impermanence of each sensation she feels. Through this awareness, she will be able to reflect the reality that everything arises and passes: itches, pains, irritations, and more. Similarly, events and experiences in life arise and pass: jobs, life stages, relationships, even life itself: everything is impermanent.

Vipassana is not merely a theory or philosophy for any kind of intellectual entertainment or devotional game. It is practical, simple, nonsectarian, result-oriented, and insight-enhancing practice. Because of this last, and most important effect, Vipassana is also known as insight meditation. It is also this quality that underscores the importance of Vipassana as a practice of becoming a better human being, and generating a peaceful and harmonious atmosphere around oneself and others.[31]

The Seven-Point Mind Training

The seven-point mind training is far more detailed and complex than Vipassana meditation. It is a way of life, requiring an entire shift in the way we allow the mind to process information and perceive the world. In this section, we will provide a concise and incomplete overview of the seven points, as they were translated from a Buddhist scholar who lived in the 12th century, Geshe Chekawa Yeshe Dorje.[32]

Point 1: Train in the Preliminaries
The meaning of the preliminaries is to reflect on the four thoughts that turn the mind toward enlightenment. These thoughts are focused on:

1. The Difficulty of Finding a Human Birth: Buddhists believe in reincarnation, and also believe that rebirth can happen in many forms, as human or nonhuman. Humans have the ability to reason, but a human birth is not always guaranteed.
2. Death and Impermanence: Thinking about our own temporariness and future death is not easy, but can help us become more at ease with this reality.
3. The Law of Cause and Effect (Karma): Here we contemplate our ability to influence our karma through our behavior and actions.
4. The Inherent Tragedies of *Samsara* (rebirth): This pertains to awareness of our eternal flaws, as there will always be things that are not quite right.

Point 2: The Main Practice
At this stage, we focus on *bodhicitta*, which is an awakened mind. Here is where we focus on helping all living beings (humans and nonhumans) to achieve complete happiness. Bodhicitta can be ultimate or relative. In its ultimate stage, the effects of the practice are more structural. Life as a whole is seen as a dream, an illusion. In its relative stage, this practice focuses on kindhearted and unselfish interactions with others.

Point 3: Transforming Adversity (negative) into the Path of Enlightenment (positive):
At this point, we focus on the conversion of the negative things of the world to become positive. We practice kindness, empathy, gratitude, protection, and the ability to apply this transformation if we encounter it.

Point 4: Applying the Practice throughout the Whole of Life:
Here, the practitioner focuses on five positive powers or forces to apply in daily life:

1. The power of goodwill in all actions
2. The power of familiarization with goals
3. The power of virtuous actions and being selective with the seeds of our mind
4. The power of remorse and releasing ego
5. The power of aspiration, which devotes attention and effort to the wellbeing of all the living[33]

Point 5: The Measure of Mind Training

At this stage, we understand the central focus of all teachings, and evaluate whether we are able to apply what we have trained our mind in. We maintain a joyful attitude and are proficient, even when distracted.

Point 6: The Commitments of Mind Training

Here, we continue to train in three basic principles:

1. Always to work for the benefit of others
2. To be kind and generous and not act in pretentious ways
3. To be neutral and fair and not partial or biased

Captured in these principles are a large number of considerations toward a righteous life, such as giving up unhealthy food, maintaining a healthy detachment (not being too strongly attached), and refraining from being competitive, from telling lies, from lashing out, and from using others' misery as a foundation to your own happiness.

Point 7: The Precepts of Mind Training

At this point, we adopt a steady set of things to reject and to accept from here onward.

We should continue to be mindful in all our actions, be aware of and empathetic to the suffering in the world, start each day with good intentions and pursue those, practice patience in good and bad circumstances, and meditate toward betterment of all life.

Mindfulness

While we all have the ability to be mindful, it takes effort and practice to enhance this ability. When we are mindful, we observe our surroundings with more attention, and live more in the moment. Our mind has the tendency to wander, and most of the time it meanders to its two favorite places: the past or the future. Being mindful of the here-and-now requires mental discipline. Fortunately, there are multiple ways to sharpen our mindfulness. Meditation is one of the most popular ways to enhance mindfulness, and Vipassana is a popular and effective one.

Mindfulness is particularly represented in all Buddhist traditions. Some authors even claim that mindfulness is the fundamental stance of attention that underlies all streams of Buddhist meditation, and that the actual practice of mindfulness is always nested within a larger conceptual and practice-based ethical framework, oriented toward non-harming.[34] An interesting way of explaining mindfulness is as a state of acute awareness, attentiveness, and perceptiveness in everything going on around oneself, while minimizing the effects of self and ego.[35] We can become more mindful when we reduce egoistic barriers to perception, and realize the existence of our interpretive filters, biases, and other internal processes, such as wants, needs, and defensive tendencies.[36] In the workplace mindfulness could lead to many advantages for the worker, such as greater concentration; more joy in the moment; the ability to remain calm in turbulent situations; and a greater aptitude to link occurrences with one another, which will help to detect patterns. A mindful person actively engages in the present and is sensitive to context as well as perspective. A mindful approach is the foundation as well as the outcome of noticing new things.[37] Mindfulness can enhance self-acceptance, which, in turn, brings greater peace of mind. When we lack self-acceptance, we may experience emotional troubles, resulting in anger and depression.[38]

Mindful people view objects as well as situations from different perspectives, and they can shift their perspectives, based on the context of an issue.[39] Mindless people, on the other hand, rigidly adhere to a single perspective without considering contexts or perspectives.[40] They compartmentalize experiences, behaviors, objects, and other people into inflexible categories. They are trapped within a single perspective, and are incapable of shifting their viewpoints in order to see the other side of a situation, story, or experience. In other words, they lack respect for others' viewpoints, because they are so caught in their own.

Aside from the mindfulness techniques so far discussed, we can also practice mindfulness by:

1. Engaging in constructive dialogues with people who have proven to be creative thinkers. If you know them well and feel comfortable doing so, ask them what qualities they see in you. What skills and talents do they think you have? What areas can they envision you in? Keep in mind that any idea is worth considering.[41]
2. Look at yourself from the other side: what are employers looking for today? Do you represent that? How? Try to put yourself in the shoes of various people you meet. Perhaps their job, their activity, their direction, may spark an idea within you that is useful toward your next career.[42]

Consider the big picture. Take some distance. Step out of the daily routine, and go, if only for one day, to a place that inspires you. It does not have to be abroad, out of state, or even outside the city. Just a place you enjoy being. Places that break the daily rhythm also help open your mind and expand your horizons (Figure 6.1).[43]

Questions

1. Considering the moral compass presented in Figure 6.1, where would you classify Ursula Burns in the Positive Psychology layer: pleasant, good, or meaningful life? Please explain your choice.
2. Consider the Seven-Point Mind Training. Based on Case 6.1, list three areas in which Ursula Burns has succeeded so far in her life.

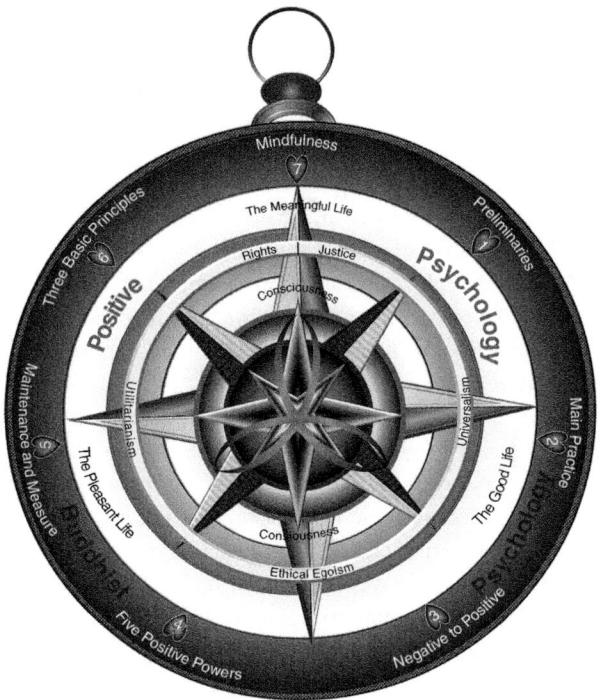

FIGURE 6.1   Polishing the Moral Compass.

Case 6.1 Maintaining Values at Xerox

From July 2009 to December 2016, Ursula Burns was the CEO of Xerox, an $11 billion American global corporation with more than 140,000 employees that sells document solutions and services, and document technology products in more than 160 countries. As Xerox CEO, Burns was the first black-American woman CEO to head a Fortune 500 company. In 2016, Xerox began a process of splitting the company into two independent companies—Xerox Corporation, comprising an $11 billion Document Technology and Document Outsourcing company, and Conduent Incorporated, a $7 billion company focused on business processing services.[44] When stepping down as CEO of Xerox in December 2016, Burns maintained the position of Chairman of the document company (Xerox Corporation). But what exactly was it that made this first-generation Panamanian immigrant so special, other than her ascent from very humble beginnings to leadership of a multibillion–dollar global corporation? It is the way she used her moral compass in decision-making.

Let's first do a quick review of the early beginnings: Burns was raised by a single parent, her mother, in a public housing project on the poor side of Manhattan. She grew up with all the perceived cultural downsides of her time: she was black, a girl, and poor. Her mother did not agree with the stereotypes, and sent Ursula to good schools. Soon, young Ursula found her educational passion: engineering. She landed at Brooklyn Polytechnic Institute, and focused on mechanical engineering as an explicit minority in an overly white male-dominated environment. The challenge was valuable in several ways: it led to her degree, and it made her more courageous and confident in the face of uncertainties and challenges.[45]

Burns started her career at Xerox in 1980 as a summer intern. She witnessed tough times with the company, and worked hard alongside previous CEO Anne Mulcahy to get the company moving forward again. Burns described her leadership and her decision-making techniques as focused on two main prongs: customers and innovation. To her, it has always been important to find out whether the customer was served well with a decision, and whether that decision was taking the company forward. She advocated parity in the organization, requesting employees to leave their department and position at the door when it was brainstorming time, and think about stakeholders: customers, competitors, coworkers, and shareholders.[46]

While she understood the importance of revenue, profits, and market share as corporate success measures, Burns made it very clear that ends did not necessarily justify means under her leadership. Her consistent aim was to do well while doing good: getting results while serving the community. When it came to making progress for Xerox, she focused on the "how" rather than on the "what": were the company's actions beneficial or destructive to the community? To the employees? To the environment? Was there also giving, or just taking? Burns was well aware that the morally responsible approach lasted much longer than a self-serving, damaging one.[47]

Integrity and values have always been high on her list of priorities. Her people focus was intact throughout her leadership career. She understood the importance of bringing talent, opportunity, and empowerment together to attain steady progress. As facilitative as her stance was toward hard and honest workers, equally hard was her stance when it came to immoral behavior. Those who disregarded the company's values were fired, even if they were star performers. This also explains why her focus was not on resumes and prior achievements, but on fit, character, and good intentions. She did not mind mistakes, as long as there was learning happening from them. She highly valued empathy and respect as critical components of emotional intelligence, and stressed that these qualities were signs of character strength rather than weakness.[48]

In her CEO days, Burns preferred input from as many sides as possible. She made it clear that she was not taking on the star CEO role as Steve Jobs did, but embracing the broad-input way. She also kept in mind the rocky road that Xerox had tread over the past decades, costing the company many customers, employees, and opportunities. She recalled the arrogance that caused customer loss, the self-centeredness that ignored employees' progress, and the unawareness that led to wrong decisions. Yet, she also remembered the turnaround days, under Mulcahy, where there was more management than leadership applied in order to get the company on track again. Once that was done, it was time for a strategy change, and that is when Burns stepped in as CEO, and shifted from a predominant managerial emphasis to a predominant leadership emphasis. This also brought about a shift from surviving to thriving.[49]

Burns feels that doing the right thing doesn't end with being kind to other people and ensuring responsible corporate performance, but it also entails being right to yourself. She recalled a time in the early 2000s when she was so focused on the company that her health was jeopardized. A hospital trip became her wake-up call, and she decided to refocus on her health, which caused her to think and perform better in the years since.[50]

3. Do you consider Burns a mindful leader? Why or why not?
4. Based on her leadership actions toward stakeholders (including employees), would you consider Burns a Utilitarianist or a Universalist? Please explain.
5. What do you admire most in Burns's leadership? Please elaborate.

Summary

- Meta-ethics explores the status, foundations, and scope of moral values, properties, and words. Rather than examining acts that are moral or immoral, meta-ethics focuses on the concept of morality itself.
  - Ethical non-naturalism, ethical naturalism, and ethical emotivism are some meta-ethical views.
- Normative ethics considers ethical action, which explains why it is also referred to as *theories of conduct*.

  - Ethical Egoism, Utilitarianism, and deontological theories (among them, Universalism) are some normative ethical views.
  - Rights theory can be critical in ensuring that moral decisions are made. The very implementation of some ethical theories may open potential doors for rights violation. Considering the aspect of rights is, therefore, an important support aspect in "mindful" moral behavior.

- Justice is yet another concept that can critically support or complement the interpretation of ethical theories. Justice distinguishes itself from rights, because there are many unfair actions that do not violate any-one's rights, such as leaving all assets to one of your children, while completely excluding another.

1. Positive Psychology studies the strengths that enable us to thrive, whether as individuals or in communities. Positive Psychology explores what makes life worth living.

    - The following elements typify Positive Psychology: flourishing, mean-ing, strengths, optimal functioning, and other people (or relationships).
    - Positive Psychology aims to augment our strengths and improve our weaknesses. It acknowledges good and bad in life as genuine, equal entities; it doesn't consider good to be the absence of bad, so good life should not be perceived as the absence of disorders, but should be em-braced as a genuine possibility.
    - Some of the critical findings of Positive Psychology are: ★ Happiness comes forth from good things in life, and has an upward spiral effect; ★ Most people are happy and resilient: ★ Crisis situations reveal our char-acter; ★ People, religious views, and engaging work are important con-tributors to meaning; ★ Money is not a great contributor to well-being and can only bring happiness when it is spent on other people; ★ There is more life satisfaction to be gained from human flourishing than from self-indulgence.
    - Positive Psychology studies happiness and its roots. Three dimensions of happiness to be cultivated:

        1. *The Pleasant Life*. We can attain a pleasant life by savoring basic life pleasures, such as companionship, the natural environment, and our physical needs.
        2. *The Good Life*. We can achieve this by discovering our unique virtues and strengths, and utilizing them creatively to enhance our lives.
        3. *The Meaningful Life*. We acquire this when we manage to employ our unique strengths to a purpose greater than ourselves. This gives the highest sense of meaning and, thus, fulfillment.

2. Buddhist psychology offers the West an important new perspective on hu-man interaction and mental processes. Buddhist teaching focuses on peace, and drawing a mental bridge from internal peace with peace in the world.

    - Similar to Western psychology, Buddhist psychology teaches that our mind is the product of past impressions. These past impressions im-pacted our views, and shaped the way we perceive the world today.
    - Unlike the Western approach, however, Buddhist psychology suggests releasing our entire "self" structure, and becoming liberated from the

ego deception. Becoming a balanced person, then, means being focused on the well-being of the world.

- Two strategies often practiced in Buddhist circles to nurture a calmer, more constructive mind are (1) Vipassana or insight meditation, and (2) the Seven-Point Mind Training.

3. Mindfulness requires effort and practice. When we are mindful, we observe our surroundings with more attention, and live more in the moment. An interesting way of explaining mindfulness is as a state of acute awareness, attentiveness, and perceptiveness in everything going on around oneself, while minimizing the effects of self and ego. There are multiple ways to sharpen our mindfulness:

- Meditation (such as Vipassana).
- Engaging in constructive dialogues with people who have proven to be creative thinkers.
- Look at yourself from the other side. Try to put yourself in the shoes of various people you meet.
- Consider the big picture. Take some distance. Step out of the daily routine, and go, if only for one day, to a place that inspires you.

Reflective Questions

1. Ethical egoism promotes acting in one's own self-interest as a moral practice. Please explain how this could be the case. (Engage in additional reading on the topic if more clarity is needed.)
2. Consider the two criticisms that were posted about Utilitarianism. Which one do you consider most disturbing? Why?
3. Consider the two criticisms that were posted about Universalism. Which one do you consider most troubling? Why?
4. Consider Martin Seligman's three dimensions to cultivate happiness. In which dimension are you now? Please explain.
5. Do you consider yourself a mindful person? How do you maintain or sharpen your mindfulness? Please explain.

Notes

1 Hospers, J. (1980). Ethics in the 20th century: A bibliographical essay. *Bibliographical Essay in Literature of Liberty* 3(3).
2 Ibid.
3 Ibid.
4 Ibid.
5 Ibid.
6 Ibid.
7 Ibid.
8 Ibid.
9 Ibid.

10 Ibid.
11 Ibid.
12 The Trustees of the University of Pennsylvania (2017). *Positive Psychology Center.* Retrieved on January 8, 2017, from http://ppc.sas.upenn.edu.
13 Asebedo, S. D., & Seay, M. C. (2015). From functioning to flourishing: Applying Positive Psychology to financial planning. *Journal of Financial Planning 28*(11), 50–58.
14 Peterson, C., & Park, N. (2003). Positive Psychology as the even-handed Positive Psychologist views it. *Psychological Inquiry 14*(2), 143–147.
15 Pennock, S. F. (April 3, 2015). What is Positive Psychology? 7 definitions + PDF. https://positivepsychologyprogram.com/what-is-positive-psychology.
16 Peterson, C. (May 16, 2008). The good life: What is Positive Psychology, and what is it not? Positive Psychology studies what makes life most worth living. *Psychology Today.* www.psychologytoday.com/blog/the-good-life/200805/what-is-positive-psychology-and-what-is-it-not.
17 Ibid. for all bullet points in this section.
18 Asebedo & Seay, From functioning to flourishing, 50–58.
19 Seligman, M. (2016). The pursuit of happiness: Bringing the science of happiness to life. *The Pursuit of Happiness.* www.pursuit-of-happiness.org/history-of-happiness/martin-seligman-psychology.
20 Ibid.
21 Ibid.
22 Ibid.
23 Tariki Trust Learning Community (2010). *Buddhist Psychology.* http://buddhistpsychology.typepad.com/buddhist_psychology.
24 Institute for Zen Therapy in Association with Amida Trust (2011). *Buddhist Psychology.* www.instituteforzentherapy.com/buddhist-psychology.html.
25 Ibid.
26 Ibid.
27 Marques, J., & Dhiman, S. (2009). Vipassana meditation as a path toward improved management practices. *Journal of Global Business Issues 3*(2), 77–84.
28 Wrye, H. K. (2006). Sitting with Eros and Psyche on a Buddhist psychoanalyst's cushion. *Psychoanalytic Dialogues 16*(6), 725–746.
29 Bercholz, S., & Kohn, S. C. (1993). *An Introduction to the Buddha and His Teachings.* New York: Barnes & Noble, Inc.
30 Marques & Dhiman, Vipassana meditation *3*(2), 77–84.
31 Ibid.
32 Pearcey, A. (transl. 2012). The Seven Points of Mind training by Geshe Chekawa Yeshe Dorje (1101–1175). www.lotsawahouse.org/tibetan-masters/geshe-chekhawa-yeshe-dorje/seven-points-mind-training.
33 Khenchen Thrangu Rinpoche. (January 11, 2017). The Seven Points of Mind Training (translated by Maruta Stern and Erik Pema Kunsang). www.rinpoche.com/teachings/sevenpoints.htm.
34 Kabat-Zinn, J. (2003). Mindfulness-based interventions in context: Past, present, and future. *Clinical Psychology: Science and Practice 10*(2), 144.
35 Hays, J. M. (2007). Dynamics of organizational wisdom. *Business Renaissance Quarterly 2*(4), 77–112.
36 Ibid.
37 Carson, S. H., & Langer, E. J. (2006). Mindfulness and self-acceptance. *Journal of Rational-Emotive & Cognitive-Behavior Therapy 24*(1), 29–43.
38 Ibid.
39 Ibid.
40 Ibid.

41 Marques, J., Dhiman, S., & King, R. (2009). What really matters at work in turbulent times. *Business Renaissance Quarterly 4*(1), 13–29.
42 Ibid.
43 Ibid.
44 January 14, 2017. The World's 100 Most Powerful Women. #34: Ursula Burns, CEO-Chairman, Xerox. *Forbes*. www.forbes.com/profile/ursula-burns.
45 Ursula M. (January 14, 2017). Burns, Chairman & CEO. *Lean In*. https://leanin.org/stories/ursula-burns.
46 Vanourek, B., & Vanourek, G. (2012). Triple Crown leadership: Building excellent, ethical, and enduring organizations. *McGraw-Hill Education*, CA. http://triplecrownleadership.com/a-vision-of-great-leadership.
47 Ibid.
48 Ibid.
49 Ibid.
50 Ibid.

PART III

Moving Forward While Doing the Right Thing

7

ABOUT CHOICE AND REALITY

Abstract

In professional as well as in private life, we make many decisions daily. Some are simple, others complex. Our decisions are based on our perceptions, which, in turn, are based on various factors that contributed to who we are today. This chapter will highlight the importance of understanding the complexity of choice and reality, both phenomena that are individually geared. In understanding that there are always choices and that there are multiple realities, this chapter aims to solidify the foundation for greater understanding and compassion needed in leadership.

Choice and Leadership

The ability to make good and responsible choices is as critical a skill to leadership as vision, directing, communicating, or being fair. Leaders make choices all the time, and they understand that every choice holds a degree of risk, because there are always factors that are not known or cannot be foreseen when making choices. And yet: choices are foundational in leading. In order to clarify this, let's take a step back, and consider the way we define *leadership* here. Some people see leadership as an act that involves a leader, followers, and a situation. Here, however, leadership starts at an earlier stage: before followers or others are involved. Facing different situations, we have to make decisions, and whenever that happens, we are engaging in leadership, with or without others included. Call it self-leadership, if you wish to distinguish between the traditional interpretation and this one, but it is leadership nonetheless.

Decision-making entails choices. In order to make a decision, we weigh alternatives, and select one option. That is a choice. Our life is filled with choices, and not only simple ones such as what clothes we will put on today, or whether we will take the bus, bike, or train to work. Who and what we are today is largely based on the choices we made in the past. Where we will be in the future is also largely dependent upon the choices we make today. Leaders are particularly aware of that. Choices are not always easy to make. They require skills that we often take for granted, but that can enhance the quality of the choices we make. Some of these skills are:

- Mindfulness: This refers to our ability to be aware of all the factors that matter in the choice process. In making choices, especially those with high impact, there is no room for neglecting factors that could be critical for the outcome. We will, therefore, have to be attentive to details, but also to the bigger picture.
- Reflection: Oftentimes, when we are facing choices, we have to tap from past experiences, but also use our imagination to envision possible outcomes. This reflective process can help us eliminate some choices that may seem appealing, but could carry consequences we may not want to deal with.
- Courage: No matter how much information we have at hand, there will always be unknown factors. Every choice is, therefore, a courageous act, a leap in the dark that may require smart adjustments when complications arise that we had not foreseen.
- Intelligence: Some choices require intellectual intelligence, such as knowledge, design thinking, and strategic insight, whereas others ask for emotional intelligence, including empathy and deep listening. This often depends on the nature of the choice and who or what is involved.
- Consideration: While reflection and intelligence do a decent job in getting to the choice to be made, it is consideration that can be seen as the final aspect. *Consideration* is the process of weighing all the options, just before making a decision.

In spite of its importance in the leadership process, choice is not often listed as a leadership skill. It is one of those qualities we take for granted, just like our breath, because we all have made choices for the longest time in our lives. But choices can lead to wonderful or disastrous outcomes. It is, therefore, equally important for leaders to know that the choice is highly important, but also that the action implemented after a choice has been made underscores the ability of a leader to think creatively, show perseverance, and remain balanced.

Choice and Mental Models

Mental models were discussed in Chapter 5, but it may be useful to briefly review the relationship between our mental models and the choices we make. Mental models are critical in making choices. They affect all aspects surrounding choice and decision-making. Earlier, we stated that choices are driven by mindfulness, reflection, courage, intelligence, and consideration. Our implementation of each of these aspects is determined by our mental models.

- Without mindfulness, we will most likely adhere to mental models that were embedded in us long ago, without caring to question them.
- Without reflection, our mental models will also be rather stale, as we will rarely (most likely never) scrutinize them.
- Without courage, we will not confront our mental models, because it is always easier to remain in a comfort zone than to tread new, unfamiliar paths. (In the next section of this chapter, we will elaborate further on the aspect of courage.)
- Without intelligence, we will not entertain the option of reflecting on and questioning our mental models, and thus base our choices, followed by our decisions, on established, possibly invalid mind-sets.
- Without consideration, we will not weigh the option of our mental models potentially needing examination prior to making choices and decisions.

Figure 7.1 demonstrates the relationship between mental models, the five factors toward choice and decision-making.

Courage

Courage has been listed above as an important aspect in making the right choices. Yet, just like the other four aspects, courage is a powerful foundational skill itself, in our private as well as our professional performance. Without

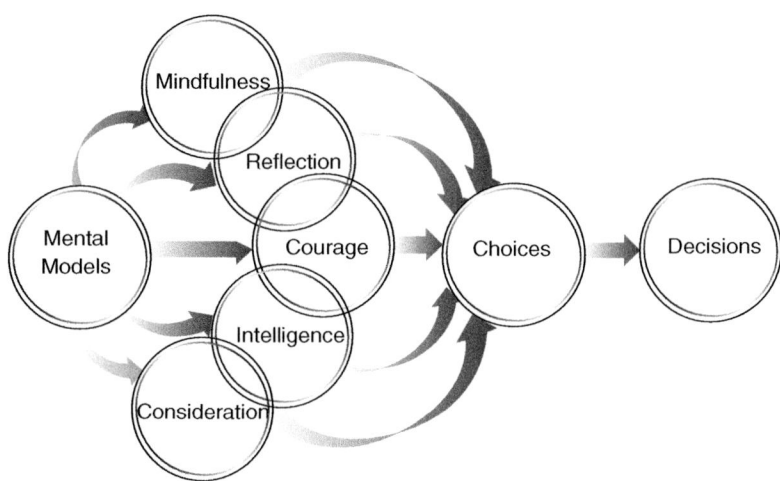

FIGURE 7.1 How Mental Models Relate to Choices and Decisions.

courage, we will have a difficult time succeeding through times of changes, and will be unable to embark upon new personal and professional journeys.

The word *courage* itself is foundational for making the bold moves that life increasingly requires from us. We, human beings, are risk-averse by nature. We try to dwell in our comfort zones as long as we can, even when those comfort zones are not pleasant, productive, or rewarding at all. And when we try to step out of them, there will always be others who, for some reason, will tell us why we should stay where we are.

Sometimes, people want us to stay in our comfort zones because they don't want us to make progress: they are envious. This brings to mind the story of Marina, a young woman, who always surrounded herself with lots of friends. Unfortunately, as it usually goes, not all of these "friends" turned out to have genuine intentions. Aside from all the jokes, support, and confidential sharing sessions, there was also a lot of hidden envy among them, as well. One time, Marina, who was also an aspiring actress, landed a role in a television show, for which she would have to move out of state for a while. All her friends seemed happy, but two of them kept casting doubt within her about this opportunity: "What if things don't work out?" "Would you really want to consider living alone in this distant state without your family and friends?" "Wouldn't it be better to just find something locally?" Fortunately, Marina could see right through her so-called friends' "concerns," and accepted the opportunity. She had a wonderful time while filming the show, and returned after several months with much more confidence than before. Had she listened to her friends, she would have always wondered what life was like on the other side of the fence.

Sometimes, those around us may be fearful that we will fail if we move on, so they try to keep us where we are. Another story, about a lady we shall call Sharma, illustrates this very well. Sharma decided one day that she needed to move away from her old hometown. Her decision was not an overnight one: she had felt burnt out in her job for quite some time, and her personal life was not too rosy either: she was in a bad relationship and had very few friends. She kept feeling as if she had reached the ceiling of her performance and endurance in the town where she was born and raised, and was yearning for a new outlook on life. Being the meticulous character she was, she traveled, investigated, and explored several potential locations, until she finally made up her mind to move to a state to the far north of her old hometown. Filled with good thoughts and excitement, Sharma started planning for the transition. When the time came to break the news of her pending move to her mother, she couldn't believe her ears. Her mom was actually trying to discourage her from leaving. And this, while the mom was well aware how unhappy Sharma had been in the past few years. The mother's reasoning was, "You know what you got here. There's no telling what you will encounter in that faraway place!" Fortunately, Sharma understood that her mom was just fearful of letting her move to a place where they would not be able to have daily visits with each other. Sharma left and started a successful, fulfilling life in her new location.

There are also times when people want to prevent us from moving ahead because they don't want to be left behind. They may not have the courage to move on, so they try to keep their friends stagnant, as well. John's case (another story by way of example) may demonstrate this. John had a best friend Leo, who turned out to be a great example of this dynamic. When John received a job offer in another city, and had to move for that purpose, Leo did everything to prevent John from going. They had been in the same dead-end job for the last seven years, and while they had both been complaining every night after work, Leo simply didn't seem to have the drive to snap out of his situation. John, on the other hand, engaged in networking, went to job fairs, and applied for jobs regularly. Thanks to a friend forwarding his resume to a large corporation a few cities away, he received the job offer that required him to move. Leo was devastated, particularly because he knew that he didn't have the stamina to step outside the mediocre comfort zone that was their work. John moved away and Leo stayed behind, feeling sorrier for himself than ever before.

As the examples above illustrate, comfort zones, whether pleasant or dreadful, have a powerful commonality: they are not easy to step out of. That may not even have so much to do with the comfort zone itself, as it does with our change aversion. It requires courage to move on when things don't work out anymore. And that moment comes—sooner or later—for every one of us: relationships end, jobs get lost, careers become outdated, you name it.

The aspect of morality comes into play here when we consider that many of the discouraging people in the examples above, Marina's friends, Sharma's mom, and John's friend Leo, may not have considered their acts immoral, and they may, indeed, be difficult to compare. Marina's friends, who had no stake in her departure other than that she was moving on and they felt "left behind," were engaging in selfish behavior, trying to withhold a friend from moving on in life. This was also the case with John's friend Leo, who lacked the courage to move away himself. In both cases, the attitudinal cues came forth from an ego that was unwilling to allow another individual to do better than the one raising all doubts. In the case of Sharma's mom, the driving motive was fear. As described in Chapter 5, David Hawkins has categorized fear as a driving motive with a consciousness of 100, just above grief and just under desire.[1] Fear is not the most constructive driver for our actions, and it can also lead to immoral behavior. While Sharma's mom may not have intended any immoral act with her doubt-casting, she would have created a mental obstruction to her daughter's future well-being, had she succeeded.

Courage could serve as a morally responsible platform to unite a number of things we all know, but rarely think about when we go through our daily swings, or even when we consider the entire scope of our lives. Courage is not only a meaningful word, but it can also be a powerful acronym, aimed at shaping and sustaining a strong mind-set on our path from here to the future. This section discusses the elements of the acronym "COURAGE": Choice, Open-Mindedness, Usefulness, Reality-Check, Attitude, Genius, and

Education.[2] Each of these aspects will briefly be evaluated from one or more angles that could contribute to a more rewarding, meaningful, and morally balanced life. Courage is one of those terms that seems to be self-explanatory when we think about leadership. Whether we perceive it as an act toward our own behavior or in interaction with others, leadership requires courage.

Choice: The two most important facts every leader should remember in this regard are: (1) there is always a choice, and (2) success often depends on what we do after we have made our choice. Regarding the first fact: while the alternatives may not always be attractive, they still exist, so when we say that we don't have a choice it merely means that we don't consider the alternatives viable. More important, however, is the fact that we always make choices with insufficient information, so it is not the choice itself that leads to success or failure, but the actions we undertake afterward. This entails that even a poor choice can become useful in the long run, based on our follow-up actions. There is quite some moral weight in making choices because, oftentimes, the options bring their own degree of moral soundness. Usually, the choices that seem easiest are not the most morally sound. This is the eternal trade-off in life: whatever sounds easy is not always right, and whatever is right is usually not easy.

> As an illustration to the moral weight of making choices: The CEO of a company faces an ongoing reduction of customer-base and interest in the company's products and services. He sends out a note to all department supervisors to consider strategies toward reducing overhead. The supervisor of the engineering department knows that all his employees work hard. His most obvious choices are to either lay off three of his engineers in order to reduce overhead and keep the other seven secured, or to ask everyone to take a cut in income for six months, or until the crisis is resolved.

Open-Mindedness: Leading without an open mind has always been an inhibiting process, but in our times, it is a downright disaster. Those who want to remain closed-minded will find it hard to establish connections with most forward-thinking people in today's professional settings, and may find themselves fallen by the wayside, chasing a dream or opportunity that never materializes. Closed-mindedness means that a person has settled for a certain mind-set and refuses to entertain alternative ways of perceiving reality. As you can gather, this is a risky and unfulfilling way of behaving these days. When we practice open-mindedness, we dare to accept options that we previously failed to consider, because we may have considered them to be above or below our level, outside our comfort zone, or against our traditional perceptions. Practicing open-mindedness means that we must regularly inspect our principles in order to find out whether they are built on convictions that matter to us here and now, or were adopted along the way without deeper considerations.

You would be amazed to find out how many biases we hold, and how limiting those are to our perceived options.

> A good way to illustrate the moral weight of open-mindedness is the issue that exists in some workplaces when it comes to employees' preferred religions. Some leaders see themselves as spiritual, by engaging in specific practices (prayers, songs, a morning service, etc.), tied to their own religion. Meanwhile, they may make employees who adhere to a different religion (or no religion at all) uncomfortable, and even make these employees feel that they are part of an outgroup. Such stern adherences to cultural, religious, or other specific viewpoints may cause good co-workers to leave, as they increasingly feel as if they perform under mental and emotional pressure. This, then, makes for an unpleasant work environment that could be labeled discriminatory toward those with other ways of thinking. That is immoral.

Usefulness: In his now-famous Stanford speech, Steve Jobs talked about the concept of usefulness in life. He reminisced about his youth and the fact that he was an early college dropout, who decided to enroll only in courses that he was passionate about. One of those courses was calligraphy. This course turned out to be the foundation for his idea of creating fonts on computers much later: a concept that we all now enjoy. Jobs took the topic of usefulness a step further: referring to his notion as "connecting the dots," he stated that everything in our life has a purpose. Sometimes we understand the purpose early on, but sometimes it takes years before we realize why something had to happen: being laid off from a job, losing a loved one, having to forego a seemingly great opportunity—even the most tedious, ridiculous, or useless-seeming things in our lives today will turn out to have a purpose.

There is a statement that has been attributed to Ralph Waldo Emerson (with some hesitance as to whether it is actually an Emerson quote) that states, "The purpose of life is not to be happy. It is to be useful, to be honorable, to be compassionate, to have it make some difference that you have lived and lived well."[3] There is food for thought in this statement, since it seemingly contradicts the mind-set that we all strive to be happy. The way this could be interpreted, however, is that happiness is often misunderstood as a moving target: one that depends on external factors, such as wealth, position, power, or relationships. Yet, having a purpose awakens our passion, and entices us to engage in something that evokes an inner sense of being useful. Having this sense of being useful is rewarding, and does not depend on external forces. The reward from being useful sparks happiness that is more genuine, more lasting, and deeper than the fleeting concept that we so often hold of it. When considered this way, usefulness is a powerful foundation for happiness, and therefore a critical element to reflect upon, because no one can determine the area in which we consider ourselves useful. This is a personal conclusion to be drawn based on our experiences, insights, character, desires, and willpower. Here is another illustrative story:

> From a young age on, Tamika loved writing. She considered that her passion, and the drive behind her very being. She discussed this with Lea, one of her mother's friends, who was a writer, and asked how she could start toward becoming recognized. Lea suggested that she start writing short articles, which she could post to public article databases online. She also suggested that she start a blog, and post her writing to any place she considered appropriate for the topics she wrote about. Within two years, Tamika received an invitation to submit some sample work to a well-known online source. This led to her becoming a regular contributor, and her name began to resonate among several reader audiences. Fast-forward two more years, and Tamika landed her first book contract. Her work, invested in her self-determined sense of purpose, had paid off. Tamika is now a well-established author. She is not fond of traveling, and will only sporadically participate in social events. This has led several of her family members and other close relatives to tell her that she was letting her happiness pass her by. Yet, Tamika disagrees. She is happy when she writes, because she feels connected to her purpose, to her sense of usefulness, and she chooses not to worry about what others think in that regard.

Reality Check: Within the context of reality check, we can also consider multiple stances. It is important to pause our actions at some point and take a critical look at what we are doing: does it still matter to us, or are we engaging in something that has long lost its luster in our lives? In other words: are we just going through the motions, just as so many people do, without wondering whether our activities actually matter to the person we are today? Realities change over time, and what we considered wonderful, important, or interesting in the past may no longer have that effect on us, if we assess our feelings. In Chapter 3, we discussed the concept of apoptosis: the process of programmed cell death. Because there are cells constantly dying in us, and others being generated, our very substance changes, and not merely at the physical level. We also change mentally, as we get exposed to the ups and downs of life. This further explains why we should take the time to examine our reality today, and consider whether our actions still matter within that framework.

Another way of considering reality check leads us back to the concept of mental models: we all have our own reality. With a world of almost eight billion people (at the time of writing this book), it is important to know that even those close to us may perceive things differently than we do, let alone those whose views are further influenced by a different culture, location, focus points, generation, or life philosophy. Leaders, especially, should realize this fact at all times, because it can help them to better understand others' viewpoints. The difference in views of reality explains why some people can smile about something while others feel offended or disinterested about the same thing. Understanding that we all have our own mental model, which we call "reality," can make us more open and understanding to viewpoints from others, and can therefore guide us to a broader spectrum of alternatives.

There is a beautiful song by Adele, titled "Million Years Ago." In this song, which I invite you to listen to on YouTube or any other available social medium, the singer bemoans her life, which seemed to have slipped through her fingers, filling her with regret for many of the things she did or did not do. She laments, in a touching way, that she realizes she is not the only one with feelings of being a failure for not having become what she thought she would be. The song has given rise to deep emotions and even deeper thought to many. Indeed, we can regret the missed chances in our lives, and dwell on our disappointments, but that makes for a grim reality today. We can also consider the usefulness of all our experiences, as discussed earlier in this chapter, and the wisdom they brought us today. By doing that, we can try to find the purpose of our current circumstances, envision an improved future, and start working toward it.

Attitude: The way we perceive and approach things has much to do with our general attitude toward life. Attitude is one of the strongest assets of a leader. In times when all runs smoothly, it is easy to maintain a positive attitude, but in difficult times, maintaining an upbeat attitude can be a challenge. Yet, our attitude is the only thing we really control. It is the single thing that cannot be determined by others; it is our own, no matter what is being added to or taken away from us. Our attitude is affected by our mental models and the choices we make. Attitude is very much a choice: how shall we perceive the circumstances we face? Do we allow them to bog us down, or do we take them as opportunities to create a better future? In other words, do we have a glass-half-full or glass-half-empty attitude? Do we focus on the dark clouds before the sun, or on the sun behind the dark clouds? The gist of the matter is that we cannot change the surprises that life presents us, but we can decide how we will approach them once they have surfaced.

Viktor Frankl, a Jewish-Austrian neurologist and psychiatrist, is one of the frequently cited authors on attitude. Frankl, his wife, parents, and brother were deported to concentration camps in the early 1940s under the German Nazi regime. For most of his years in the various concentration camps where he was imprisoned, he was utilized as a physician or a therapist. Upon liberation, in 1945, he learned that his entire captured family had died. The only surviving member was his sister, who had escaped the concentration camps by migrating to Australia. Through his years as a concentration camp prisoner, Frankl found confirmation of his viewpoint that human beings are mainly motivated by a desire to find the meaning of their lives, and that finding this meaning can serve as a beacon to overcome even the grimmest situations. Reflecting on a very grim experience in the concentration camp, and recalling how thoughts of his wife kept him focused, Frankl wrote,

> In a position of utter desolation, when Man cannot express himself in positive action, when his only achievement may consist in enduring his sufferings in the right way—an honorable way—in such a position Man can, through loving contemplation of the image he carries of his beloved, achieve fulfillment.[4]

Genius: We don't often think of ourselves as geniuses, and some of us never do, but each of us harbors distinct qualities that reflect genius allure. Over the course of our life, however, our inner-genius has received many blows: it has been belittled, discouraged, and demoralized through a large range of rejections, pressures, corrections, rules, and negative feedback. We can all recall several instances in our schooldays, at work, or even at home, where we were reprimanded for doing something wrong, and sternly corrected, leaving us with a feeling of being good for nothing. Still, in spite of all these discouragements, we can revive our inner-genius if we choose to do so. The first step in doing so is accepting that we have an inner genius. The second step is accepting it, and the third is to start exploring it. Here is where our attitude reenters the picture: do we want our inner-genius to thrive? Or are we too skeptical to allow it another chance? Our inner-genius can help us to realize the many opportunities that are captured in every day, the many avenues we don't take, as we allow ourselves to be stuck in a monotonous pattern of existing. We can revive our inner-genius by starting to talk to people outside of our comfort zone, reading books that are different from the ones we always read, taking a different path to do the things we always do, in other words, start applying changes in our daily pattern where possible. Gradually, the fountain of creative thinking will come alive again.

> One of the strongest pieces of evidence about the existence of genius in most people was delivered by the National Aeronautics and Space Administration (NASA). In 1968, as part of an effort to unlock the mystery of innovation, this prestigious organization decided to administer a creativity test to 1,600 five-year-olds to find out how creatively they were able to think. The results were astonishing: 98 percent of these children met the standards of "creative genius." Fascinated by this finding, George Land, the study developer, and his team of NASA-contracted researchers, decided to continue tracking these young creative geniuses over time. Five years later, the children, now ten years old, delivered an entirely different result: only 30 percent could still be labeled as creative geniuses. Another five years later, now 15 years old, only 12 percent of the children

met the criteria of creative geniuses.[5] After that test, Land and his team tested more than 300,000 adults, and found out that at the average age of 31 years old, only 2 percent of adults remain creative geniuses. Analyzing the findings of their study, Land and his team found out that we need two different types of creative thinking in order to be creative and innovative: divergent and convergent thinking. *Divergent thinking* allows us to brainstorm in unusual, nontraditional, envisioning ways, or "out of the box." Subsequently, however, we need *convergent thinking*, to match our visions and ideas to reality and fit them within the parameters of our abilities. So, developing ideas is one thing, but matching the ideas to an action plan is another story. The art is to use both types of thinking in a useful sequence and not simultaneously. A simultaneous use of these ways of thinking causes a decline in creative thinking.[6]

Education: Regardless of the type of education we choose, whether formal or informal, it is important to keep our education alive in some form. Our brains need regular challenging to remain intact. Therefore, we should continue seeking ways to maintain our mental exercise, be it by following a course (there are many available online—a large part of them free), through teaching ourselves by reading up on topics of interest, or through talking with people from whom we can learn things. Education is the vehicle to keep leaders ahead of the crowd. The more we learn, the sharper our critical and creative thinking skills will get, the broader our scope will become, and the more possibilities we will see and create for ourselves. These are exponential times, where continuing our education is no longer considered something reserved only for the affluent or the young: it is accessible to all of us. Therefore, failing to continuously educate ourselves will prevent us from seizing opportunities that others learn about.

When we consider the advantages of education, we often think of external features, such as having the knowledge to acquire more prestigious jobs, thus earning more admiration from others; having more and better choices in the job market; and increasing one's network with influential friends and acquaintances. Yet, there are also very powerful advantages tied to obtaining as high an education as possible, such as acquiring the ability to engage in more responsible time and money management, the ability to make more prudent and responsible choices, and, perhaps most importantly, the skill of critical thinking, oftentimes resulting in changed ways of looking at life and changed habits.

It is also important to realize that the stories we hear of successful college dropouts, such as Bill Gates (Microsoft), Mark Zuckerberg (Facebook), Steve Jobs (Apple), Larry Page and Sergey Brin (Google), and Michael Dell (Dell Computers), are stories of an extreme minority in the world of professionals. By far, we still live in a world where the level of education makes a tremendous difference in many regards. It has even been proven that there is a direct link between education and health: people who are better educated make more conscious decisions about their life and health as well, and suffer fewer cumbersome health issues, on average. Among the many sources that attest to this fact is a 2015 article by Zimmerman, Woolf, and Haley, in which the authors share some compelling statistics regarding life expectancy.[7] Studies demonstrated that people without a high school diploma had a higher chance of dying earlier than their fellow citizens with college degrees, and that those who had professional degrees had a higher chance of living longer than those with only a bachelor's degree. Additionally, the chance for getting diabetes was 15 percent higher for adults without a high school education than for those with a college degree.

Several of the behaviors and mind-sets in the seven elements of COURAGE are interrelated. Education helps reignite our inner-genius, which can make us more receptive to the differences in mental models (reality check). Practicing open-mindedness reveals more choices, and can help us see the usefulness of experiences more clearly. An open mind is a great foundation for a constructive attitude, which can encourage us to explore more choices, and revive our inner-genius.

Choice Theory

Developed by renowned psychiatrist William Glasser, Choice theory explains that our current circumstances are based on the choices we have made so far, and that we, therefore, have no one else to blame for our circumstances. Glasser's theory states that through understanding one's needs and power to make personal choices, people may increase happiness and improve their relationships.[8] While people have a tendency to accuse others of their misery, the feelings are still their choice. We humans obtain information from others, but the feelings we get from this information, whether these are of the happy or miserable kind, are our own choice. Glasser firmly states that we choose our actions and thoughts and, therefore, practically all our feelings, as well as our physical state. He clarifies this by stating that much of what happens with our body is the result of what we have done to it.[9] In fact, Choice theory aims to teach us to take more responsibility over our life by placing our behaviors at the center of our existence and the things that happen therein. Similar to Maslow's theory of needs, Glasser breaks the driving motives of our behaviors into multiple categories. He distinguishes two main category clusters: genetically driven needs, and psychological needs. Under "genetically driven needs," he lists food, clothing, shelter, breathing, personal safety, and security. Under fundamental "psychological needs," Glasser lists belonging/connecting/love; power/significance/competence; freedom/autonomy, and fun/learning.

On the website of the Glasser Institute, Choice theory is explained as follows:

- All we do is behave,
- Almost all behavior is chosen, and
- We are driven by our genes to satisfy five basic needs: survival, love and belonging, power, freedom, and fun.[10]

Love and belonging are explained as the most important needs, since our closeness with those we care about enables the satisfaction of all other needs.

Very much in line with our entire stance in this book, Glasser's Choice theory identifies seven caring habits that we should develop and nurture, and seven deadly ones, which we should overcome.

The seven caring habits are support, encouragement, listening, acceptance, trust, respect, and the skill of negotiating differences. The seven deadly habits are criticizing, blaming, complaining, nagging, threatening, punishing, and bribing.[11]

As a final note on Choice theory, here are ten axioms to keep in mind:

1. The only person whose behavior we can control is ourself.
2. All we can give another person is information.
3. All long-lasting psychological problems are relationship problems.
4. The problem relationship is always part of our present life.
5. What happened in the past has everything to do with what we are today, but we can only satisfy our basic needs right now and plan to continue satisfying them in the future.
6. We can only satisfy our needs by satisfying the pictures in our current World.
7. All we do is behave.
8. All behavior is Total Behavior (everything invested here and now) and is made up of four components: acting, thinking, feeling, and physiology.
9. All Total Behavior is chosen, but we only have direct control over the acting and thinking components. We can only control our feeling and physiology indirectly through how we choose to act and think.
10. All Total Behavior is designated by verbs and named by the part that is the most recognizable.[12]

It is important to realize that Choice theory points out the need for us to take responsibility for our lives, because only then will we find gratification and purpose in what we do. Moreover, responsibility will help us to rid ourselves of senses of regret and anger when we realize that every situation we land in is ultimately the result of the choices we made.

Case 7.1 Wells Fargo: The Challenge of Making Responsible Choices

In 2016, one of America's most respected banks, Wells Fargo, made the news in a less-reputable way. Founded in 1852 by Henry Wells and William G. Fargo, the institution had seen more than 150 years of expansion and generally excellent standing before a scandal surfaced involving the alleged creation of more than 2 million bogus bank accounts by thousands of Wells Fargo employees. This was particularly shocking when we consider Wells Fargo's position in the US and global society: up till the news of the scandal in September 2016, Wells Fargo was the world's largest bank by market capitalization. It was also the third-largest US bank by assets at the end of 2015, and the second largest bank in deposits, home mortgage servicing, and debit cards.

Yet, not its age, size, standing, stakeholders' trust, or its popularity could protect this company from falling prey to unethical choices by its leaders, leading to the order to pay a fine of $185 million and return to its customers $5 million in wrongly charged fees. The reason for the bank having to pay these fines lay in a whopping two million bank- and credit card accounts that were created by Wells Fargo employees without customers' permission.[13] So, why were these immoral choices made? They were made to reach the company's aggressive standards in meeting sales quotas and earning incentives. Employees were valued on basis of reaching targets that were translated into incentives. In order to meet those targets, employees became "creative," initially with minor transgressions, such as pushing customers to open unneeded accounts, but gradually progressing to opening accounts in their family members' names, to be closed shortly after the quota was reached, and subsequently declining into the act of opening unpermitted accounts in customers' names, and closing those again once the numbers were made.[14]

In the aftermath of this immense scandal, Wells Fargo fired more than 5,000 employees for their inappropriate sales actions, and in an attempt to regain customers' trust, the bank revised its quota system to eliminate sales goals. Yet, the question remains whether these actions will really boost morale and will actually lead to more responsible choices made by Wells Fargo's top managers in leading their workforce. After all, the first manifestation of this problem dated back five years before it reached scandal magnitude: from 2011 on, Wells Fargo fired about 1,000 employees every year for exactly the same reason, but nothing seriously was undertaken until 2015, when media reports started appearing, and the culture remained unchanged.[15] Considering Wells Fargo's external climate, there is reason for concern as well: nothing has changed in the highly competitive climate in which the bank operates, so one may wonder how the bank will keep itself in the running if it tones down its aggressive goals and incentives based practices.[16]

As part of the aftermath of Wells Fargo's fraudulent practices, the bank came under investigation by federal prosecutors and congressional overseers, while several states, such as California and Illinois, suspended parts of their business relationships with the bank.[17] Critics who meticulously followed the testimonials from now-former CEO John Stumpf and his team have predicted an emergence of new scandals if Wells Fargo does not take a hard look at its culture and management mind-sets. Wells Fargo has systematically distinguished itself from its peers, claiming a culture of caring since 1852. Top management, therefore, refused to accept that there were systemic flaws within the organization's strategic choice processes. The CEO maintained that the percentage of employees involved in unethical practices as well as the percentage of fake accounts were minor in comparison to the company's overall workforce and customer base. He marginalized the problem by claiming that only 1 percent of employees were fired per year, and only 1.9 percent of deposits were fraudulent. Stumpf also stated that the bank undertook action once it realized that customers could be charged for the fake accounts opened. This led to the insight that the *only* motive for taking action was the financial consequence that these false accounts had on customers, and not the immoral practice at its foundation.[18]

As Wells Fargo tries to move on from this dark page in its history, critics remain skeptical about the bank's ability to change the aggressive culture that has been upheld so long in the company, especially in light of the realization that many warning signs were systematically ignored by the company's top managers. Employees who tried to voice their concern about the immoral culture were ignored, silenced, and sometimes even fired. A petition signed by about 5,000 employees to lower the aggressive quota was ignored, and whistle-blowers were fired, all signs indicating leading intimidation and keeping the current workforce silent.[19]

Indeed, corporate leaders seem to continue to slide from the moral path of performance as they try to elevate their business to higher performance plains. In a thought-provoking article about the unethical choices people tend to make in business environments, Ron Carucci contemplates the beautiful values statements that many corporations formulate, after which they promptly engage in the most blatant immoralities. Enron is the first to come to mind in that regard, as their values statement was well articulated and compelling. Yet, their blatant disregard of ethical performance placed an immoral smudge on the first decade of the 21st century, soon followed by several others.[20]

Carucci points out the fact that unethical corporate choices are not merely disturbing and disheartening for stakeholders, but they are also expensive. And while leaders have been progressing in their responsible choice-making, the number of unethical practices remains of concern today. There are, unfortunately, still legions of employees in small, mid-sized and large companies, that feel pressured to do the wrong thing. Carucci lists the following five organizational practices that push employees into unethical choices:

1. Open-door policies are limited to certain topics, from which moral concerns are excluded. Some corporate leaders simply discourage employees from speaking up, effectively making those employees who try to voice concerns feel incompetent and futile, and thereby discouraging others from doing the same.[21]
2. Unrealistic goals, such as in Wells Fargo's case, force employees to do whatever they see useful to maintain their jobs. Oftentimes, this will lead to teaming up in unethical actions to prevent the loss of their livelihood.[22]
3. The phenomenon of conflicting goals is also a frequent problem in damaging employees' morale: when workers find out that their department is curtailed for the growth of another, and that they have to do more with less, while other departments flourish, they start experiencing a sense of inequality, which can cause major resentment.[23]
4. Merely talking about ethics, and then failing in the moral walk is yet another frequent error in corporate managerial performance. Ethical behavior can only be taught by ethical behavior, and not merely by an annual talk about moral performance or a values statement.[24]
5. Withholding the truth from employees is a clear indicator of hypocritical behavior and is rapidly spotted by subordinates, who then lose trust in their leader. Even if a lie was presented for a good reason, it will not be appreciated overall, and exude the message that being untruthful is okay.[25]

Questions

1. What wrong choices did Wells Fargo's top management make leading up to the 2016 scandal?
2. Do you think CEO Stumpf made a good point when he stated that *only* 1 percent of employees engaged in immoral behavior, and only 1.9 percent of accounts were false? Why or what not? Please share your reasoning.

3. Do you think Wells Fargo will be able to eradicate quotas and incentives from its culture? Why or why not?
4. Which of Carucci's five sources of unethical corporate behaviors disturbs you most? Why?

Summary

*   The ability to make good and responsible choices is as critical a skill for leadership as vision, directing, communicating, or being fair. Leaders make choices all the time, and they understand that every choice holds a degree of risk, because there are always factors that are not known or cannot be foreseen when making choices.
*   Choices are not always easy to make. They require skills such as:
    *   Mindfulness: Our ability to be aware of all the factors that matter in the choice process.
    *   Reflection: Tapping from past experiences, but also using our imagination to envision possible outcomes.
    *   Courage: A choice to leap in the dark, which may require smart adjustments when unforeseen complications arise.
    *   Intelligence: Of two kinds: some choices require intellectual intelligence, while others ask for emotional intelligence. This often depends on the nature of the choice and who or what is involved.
    *   Consideration: The process of weighing all the options, just before making a decision.
*   Mental models are critical in making choices. They affect all aspects surrounding choice and decision-making.
*   Courage is foundational for making the bold moves life increasingly requires from us. It helps us to get outside our comfort zone. COURAGE is also a powerful acronym, aimed at shaping and sustaining a strong mindset on our path from here to the future:
    *   Choice: The two most important facts every leader should remember in this regard are (1) there is always a choice, and (2) success often depends on what we do after we have made our choice.
    *   Open-Mindedness: Leading without an open mind has always been an inhibiting process, but in our times, it is a downright disaster. Those who want to remain closed-minded will find it hard to establish connections with most forward-thinking people in today's professional settings, and may find themselves fallen by the wayside.
    *   Usefulness: Everything is useful, no matter how tedious, aggravating, or useless it seems at the moment. Sometimes we understand the purpose early on, but sometimes it takes years before we realize why something had to happen.

- Reality Check: Realities change over time, and what we considered wonderful, important, or interesting in the past may no longer have that effect on us, if we assess our feelings. Another way of considering reality check leads us back to the concept of mental models: we all have our own reality.
- Attitude: The way we perceive and approach things has much to do with our general attitude toward life. Attitude is one of the strongest assets of a leader. In times when all runs smoothly, it is easy to maintain a positive attitude, but in difficult times, maintaining an upbeat attitude can be a challenge.
- Genius: We don't often think of ourselves as geniuses, and some of us never do, but each of us harbors distinct qualities that reflect genius allure.
- Education: Regardless of the type of education we choose, whether formal or informal, it is important to keep it alive in some form. Our brains need regular challenging to remain intact.
- Choice theory was developed by renowned psychiatrist William Glasser. Choice Theory explains that our current circumstances are based on the choices we have made so far, and that we, therefore, have no one else to blame for our circumstances.
  - While people have a tendency to accuse others of their misery, the feelings are still their choice.
  - We choose our actions and thoughts and, therefore also, practically all our feelings, as well as our physical state.
  - Glasser's Choice theory identifies seven caring habits, which we should develop and nurture, and seven deadly ones, which we should overcome.

Reflective Questions

1. In the first part of the chapter it is stated that "choices are foundational in leading." Do you agree with this statement or not? Please explain.
2. Why are mental models critical in making choices?
3. Courage is explained as an enabler for making bold moves: courageous moves. Reflect on your life and possibly your career and share a courageous move you made that you feel proud of today.
4. At several instances in this chapter, it is stated that most of your current circumstances result from the choices you made in the past. Do you agree or disagree? Please explain.
5. "Choice theory aims to teach us to take more responsibility over our life by placing our behaviors at the center of our existence and the things that happen therein." Please share your interpretation of this statement in about 100 words.

Notes

1 Hawkins, D. R. (1995). *Power vs. Force: The Hidden Determinants of Human Behavior.* Carlsbad, CA: Hayhouse, Inc.
2 Marques, J. (2013). *Courage in the Twenty-First Century: The Art of Successful Job Transition.* New York: Palgrave-MacMillan (Palgrave Pivot).
3 Ralph Waldo Emerson. (February 12, 2016), www.wisdomquotes.com/quote/ralph-waldo-emerson-169.html.
4 Frankl, V. (2006). *Man's Search for Meaning,* Part One, "Experiences in a Concentration Camp." Boston, MA: Beacon Press, pp. 56–57.
5 Wilson, L. (2017). You were once a creative genius. *Len Wilson.* http://lenwilson.us/you-were-once-a-creative-genius.
6 Rembach, J. (2017). Innovation secret discovered at NASA. *Beyond Morale.* www.beyondmorale.com/innovation-secret-discovered.
7 Zimmerman, E. B., Woolf, S. H., & Haley, A. (2015). Population health: Behavioral and social science insights understanding the relationship between education and health. *Agency for Healthcare Research and Quality.* www.ahrq.gov/professionals/education/curriculum-tools/population-health/zimmerman.html.
8 Mental health; choice theory education conference: Sacramento, Saturday, May 30. (2009). *Biotech Week*, 3410. Verify.
9 Glasser, W. (1999). *Choice Theory: A New Psychology of Personal Freedom.* New York: HarperCollins Publishers.
10 The Glasser Approach. (2017). *wglasser.com.* www.wglasser.com/the-glasser-approach/choice-theory.
11 Ibid.
12 Ibid.
13 Zoltners, A., Sinha, P., & Lorimer, S. (September 20, 2016). Wells Fargo and the slippery slope of sales incentives. *Harvard Business Review.* https://hbr.org/2016/09/wells-fargo-and-the-slippery-slope-of-sales-incentives.
14 Ibid.
15 Ochs, S. M. (October 2016). The leadership blind spots at Wells Fargo. *Harvard Business Review.* https://hbr.org/2016/10/the-leadership-blind-spots-at-wells-fargo.
16 Zoltners, A., Sinha, P., & Lorimer, S. (September 20, 2016). Wells Fargo and the slippery slope of sales incentives. *Harvard Business Review.* https://hbr.org/2016/09/wells-fargo-and-the-slippery-slope-of-sales-incentives.
17 Ochs, S. M. (October 2016). The leadership blind spots at Wells Fargo. *Harvard Business Review.* https://hbr.org/2016/10/the-leadership-blind-spots-at-wells-fargo.
18 Ibid.
19 Ibid.
20 Carucci, R. (December 16, 2016). Why ethical people make unethical choices. *Harvard Business Review.* https://hbr.org/2016/12/why-ethical-people-make-unethical-choices.
21 Ibid.
22 Ibid.
23 Ibid.
24 Ibid.
25 Ibid.

8

FIVE MORAL PITFALLS TO AVOID

Abstract

This chapter highlights five generally accepted mind-sets that can become moral pitfalls, and which oftentimes happen simultaneously: greed, pride, excessive end-focus, moral rationalization, and apathy. An in-depth review of these five factors will be presented, including the cognitive dissonance that is oftentimes embedded in such moral pitfalls, the ease of adhering to them, and the disastrous outcomes they can cause.

About Pitfalls and Cognitive Dissonance

Every behavior can serve as an advantage or a pitfall, depending on the intensity we invest in it. Perseverance, usually considered a strong quality, could evolve into blind persistence long after the sense of achieving our goal has waned. The desire to ensure growth and profitability could morph into selfish greed, the aim to gain prominence may turn into damaging pride, the wish to achieve a goal could degenerate into an excessive end-focus, the desire to realize a potentially noble initiative may lead to the rationalization of unacceptable acts, and the quality of being patient, lax, or understanding may dilute into apathy.

Cognitive dissonance is a state of having inconsistent thoughts, beliefs, or attitudes, especially as relating to behavioral decisions and attitude change. It often conjures up a sense of uneasiness, due to the desire to restore the balance between our perceptions and our actions.[1] One simple example of cognitive dissonance is a person who smokes while knowing it's a hazard to his or her health. Human beings always want consistency in their beliefs and behaviors. The concept of cognitive dissonance was first studied by Leon Festinger. His 1957 theory of cognitive dissonance explains that an individual who experiences such inconsistency has a tendency to become psychologically uncomfortable, and will try to reduce the cognitive dissonance occurring, while also actively avoiding situations and information likely to increase the psychological discomfort.[2] Indeed, people who get confronted with a discrepancy between their behavior and the reality may want to seek reasons to justify their behavior, nonetheless.[3]

The closer to home the dissonance is, the stronger it is. When we believe something about ourselves and discover that we act against that belief, then we will face a strong level of dissonance. It is this strong sense that also encourages us to change and work on ourselves.

In this chapter, we will review some of the pitfalls that can cause leaders to lose sight of their moral path and fall prey to some of the most common downsides of performance orientation, along with the cognitive dissonances that could be at the foundation of such pitfalls. Keeping track of these moral pitfalls may keep us more on our leadership toes, and assist us in becoming the role models we aspire to be for upcoming generations.

Greed

When we stand at the bottom of the career ladder, we are usually filled with good intentions. In my many years as a facilitator of seminars with upcoming business leaders, I have yet to meet one who said she or he would become a greedy, ruthless executive. Greed grows on us when we fail to closely observe ourselves. It is a notorious by-product of the desire to be a winner. Corporate leaders, but also those with fighting spirit in different settings, can relate to this: as you fight your way to the top, you focus so much on your own victory that you may become blind to the needs of others, and ignorant of the way you are perceived. By the time you realize what happened, you may find yourself too anchored in the behavior of selfish gain to find a way out.

Greed is a recurring problem among leaders, and not only those serving for-profit entities. It seems, especially in the US, that the established focus on accruing wealth repeatedly causes people with brilliant minds to behave mindlessly, and oftentimes in ways that harm them, as well as many others.[4] The 2008 economic recession was a clear example of greed, and how it has seeped into many layers of financial institutions. The cases of corporate fraud, insider trading, and investment swindles are numerous, and, oftentimes, executives at reputable companies such as IBM, McKinsey, and Berkshire Hathaway fall prey to this destructive behavior.[5] The most concerning issue here is that many of the manifestations of greed are not sporadic acts from isolated individuals, but more often collective acts that are condoned or subliminally supported by formal bodies. An example that comes to mind is the case of AIG, where corporate greed was basically rewarded by a government bailout. The foundational question we can ask ourselves in all these cases is: what does it ultimately benefit the perpetrators? They earn a lot of money, become very affluent, yet still want more, so they engage in acts driven by greed, get in serious legal trouble, and ultimately lose everything.[6] Most interestingly, however, is the fact that people seem to have a completely distorted idea of what money can do for them. They don't realize that it will not change the foundational concepts of a person's character of life perceptions: worriers will remain worriers, and unhappy souls will remain unhappy, because money cannot suffice in those areas, as is often expected. People often overlook the blessings that lie in the challenges of their work and the fulfillment it gives, even if it will never make you a millionaire.[7]

The Cognitive Dissonance in Greed

So, how is greed related to cognitive dissonance? There are multiple ways, but we will review two angles here. From the side of the predators, those aiming to take advantage of others, there may be a sense of *entitlement* regarding the wealth they should accumulate. If such wealth cannot be acquired in a virtuous way, then less-virtuous (dishonest and possibly immoral) ways are applied to balance out the existing cognitive dissonance.

From the side of the victims of greed, the picture looks somewhat different. As Festinger explained in his cognitive dissonance theory,[8] people's desire to attain cognitive consistency and get rid of the dissonance can lead them to engage in irrational behavior. In their quest to get rid of the internal discrepancy between themselves and the world, many people open themselves to a vulnerability that is senseless, and they immerse themselves in actions that they would never engage in with a rational mind[9]. This is oftentimes the case in Ponzi schemes, where people expect exorbitant returns on their investments, but end up losing all their money.[10]

Pride

Pride can be a downside of many factors. It can surface when a leader works on self-confidence, and does such a good job at it, that he or she ultimately thinks he or she has all the answers. This type of pride is also known as *arrogance*. Pride can also manifest itself in the sense of not wanting to lose face. Some leaders have so much trouble admitting that they were wrong that they would rather manipulate data, contaminate people, and risk valuable relationships to prove that they are right. Pride is an easy gateway to becoming so self-indulged that one may start thinking that he or she stands above the law and may engage in acts that are unacceptable for others.

Arrogance can be a major impediment to leadership. It does not take long for one person to detect arrogance in another, particularly because arrogant people are usually not the most pleasant ones to interact with. When they hold positions of power, they become difficult to be around, often causing their own downfall, because their mannerisms obstruct the quality of interactions in their workplaces.[11] While arrogance can easily result from excessive self-confidence, there are important differences between arrogance and self-confidence. Self-confidence is usually driven by a sense of self-worth, gathered from one's awareness of one's abilities or standing. Arrogance, on the other hand, is not always an expression of high confidence. Sometimes, it is intended to conceal exactly the opposite, insecurity.[12]

The arrogance that comes from pride is not merely limited to humans. Companies, since they are steered by human beings, can also be subject to "collective" arrogance, and lead to performance decline that can be attributed to exactly the same factors that initially caused growth.[13] Performance is no longer limited to profit maximization alone. Any person or company that focuses only on profit maximization will ultimately fall by the wayside, since a focus on continuous and creative innovation is equally as important as safeguarding revenue. Yet, as success augments, and prestige grows, people and companies get beside themselves and forget to focus on what is critical for maintenance of upward performance.[14]

The Cognitive Dissonance in Pride

So, how is pride related to cognitive dissonance? There is a simple explanation to this one. When people feel that their losses make them lose face, they will try to restore the status they feel they deserve. These people want to recover from the perception of having made poor decisions, leading to losses, and they will do whatever they feel to be needed to correct this internal discord.[15] In order to restore their sense of pride toward themselves and the world, they will, therefore, engage in actions to "save face," which can vary from finding someone else to take the blame, to engaging in immoral practices to correct their losses.

Excessive End-Focus

This moral flaw has the best chance of surfacing when critical and pressing goals need to be met. In such circumstances, it is easy to fall prey to the mindset that achieving the numbers justifies everything, even a few unethical acts. This, then, is when we can see leaders betraying their employees' psychological contracts by continuously demanding more output from them without giving any additional rewards, callously disregarding employees' work–life balance for the sake of the meeting or exceeding deadlines, and even shipping substandard or damaged products in order to justify quota.

What many goal-focused people don't realize is the pressure they place on other people when they want to realize their goals within certain time limits. Oftentimes, others have to make sacrifices beyond their normal schedule or actions to get the goal achieved. Additionally, the intense focus caused by this mentality can lead to oversights of other things that are important in the process. Focusing intensely on a goal often also leads to a heavy short-term preference and a loss of the essence of long-term achievements.[16] Then, as indicated above, achieving the goal may become such an obsession that everything seems to be justified to accomplish the goal, even if "everything" also entails immoral acts. Besides, in their desire to achieve their goal, some people may lie that they have accomplished more than they really did. Additionally, there is the fact of competitiveness: in order to reach a goal, other things must be sacrificed. In organizations, this could mean that colleagues start competing with one another for scarce resources, and collegiality may suffer.[17] At the personal level, meeting strict goals can also diminish the intrinsic motivation a person would otherwise get from completing a rewarding assignment. The goal can become so critical to be attained that the fulfillment of engaging in the task becomes secondary.[18]

The Cognitive Dissonance in Excessive End-Focus

The very concept of goal-setting can lead to cognitive dissonance. Some leaders formulate their goals in actions and others do so in outcomes.[19] And then the major issue is whether these actions or outcomes can be perceived as realistic and sensible. The most challenging aspect to overcome in focusing on any target is to get people to buy into it. If goals don't appeal to people, they will only get disengaged and demoralized, no matter how hard their leader wants them to focus on these goals. This, then, is considered a discord, which can easily digress into cognitive dissonance for either the employees or the leaders who have set the goals. Employees may dislike the way they are being pushed toward the end-focus of their leader, and either massively revolt or exit in order to find a better fit between their notions of the world and themselves therein. Similarly, leaders may get discouraged if their goals are not met or supported by their team, which may lead them into seeking alternative ways (massive layoffs and workforce replacement, outsourcing, automatizing, etc.) in order to restore their cognitive consonance.

Moral Rationalization

Rationalization is yet another quality that sounds good, but can also have its dark side. In dire times, leaders can begin to rationalize why engaging in less-than-rosy practices could be justified. For years, now, I have presented business students a dilemma that boils down to the following: should you use illegally acquired data from a competitor to win a bid, or forego the opportunity and risk going out of business? So far, the responses have been even: half of the participants stated that they would not use the data, as it would be blatantly immoral, and half came up with all sorts of rationalizations as to why they would use the information, even though they knew it was unethical. Some of the most common rationalizations of immoral acts are: everyone does it, this is my fair right in an unfair world, or it's part of my responsibility to my job, family, culture, or any other group I affiliate with.

Moral rationalization is an individual's ability to reinterpret his or her immoral actions as, in fact, moral. It arises out of a conflict of motivations and a need to see the self as moral.[20] Some people remain ignorant of the discrepancy between what they claim to stand for and what they actually do in their actions. When confronted with the immoral elements of their actions, most people can come up with the most interesting rationalizations that are supposed to illustrate why their reason for doing what they do, even if perceived as immoral, is actually perfectly fine. Moral rationalization is a cognitive process that human beings use to convince themselves that their behavior is in line with, and therefore does not violate, their moral standards. We justify small and large things, varying from tax reporting to dangerous patterns.[21] Some examples of how people justify immoral behavior are: when they can hide behind others' authority and claim that they were just complying, just as in the Milgram obedience studies, a case where several people obeyed an unknown figure in authority in supposedly sending large dosages of electricity to a human subject.[22] Fortunately, the "victims" to which the electricity was sent in the Milgram Experiment were actors, who were not really being electrocuted. However, even though there was severe screaming, many of the study participants kept pressing on the electrocution button when ordered to do so, even though they felt bad about doing so. When we assign people roles, they may also get so absorbed in fulfilling the roles that the immoral aspects of those roles are left unconsidered. This happened during the Stanford prison experiment, whereby Stanford University students that were assigned guard roles became increasingly arrogant and mean toward their fellow students that had accepted prisoner roles.[23]

The Cognitive Dissonance in Moral Rationalization

So, how is moral rationalization related to cognitive dissonance? If we consider that people always seek to obtain consonance rather than dissonance in their behaviors, it is easy to infer that they will change their behavior, trivialize the situation, or rationalize their actions. This last option, rationalizing actions, is what occurs in moral rationalization. The individual in this case will either try to explain that their actions have a special, valuable serving focus, or they will minimize their role in the action. They may also downplay potential negative effects, or blame others for undesirable outcomes.[24] As a matter of fact, there is a reverse effect going on here: the more there is at stake, the smaller will the issue be made (trivialization).

Apathy

Knowing that others are engaging in something immoral and not doing anything about it, even if you can, is as immoral as being fully involved in the act. Apathy is the less-attractive side of acceptance. While acceptance is usually a positive quality, we can push it too far, just as we could any other good quality, and become complacent about the status quo, even if it is an undesirable one. Being apathetic is inexcusable in leadership, because leaders are supposed to know what is going on in their environments.

Apathetic leaders are indifferent to the trends and developments in their organizations, a fact that is quickly picked up by employees, who then promptly get demoralized and become less engaged. It is easy to construe, then, that diminished employee engagement will have a negative effect on the organization's performance.[25] When placed within that scope, apathy could be considered the opposite of passion. In many workplaces today, you will find leader teams that are quick to blame all the wrongs in their processes, output, and Return on Investment (ROI) on external factors outside of their influence: the economy, the government, the market, global volatility, you name it. These leaders are so busy proving that things are bad that they forego great opportunities to turn the tide by mobilizing their workforce into a "can-do" mind-set. Apathy has been likened to weed: it can spread with dazzling speed throughout an organization, converting people who were once passionate and energetic into lethargic and uncaring sluggards. Once apathy is in, creativity and innovation are out, and the focus shifts from solution-based to problem-based.[26]

Some steps leaders can consider if they want to snap out of an apathetic mode include:

1. Self-reflection and understanding that you, as the leader, carry the responsibility to set a go-getter tone.
2. Discover the sources of apathy in your organization, and address them.
3. In addressing the sources, avoid blame, and try to understand how this mind-set came about.
4. Explain the effects of apathetic behavior to those engaging in it, and suggest collaborative ways to bring about a change.
5. Acknowledge positive changes, even if they are small to start with.[27]

The Cognitive Dissonance in Apathy

Apathy is an effective way to increase an already extant level of cognitive dissonance. By being apathetic about organizational activities, constructive feedback and encouragement will remain absent. That is, unless a leader's apathy is interpreted as approval. Either way, an apathetic approach implies a leader with an external locus of control: the main responsibility for whatever happens, especially when it's negative, is placed in the shoes of co-workers. In the case of Enron, for instance, the chairman, Ken Lay, took an apathetic stance while his employees were engaging in the most unethical ways to make profits. As long as profits were made, he seemed to be fine with looking the other way and acting as if he was unaware of what was going on. In the case of Enron, one could deduce that an apathetic approach may have been useful to Lay, as it allowed employees' immoral practices to bring in the dollars he considered important to restore his cognitive consonance.

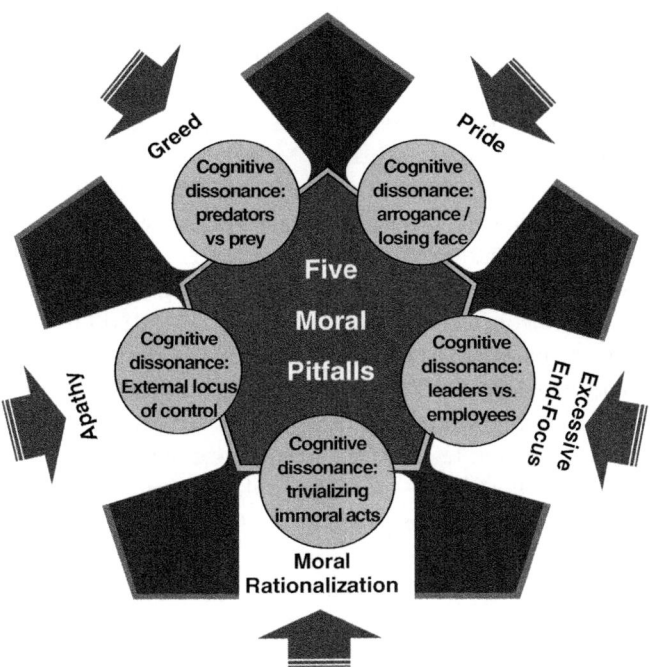

FIGURE 8.1 Five Moral Pitfalls.

Case 8.1 The Brazen Business Dealings of Martin Shkreli

A young, intelligent, and promising entrepreneur, Martin Shkreli made a name for himself as an American entrepreneur and a pharmaceutical executive, and subsequently as a price gouger and securities fraudster. After earning a business degree from New York's Baruch College in 2004, he explored a path that seemed promising to him: the financial industry. He had earned some early successes in predicting biotech stock at Cramer, Berkowitz and Company, and Regeneron Pharmaceuticals in the early 2000s, then worked at UBS and Intrepid Capital Management prior to cofounding a hedge fund called MSMB Capital Management in 2009.[28] MSMB Capital Management LLC provided investment services, particularly specializing in long-term investments in both private and public healthcare and biotechnology businesses. Shkreli quickly became known and feared for shorting biotech stocks and berating those companies on social media.

In 2011, Shkreli expanded his horizons and founded the pharmaceutical company Retrophin, and managed it as a portfolio company focusing on biotechnology to create treatments for rare diseases. Right after doing so, Shkreli, who had been labeled by critics as immature and unfocused for such a position, made some poor bets, causing him to lose $7 million for his hedge fund, and an additional $1 million in other trading losses. Having reached an all-time low in assets, MSMB discontinued its trading. However, Shkreli continued to communicate with investors as if all was still flourishing at MSMB. According to the federal indictment and the SEC, Shkreli's string of losing money and lying to investors had been going on almost from the moment he started MSMB. Still in his twenties at the time, Shkreli convinced nine investors to place $3 million with him, and mismanaged it to a point where he had a little over $300 left. He had a habit of paying himself lavishly, merrily ignoring the agreed-upon 1 percent management fee and 20 percent profit incentive.[29]

As with most Ponzi-like swindlers, Shkreli started robbing Peter to pay Paul: for the next three years, he took money from Retrophin to pay for his personal debts and those of MSMB.[30] He falsified documents to make it appear as if MSMB had invested in Retrophin. Investors at Retrophin started becoming concerned and demanded money from Shkreli. As Shkreli continued his unapproved settlements, disguised as (fake) consulting agreements, the members of the Retrophin board became so disconcerted that they voted him out as CEO in 2014.[31] Shortly before he was ousted from Retrophin, the company acquired the rights to market Thiola, a drug used to treat the disease cystinuria, and raised the price of this medicine from $1.50 to $30 per pill, a 2,000 percent price increase for a pill often taken 10–15 times per day by one patient.

Undaunted by his previous experiences, Shkreli started another pharmaceutical company, Turing Pharmaceuticals, within a year. Turing bought the rights to market Daraprim, a popular and highly demanded medical treatment for AIDS patients. As he got sued by Retrophin for $65 million for using the company's money to pay off MSMB investors, Shkreli unscrupulously gouged the price of Daraprim by raising the price per pill from $13.00 to $750.00, a raise of 5,000 percent,[32] claiming that he did what his investors wanted: maximized profits. In fact, this recurring act of price gouging on medicines has revived the discussion about capitalism and human well-being. "When allowing pharmaceutical companies to arbitrarily decide prices, especially for those medications that do not simply relieve symptoms but rather sustain life, many believe that dangerous territory is entered: 'The more definitive the cure, the closer we are to asking, 'What's the value of a human life?'"[33]

With such despicable abuse of power, Shkreli became a focus point of criticism for presidential candidates Bernie Sanders, Hillary Clinton, and

Donald Trump. Shkreli soon acquired the reputation of being the most hated man in America, not necessarily because of the size of his securities fraud, which was nowhere in comparison to major predators such Bernie Madoff, but far more because he engaged in such distasteful price gouging with products that were meant to assist sick people. At the end of that year, Shkreli's game of greed, manipulation, and fraud was over. He was arrested by the FBI, and was accused of running a Ponzi-like scheme. He resigned as CEO of Turing, and was replaced by the chairman of the company's board, Ron Tilles. As of this book's publication date, the price of Daraprim remains high in the US, for reasons that are considered unacceptable by medical doctors.[34]

In an interesting point-counterpoint article, Shkreli's status of being an entrepreneur is debated.[35] While two of the three authors feel that Shkreli cannot be labeled an entrepreneur, because entrepreneurs create new value, and Shkreli just bought the rights to existing drugs and gouged their prices, the other author asserts that Shkreli is an entrepreneur, albeit an immoral one, since he did engage in product exchange with the aim of (successfully) obtaining a profit, and therefore engaged in value creation for his investors. The opposing authors feel that it is important to refrain from labeling Shkreli an entrepreneur, because upcoming generations are encouraged to become entrepreneurs, and we have to safeguard who their role models are. The proponent author affirms that it may be critical for upcoming generations to be aware of the various types of entrepreneurs there are, understand the consequences, and make a conscious choice in what type they would like to be.[36]

Questions

1. Which of the five pitfalls can you detect in this case? Please explain.
2. Please discuss at least two instances of cognitive dissonance in the case.
3. Please engage in some update research: what is Martin Shkreli doing now?
4. Do you think Shkreli will cease his brazen acts? Why or why not?

Summary

- Every behavior can serve as an advantage or a pitfall, depending on the intensity we invest in it. Keeping track of moral pitfalls may keep us more on our leadership toes, and assist us in becoming the role models we aspire to be for upcoming generations.
- Cognitive dissonance is a state of having inconsistent thoughts, beliefs, or attitudes, especially as relating to behavioral decisions and attitude change.

It often conjures up a sense of uneasiness, due to the desire to restore the balance between our perceptions and actions.

- Greed grows on us when we fail to closely observe ourselves. It is a notorious by-product of the desire to be a winner.
  - Greed is a recurring problem among leaders, and not only those serving for-profit entities. The cases of corporate fraud, insider trading, and investment swindles are numerous, and oftentimes, executives at reputable companies fall prey to this destructive behavior.
  - The cognitive dissonance in greed can be explained in multiple ways. From the side of the predators, those aiming to take advantage of others, there may be a sense of entitlement regarding the wealth they should accumulate. From the side of the victims of greed, those who are taken advantage of, the problem also surfaces as a desire to get rid of the internal discrepancy between themselves and the world, leading people to immerse into actions that they would never engage in with a rational mind.
- Pride can surface when a leader works on his or her self-confidence, and does such a good job at it, that the leader ultimately thinks that he or she has all the answers (arrogance). It can also manifest itself in the sense of not wanting to lose face. Pride is an easy gateway to becoming so self-indulged that one may start thinking that leaders stand above the law.
  - Difference between arrogance and self-confidence: Self-confidence is usually driven by a sense of self-worth, gathered from one's awareness of one's abilities or standing. Arrogance is not always an expression of high confidence. Sometimes it is intended to conceal insecurity.
  - The cognitive dissonance in pride can manifest itself when people feel that their circumstances make them lose face. They may then want to recover the perception of having made poor decisions, and they will do whatever they feel to be needed to correct this internal discord.
- Excessive end-focus has the best chance of surfacing when critical and pressing goals need to be met. In such circumstances, it is easy to fall prey to the mind-set that achieving the numbers justifies everything, even a few unethical acts. What many goal-focused people don't realize is the pressure they place on other people when they want to realize their goals within certain time limits.
  - Focusing intensely on a goal often also leads to a heavy short-term preference and a loss of the essence of long-term achievements. Achieving the goal may become such an obsession that everything seems to be justified to accomplish the goal, even if "everything" also entails immoral acts.
  - The cognitive dissonance in excessive end-focus lies in goal setting. The most challenging aspect to overcome in focusing on any target is to get people to buy into it. If goals don't appeal to people, they will only get disengaged and demoralized, no matter how hard their leader wants them to focus on these goals. Leaders may get discouraged if their

goals are not met or supported by their team, which may lead them into seeking alternative ways (massive layoffs and workforce replacement, outsourcing, automatizing, etc.) in order to restore their cognitive consonance.

- Moral rationalization is an individual's ability to reinterpret his or her immoral actions as moral. It arises out of a conflict of motivations and a need to see the self as moral. Some people remain ignorant of the discrepancy between what they claim to stand for and what they actually do.
  - When confronted with the immoral elements of their actions, most people can come up with the most interesting rationalizations that are supposed to illustrate why their reason for doing what they do, even if perceived as immoral, is actually perfectly fine.
  - The cognitive dissonance in moral rationalization comes from the fact that people always seek to obtain consonance rather than dissonance in their behaviors: they either change their behavior, trivialize the situation, or rationalize their actions. The act of rationalizing actions is what occurs in moral rationalization.
- Apathy is the less-attractive side of acceptance. Being apathetic is inexcusable in leadership, because leaders are supposed to know what is going on in their environments.
  - Apathetic leaders are indifferent to the trends and developments in their organizations, a fact that is quickly picked up by employees, who then promptly get demoralized and become less engaged. When placed within that scope, apathy could be considered the opposite of passion.
  - The cognitive dissonance in apathy can be detected in the leader's behavior and its effects: by being apathetic about organizational activities, constructive feedback and encouragement will remain absent.

Reflective Questions

1. Of the five moral pitfalls discussed in this chapter, identify one that you feel you could mostly fall prey to. Why did you select this pitfall? Reflect on how you aim to avoid falling prey to it.
2. Identify a cognitive dissonance that you have struggled with or are currently struggling with. Do you consider it a moral dilemma? Please explain.
3. The chapter mentions a trend of corporate fraud, insider trading, and investment swindles in which executives at reputable companies are involved. What do you consider to be the foundation to this trend? Please explain.
4. Consider greed from the stance of Utilitarianism (see Chapter 2 for a more detailed explanation of this theory). Could greed be justified in the Utilitarian viewpoint? Why or why not?
5. Consider pride from the stance of Universalism (see Chapter 2 for a more detailed explanation of this theory). Could pride be justified from the Universalist viewpoint?

Notes

1 McLeod, S. (2008, 2014). Cognitive dissonance. *Simply Psychology*. www.simply psychology.org/cognitive-dissonance.html.

2 Festinger, L. (1957). *A Theory of Cognitive Dissonance*. Redwood City, CA: Stanford University Press.

3 McLeod, S. (2008, 2014). Cognitive dissonance. *Simply Psychology*. www.simply psychology.org/cognitive-dissonance.html.

4 Gaughan, A. J. (April 25, 2016). How America's rich betrayed their fellow citizens. The Guardian: Money. Retrieved from https://www.theguardian.com/commentisfree/2016/apr/25/america-wealthy-class-betrayed-inequality.

5 Taylor, B. (May 17, 2010). Money and the meaning of life. *Harvard Business Review*. https://hbr.org/2011/05/money-and-the-meaning-of-life.

6 Ibid.

7 Ibid.

8 Festinger.

9 Ibid.

10 Harris, D. (August 15, 2016). China, the world, greed, cognitive dissonance, the best and the brightest, and why people seem to encourage/almost enjoy getting scammed. *China Law Blog*. www.chinalawblog.com/2016/08/china-the-world-greed-cognitive-dissonance-the-best-and-the-brightest-and-why-people-seem-to-encouragealmost-enjoy-getting-scammed.html.

11 Silverman, S. B., Johnson, R. E., McConnell, N., & Carr, A. (2012). Arrogance: A formula for leadership failure. *TIP: The Industrial-Organizational Psychologist 50*(1), 21–28.

12 Ibid.

13 Anthony, S. (November 13, 2012). How arrogance can blind your transformation efforts. *Harvard Business Review*. https://hbr.org/2012/11/how-arrogance-can-blind-your-t.

14 Ibid.

15 Chang, T. Y., Solomon, D. H., & Westerfield, M. M. (2016). Looking for someone to blame: Delegation, cognitive dissonance, and the disposition effect. *Journal of Finance 71*(1), 267–302.

16 Williams, R. (July 11, 2014). Why goal-setting doesn't work. *Psychology Today*. www.psychologytoday.com/blog/wired-success/201407/why-goal-setting-doesnt-work.

17 Ibid.

18 Ibid.

19 Jinks, D., & Dexter, J. (2012). What do you really want: An examination of the pursuit of goal-setting in coaching. *International Journal of Evidence Based Coaching & Mentoring 10*(2), 100–110.

20 Tsang, J. (2002). Moral rationalization and the integration of situational factors and psychological processes in immoral behavior. *Review of General Psychology 6*(1), 25–50.

21 Ibid.

22 Read about the Milgram Experiment at: McLeod, S. (2007). The Milgram Experiment. Simply Psychology. Retrieved from https://www.simplypsychology.org/milgram.html.

23 Read more about the Stanford Prison Experiment in Zimbardo, P. (2017). The Stanford Prison Experiment: A simulation study on the psychology of imprisonment. Retrieved from http://www.prisonexp.org/.

24 Peters, R., & Filipova, A. (2009). Optimizing cognitive-dissonance literacy in ethics education. *Public Integrity 11*(3), 201–219.

25 Jenkins, J. (June 16, 2013). Apathy and leadership. *Leadership & Teambuilding*. www. managingamericans.com/BlogFeed/Leadership-Teambuilding/Apathy-and-Leader ship.htm.

26 Ibid.

27 Ibid.

28 Goldman, D. (December 18, 2015). Who is Martin Shkreli? A timeline. *CNN Money*. http://money.cnn.com/2015/12/18/news/companies/martin-shkreli.

29 Smythe, C. (December 17, 2015). Shkreli, drug price gouger, denies fraud and posts bail, arrested Thursday, accused of Ponzi-like scheme. *Bloomberg*. www.bloomberg. com/features/2015-martin-shkreli-securities-fraud.

30 Goldman, D. (December 18, 2015). Who is Martin Shkreli? A timeline. *CNN Money*. http://money.cnn.com/2015/12/18/news/companies/martin-shkreli.

31 Ibid.

32 Ibid.

33 (2015). Martin Shkreli and the increased cost of Daraprim. *Penn Bioethics Journal 11*(2), 6.

34 Court, E. (Feb 4, 2016). Here's why Daraprim still costs $750 a pill. *MarketWatch*. Retrieved from http://www.marketwatch.com/story/heres-why-daraprim-still-costs-750-a-pill-2016-02-03.

35 Plummer, L. A., Mitchell, J. R., & McMullen, J. S. (2017). What exactly IS Martin Shkreli? *Business Horizons 60*(1), 19–24.

36 Ibid.

9

MORAL THEORIES

Some Pros and Cons

Abstract

This chapter will review four of the most commonly discussed moral theories: Utilitarianism, Universalism (Kantian Ethics), the Golden Rule, and Virtue Ethics, and present a dialogue about the most common strengths and weaknesses of each theory, with the aim to underscore that adhering to one single moral theory is not an easy task. This chapter will also discuss some of the challenges leaders may face in their efforts to do the right thing.

The Challenge with Moral Theories

Moral theories can be complicated and confusing. Some of them overlap, while others complement one another, and yet others completely contrast each other in the decisions and actions they recommend. Some moral theories are rather inflexible, while others provide ample room for interpretation and implementation variance. There are moral theories that date back more than two millennia, such as the Golden Rule, which can be traced all the way to biblical times, and Aristotle's Virtue Theory (Virtue Ethics), which also dates back several centuries BCE. Other theories were developed in more recent centuries, such as Kant's Universalism and Bentham's Utilitarianism (18th century). The most interesting thing about moral theories is that all of them make sense when perceived against certain backgrounds, circumstances, and mind-sets.

Many people make moral decisions without knowing which theory lies at the foundation of those decisions. They go with what we conveniently refer to as their "gut feeling." Many business leaders make critical decisions in their business operations that way. They may just do what has been referred to as the family and newspaper text: would I mind that my family knew about this, and would I mind if it were to be published in tomorrow's newspaper? Some leaders may take their personal moral decisions a step further by asking themselves if they would still make the decision if their child (or other loved one) would be on the receiving end of it. (We'll discuss these types of decisions in Chapter 10.)

When making quick moral decisions, one of the quickest theories that can be used is the Golden Rule. The example of substituting a loved one at the receiving end of a decision has much to do with that: don't do unto others what you would not want to have done unto yourself (or your loved ones). In this same decision process, we can also discover some Universalism, because this theory suggests that we should refrain from seeing others as a means toward our selfish ends, but rather treat them as a means onto themselves. Similarly, we could use the lens of Virtue Ethics as the foundational mind-set here, as this promotes *eudaimonia* (happiness, well-being, a good life) as the main focus of human life, which should prompt us to practice good character and virtues in our daily activities.

Let us first reintroduce the moral theories in a concise way (introductory details in Chapter 2), and then engage in a comparison of their strengths and weaknesses.

Moral Theories: A Brief Recap

Universalism

Universalism is a deontological or duty-based approach to life.[1] Immanuel Kant, a German philosopher, still considered a central figure in modern philosophy to this day, is known for his theory that there is a single moral obligation, called the *Categorical Imperative*, that is derived from the concept of duty. The categorical imperative, as explained in Chapter 2, holds that every act we commit should be based on our personal principles or rules, labeled by Kant as *maxims*. Maxims are the reasons behind our actions. In order to ensure that our maxims are morally sound, we should ask ourselves if we would want them to be universal laws. A maxim should only be considered acceptable if it could become a universal law. If not, it should be dismissed.[2]

The categorical imperative can be divided in two parts[3]: (1) We should only choose for an act if we would want every person in the world, if in the same situation as we currently are, to act in exactly the same way, and (2) We should always act in a way that demonstrates respect to others and treats them as ends unto themselves rather than as means toward an end.

Utilitarianism

Utilitarianism, being a form of consequentialism, focuses predominantly on the end result or outcomes (the consequence) of any act. Considering this, we can quickly conclude that this theory forms a stark contrast with the above-summarized Universalist approach, because Universalism focuses on intentions rather than outcomes. In general, Utilitarianism holds the view that the action that produces the greatest well-being for the largest number is the morally right one. Utilitarianism has been defined as "a measure of the relative happiness or satisfaction of a group, usually considered in questions of the allocation of limited resources to a population."[4] Jeremy Bentham, the most notable promotor of this theory, reasoned that all good things should be maximized to benefit as many stakeholders as possible. Due to this focus on the happiness levels of the largest group, a significant degree of flexibility was embedded in the Utilitarian approach, simply because the greatest good today might not be the greatest good tomorrow.

The Golden Rule

The Golden Rule is one of the oldest moral theories, usually articulated as, "Do unto others as you would have others do unto you."[5] The concept of the Golden Rule seems to have arisen in several places, such as China, Greece, and Israel, around the same time, which was around 600 B.C.E. Analysts of the rule have established that it should be seen as a moral principle, but not as a fully developed, formal ethical system.[6] The Golden Rule calls for its practitioners to reflect on their own preferences, and refrain from treating others in ways they would not want to be treated. The fact that the Golden Rule was formulated so long ago may explain why it is prone to some firm criticism today. In early days, communities were close-knit, with a common culture and little diversity. Thus, one could easily assume that there were many common perspectives, common likes and dislikes. Today, humanity is exposed to immense degrees of diversity due to heavily increased global traveling trends. Placing ourselves in others' shoes is commonly a noble idea, but there should be some consideration in this act when it comes to the Golden Rule.

Virtue Ethics

Virtue Ethics focuses on virtues, or moral character, in contrast to duties or rules or consequences of actions.[7] With their strong focus on duties and outcomes, neither of the more recent moral theories (Utilitarianism and Universalism) was considering the conscious context of virtues, motives, moral character, moral education, moral wisdom or discernment, relationships, the concept of happiness, the role of emotions in moral life, and the foundational questions of what sort of person one should be.[8] It is important to emphasize that a virtue is a character trait, which means that it cannot be distinguished from one single action alone. It is consistent behavior. It is not a habit, but more a deep-rooted sense of being that gets translated in feelings, perceptions, decisions, and actions. Our virtues are the foundations of our personality. Being a truly virtuous person is admirable, because life presents us many challenges that create or increase the temptation to decide against virtuous acts.

Strengths and Weaknesses of the Theories

Universalism

Most Important Strengths

The most obvious strength of Universalism is its consistency. With this moral approach, there is no question about the decision to be made: what is right for one should be right for all. This removes any emotional considerations and guarantees a clearly outlined *modus operando*.

Another major strength of Universalism is the fact that this moral theory focuses on the intentions of the decision-maker, thus making the decision-maker his or her own moral agent, and motivating him or her to practice respect for those encountered in the decision-making processes. Furthermore, the reflective element in this theory, evoking a deep consideration for the well-being of all parties involved in our actions, exalts it moral magnitude. "Moral requirements have a special status in human life. . . . If one who has moral sentiments at all fails to act on them, one will feel guilty, regretful, or ashamed. Moral requirements are the most demanding ... standards for conduct, for interpersonal and intercultural criticism."[9]

The foundational guideline in Universalism to make our counterparts an end unto themselves instead of a means toward our ends reminds us somewhat of the Golden Rule, which states that we should not do unto others what we would not have done unto ourselves.[10] The Golden Rule, however, could be considered as having a narrower focus than the Universalist approach, since it only considers immediate stakeholders, while Universalism urges us to think in terms of universalizability.

The fact that intentions are more important than outcomes in Universalism also emphasizes its noble foundation. While we cannot influence the outcomes of our actions, we can, after all, always embark on their realization with the best of intentions.

Most Important Weaknesses

It is first and foremost the aspect of Universalizability that raises concern within the opponents of the Universalist approach: how possible is it, they question, to consider all people, all nations, all beliefs, and all cultures in every single act we implement? In addition, the equality-based approach, which Universalism proclaims, is an ideal one, but not realistic in today's world. While a good point could be made in favor of ending unfair treatment of those who are already privileged, there is a serious weakness to be detected if we start applying equal treatment when we want to resolve an existing imbalance. By utilizing the Universalist approach at all times, we would not be able to correct existing imbalances, simply because Universalism does not condone a more favorable approach to anyone, hence not even to those that are oppressed and subjugated. Similarly, it does not support a less favorable treatment of anyone, hence not even those that have been unfairly privileged in past centuries.

When we contemplate the major moral issue of human rights, we could raise an important question by comparing the Divine Command theory (not discussed earlier, but frequently applied by religious people—see brief explanation in endnotes), which proposes a Universalist approach based on religious rulings, with Kant's categorical imperative, which proposes this same approach based on autonomy.[11]

> Divine Command Theory is the view that morality is somehow dependent upon God, and that moral obligation consists in obedience to God's commands. Divine Command Theory includes the claim that morality is ultimately based on the commands or character of God, and that the morally right action is the one that God commands or requires.[12]

What makes one more acceptable than the other, if they are both aiming for universal application? The fact that non-Muslims become uncomfortable when a Muslim scholar claims that Islam has formulated fundamental rights for all of humanity, and that these rights are granted by Allah, should be a clear indication that there could be opponents to any universal law, formulated by any group or individual at any time. "The question here is whether two conflicting justifications that appeal to different foundations of human rights (divine command and autonomy) should strengthen or weaken our confidence in the universality belief."[13] Some authors point out, in Kant's favor, that the notion of autonomy assumes a rational person's capacity for free moral choice made in the spirit of enlightenment.[14] These authors defend Universalism as being secular and rational, free from superstition or divine commands, void of emotions or filial bonds, and centered on doing the right thing for the right reasons. On the other hand, these same authors candidly admit that Universalism, as Kant defined it, is void of compassion, as it mainly focuses on fulfilling a responsibility. Indeed, rigid and consistent at its core, the Universalist approach does not leave room for flexibility. What is right is right and what is wrong is wrong: no negotiation possible. This stance can become problematic when situations occur with conflicting duties among involved parties, because in such cases a mutually gratifying solution is impossible to attain.

The intention-based focus of Universalism may not always lead to desired outcomes, and may leave unwanted victims down the line. This could be seen as an unwelcome side-effect of a generally well-considered moral approach. No one enjoys disastrous outcomes, even if intentions were good. Universalism may, therefore, not always be the most desired mind-set, depending on what is at stake.

Critical Opportunities

Possible opportunities for Universalism must be considered against the backdrop of contemporary society. Given the upward trend of globalization, and the consequentially increasing cultural blend of people worldwide, the mind-set of Universalism may become more appealing in near-future moral considerations. The increased exposure to a broad range of cultures, religions, ethnicities, age groups, and education levels in one single work environment has become part of the fabric of modern-day workplaces. Universalists feel that "Our globally interdependent world . . . stands in need of an ethical perspective that transcends cultural and religious differences."[15] If this mind-set finds acceptance on a massive global scale, Universalist thinking may become the most gratifying and acceptable, hence dominant, moral philosophy.

Critical Threats

Inasmuch as globalization is an unstoppable trend, the diversity that it brings reinforces flexibility and receptiveness to multiple perceptions. In its conceptual form, Universalism is known as a rigid, inflexible moral stance. The 21st century has taught us thus far that such inflexibility cannot be upheld and tolerated in today's versatile environments. While there is much to be said about considering others as ends unto themselves and not as means toward our ends, the manifestation of conflicting duties based on opposing viewpoints is also more pertinent than ever. This may either lead to an opportunity for Universalism to be adjusted toward contemporary needs of human society, or to obsolescence of a once-laudable moral theory.

Figure 9.1 presents the above-mentioned Strengths, Weaknesses, Opportunities, and Threats (SWOT) analysis for Universalism in a nutshell.

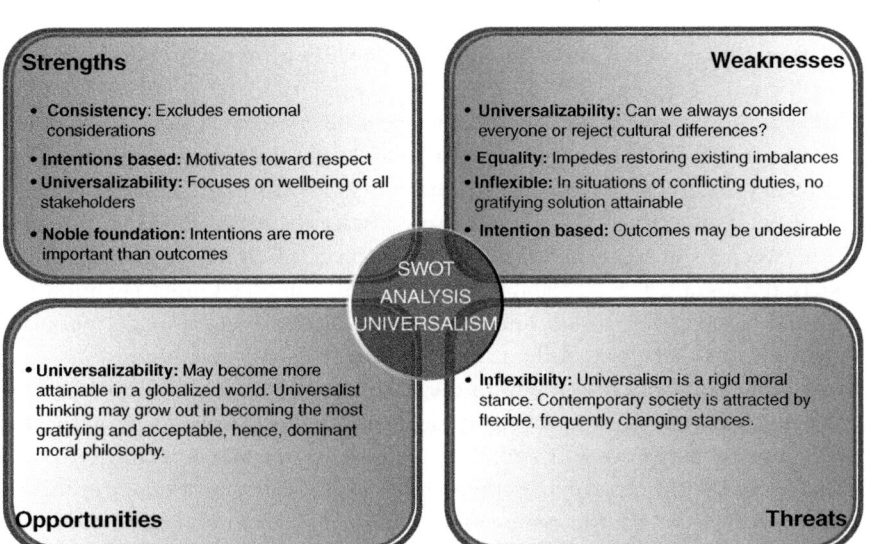

Strengths

- **Consistency**: Excludes emotional considerations
- **Intentions based:** Motivates toward respect
- **Universalizability:** Focuses on wellbeing of all stakeholders
- **Noble foundation:** Intentions are more important than outcomes

Weaknesses

- **Universalizability:** Can we always consider everyone or reject cultural differences?
- **Equality:** Impedes restoring existing imbalances
- **Inflexible:** In situations of conflicting duties, no gratifying solution attainable
- **Intention based:** Outcomes may be undesirable

SWOT ANALYSIS UNIVERSALISM

- **Universalizability:** May become more attainable in a globalized world. Universalist thinking may grow out in becoming the most gratifying and acceptable, hence, dominant moral philosophy.

- **Inflexibility:** Universalism is a rigid moral stance. Contemporary society is attracted by flexible, frequently changing stances.

Opportunities

Threats

FIGURE 9.1 SWOT Analysis of the Universalist Approach.

Utilitarianism

Most Important Strengths

The most important appeal of the Utilitarian approach is its focus on the well-being of the majority, thus ensuring a broadminded, social approach to any problem that arises. This theory also overrules selfish considerations, and requires caution in decision making processes, with a meticulous focus on the possible outcomes.

Unlike the rule-focus of universalism and the golden rule, utilitarianism is egalitarian, as it allows the practitioner to make her own decision as to what is to be considered "the greatest good" and "the greatest number".

In addition, the flexibility that is embedded in this approach makes it easy to reconsider and adjust decision-making processes based on current circumstances. As we live in an era where flexibility is the mantra for succeeding, Utilitarianism seems to be a solid way of ensuring that needs are met with consideration of the needs and desires of all stakeholders. One author's team explains this as follows: "The advantages of Utilitarianism as an ethical theory lie in its intuitive appeal, particularly in the case of 'act Utilitarianism,' and its apparent scientific approach to ethical reasoning."[16] Also, Utilitarianism focuses on establishing or enhancing happiness and well-being for as many constituents as possible.

Most Important Weaknesses

When adhering to the Utilitarian (consequentialist) approach, one should be willing to let the general welfare prevail, thus be ready to denounce personal moral beliefs and integrity in case these are not aligned with what is considered "the overall good." There is a strong point to be raised in this matter: "One's integrity cannot be simply weighed against other considerations as if it was something commensurable with them. Being prepared to do that is already to say one will be whatever the Utilitarian standard says one must be, which is to have already abandoned one's integrity."[17] We should also consider the moral dilemma that may rise between a potentially questionable "common good" and one's personal moral beliefs, the so-called "replaceability" problem.[18] Within the Utilitarian mind-set, it would be preferable to kill one healthy person in order to provide transplant organs for six others, or to kill one man in order to save dozens of others.

Another point of caution within the Utilitarian approach is its outcome focus: while the end-result may be considered admirable for any decision, there is no guarantee that an act will actually generate a desired outcome. Life is unpredictable, and with the growing complexity of our current work environments, there may be many factors we overlook. This can lead to undesired outcomes that backfire, regardless of the initial focus. If, for instance, a manager decides to lay off three employees to reduce overhead and save the livelihood of twenty other workers, he may find that several of the twenty remaining workers either become demoralized and less productive as a result of this decision, or even resign if they have the opportunity to do so.

In addition, Utilitarianism is an individual perception-based approach. Depending on the magnitude of factors involved, it may occur that different Utilitarian decision-makers come to different conclusions and make entirely different outcomes, based on the angle from where they perceived the issue at hand. One manager may, for instance, conclude that using secret data from a competitor brings the greatest good for the greatest number in focusing on his workforce, leading him to use the data; while another manager may find that using this secret data will negatively affect the well-being of the much larger workforce of his competitor, leading him not to use it.

Presented bluntly, utilitarianism can be seen as a model to exploit the minority, as it aims to benefit majorities. This, then, can lead to disastrous outcomes, especially if the majority is a group of wealthy predator-minded entities. Once they set the tone and have their way, the minority group, regardless of how admirable in intention, will have to yield. Perceived as such, Utilitarianism also approves of the behavior of major corporations, such as Wall-Mart, Nike, and others to use sweatshops in order to exploit the financially weak so that their hundreds of millions of customers can benefit from extremely low prices on the goods they purchase. Utilitarianism could thus be seen as a moral blinder to do anything possible (even stealing, robbing, murdering, enslaving, and cheating) to benefit the greatest number.

Critical Opportunities

Given its focus on circumstances at hand, and its lack of concern about consistency, the Utilitarian approach may remain a popular moral stance for a long time to come. Its prominence may even rise, due to the fact that societies are increasingly diversifying, thus in need of continuous changing considerations of what is the proper moral decision. It should also be noted that a Utilitarian approach safeguards the benefits of the majority of people involved, not merely in material sense, but also in areas of happiness, friendship, health, knowledge, and more.[19]

Critical Threats

The lack of consistency, not only seen over time, but also in the decision-making processes from various Utilitarians at the same time, based on their viewpoints and the information they have at hand, may become an increasing source of concern, leading to outcomes that bring more harm than advantage to a community. "The greatest good for the greatest number" is not as generally established as it may seem, but is a very personal perspective. This, then, entails

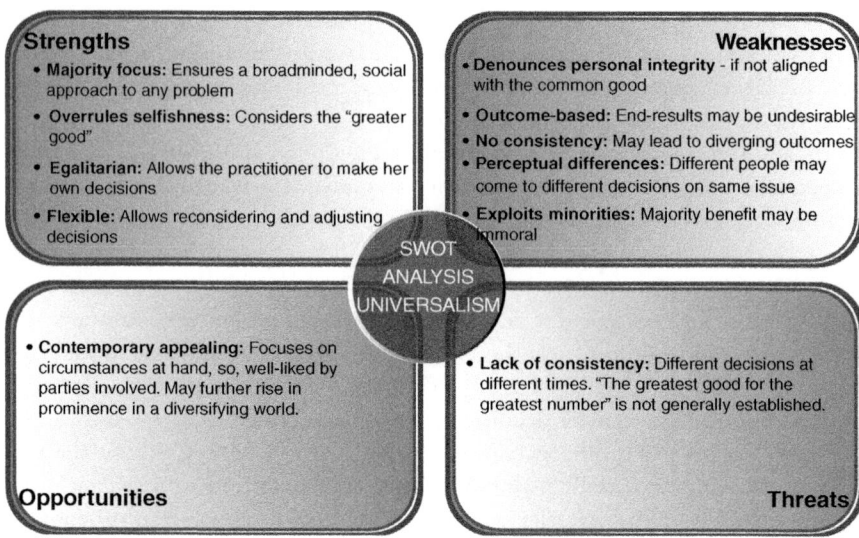

Strengths
- **Majority focus:** Ensures a broadminded, social approach to any problem
- **Overrules selfishness:** Considers the "greater good"
- **Egalitarian:** Allows the practitioner to make her own decisions
- **Flexible:** Allows reconsidering and adjusting decisions

Weaknesses
- **Denounces personal integrity** - if not aligned with the common good
- **Outcome-based:** End-results may be undesirable
- **No consistency:** May lead to diverging outcomes
- **Perceptual differences:** Different people may come to different decisions on same issue
- **Exploits minorities:** Majority benefit may be immoral

SWOT ANALYSIS UNIVERSALISM

- **Contemporary appealing:** Focuses on circumstances at hand, so, well-liked by parties involved. May further rise in prominence in a diversifying world.

- **Lack of consistency:** Different decisions at different times. "The greatest good for the greatest number" is not generally established.

Opportunities

Threats

FIGURE 9.2 SWOT Analysis of the Utilitarian Approach.

that the perceived greatest good for the greatest number for one group, organization, city, county, state, or nation may turn out to be disastrous for others.[20]

Figure 9.2 presents the above-mentioned SWOT analysis for Utilitarianism in a nutshell.

The Golden Rule

Most Important Strengths

Many people, till today, consider the Golden Rule one of the most powerful moral approaches toward global peace, respect, and understanding.[21] Especially among people with strong religious beliefs, this rule seems to be considered a strength. In the 16th century, the rule obtained the prefix "golden" in order to indicate its superiority over other rules.[22] As a "rule," this moral behavioral concept dictates a practice of self-reflection, in order to ascertain how one would, and would not, like to be treated, and subsequently, adjust his or her behavior toward others accordingly.[23] Herein, then, lies one of the Golden Rule's major strengths: it grants the actor full autonomy in regards to what she or he considers the most appropriate treatment of others. There is no dictation on specific behavioral patterns, other than through reflectivity.

Through this very requirement of reflection, the Golden Rule effectively cures self-centeredness, as it invites the actor to place others in his or her own shoes, and thus be more empathetic to those others.[24]

Most Important Weaknesses

In today's world, where a lot of the behavioral cues are dictated by reciprocity, the Golden Rule is sometimes considered a weakness, because it dictates unconditional altruism toward others, regardless of who they are and what their intentions are toward us.[25] Critics of the Golden Rule therefore claim that, by engaging in the reflective behavior of treating others the way we would like to be treated, we subject ourselves to being taken advantage of on a continuous basis in today's diehard world,[26] as it is unrealistic to assume that everyone around us will engage in similar reflections toward others. Many also claim that conditional altruism (only doing well to those we consider capable of returning the favor) is typical human behavior, even though great thinkers, among them Charles Darwin, consider it a conscious, and therefore even more regrettable and immoral, human tendency.[27] What happens, in general, is that very few people are entirely selfless or entirely selfish. Many will practice both, conditional and unconditional altruism, depending on their personal assessment of the circumstances, and not necessarily because they have any concern about being right or wrong.[28]

Another frequently presented concern with the Golden Rule is the case of people with warped mind-sets. There is always the danger that masochists, who prefer to be hurt by others, might consider that others would like the same, or that sexual predators may feel that they would enjoy being in their victims' place. Even though there may be correcting arguments brought up for such cases, it remains that practitioners of the Golden Rule are expected to reflect on their own feelings and desires, and behave accordingly, while these feelings and desires may be considered very unwelcome by others.[29] In response to such concerns, some people recommend the "Platinum Rule," which suggests treating people the way *they* want to be treated. Unfortunately, the Platinum Rule brings its own challenges, because the other party may also have wishes that are undesirable and immoral in their fulfillment.[30]

Critical Opportunities

The Golden Rule has been cited and promoted by a variety of religions and cultures throughout the world: Christianity, Confucianism, Judaism, Buddhism, Hinduism, Islam, Zoroastrianism, and Taoism are known to promote it, while many secular thinkers in different cultures have also confirmed this rule, considering it the core of ethical thinking.[31] Since this rule is honored by so many different groups globally, it could be seen as a common bond among many different peoples of the world, thus reducing disagreements and aversions, and cultivating increased tolerance and respect.

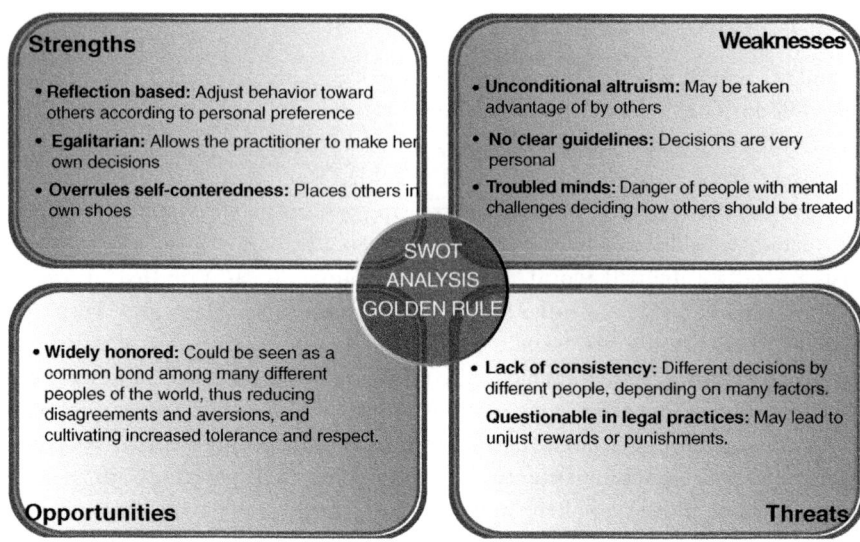

FIGURE 9.3 SWOT Analysis of the Golden Rule.

Critical Threats

The reflective argument in the Golden Rule can also become a breaking point in inter-human, bilateral, or multilateral relationships, because what one may consider the ideal treatment for the self may drastically conflict with what another considers so, due to diverging circumstances. A rich person may consider not wanting to be paid for a favor done to others, because money is not of the essence to him or her. Yet, a poor person who has a hard time making ends meet may consider money the ultimate reward to alleviate some of his or her urgent needs.

In court systems, there is divergence in perception of the Golden Rule as a proper decision guide. "Although there is universal agreement among federal courts that Golden Rule arguments are improper in the context of damages, there are divergent opinions regarding the use of Golden Rule arguments towards ultimate liability."[32] Courts are generally in agreement about the fact that a Golden Rule argument could create a substantial risk that a jury would award unequal damages based on unfairly aroused sympathy or other improper emotion.[33]

Figure 9.3 presents the above-mentioned SWOT analysis for the Golden Rule in a nutshell.

Virtue Ethics

Most Important Strengths

Virtue Ethics are character based, and focus on living a good life. This means that Virtue Ethics leans more to the intuitive practice of a person, rather than considering the universal rule of Kantian ethics (Universalism), or the calculation of greater good for greatest number, as captured in Utilitarianism.[34] The Virtue Ethics practitioner will turn inward, reflect, and consider what would be considered "good character," even if it may be in contrast with his own desires. Yet, while acting personally and intuitively, Virtue Ethics also aims at social flourishing (*eudaimonia*). The "other" person is not considered a moral object, as is the case with Universalism and Utilitarianism, but a reflection of the self, which, some could argue, places it within the ideology of the Golden Rule.

The difference here may be, however, that the Golden Rule purely reflects on our own behavioral preferences, while Virtue Ethics prompts us to become better people by reflecting on characteristics such as generosity, honesty, compassion, friendliness, and other admirable qualities,[35] *in spite of* our own behavioral preferences. To that end, Virtue Ethics focuses on relationships and encourages people to cultivate their sense of community.

Because of its social considerations, Virtue Ethics aims for a state of happiness that is sustainable and doesn't happen at the expense of other persons or groups.

Most Important Weaknesses

One of the major problems with Virtue Ethics is that, just like Utilitarianism, it is subjective, in that not everyone agrees on what a virtue is, just as not everyone considers the same "greatest good for the greatest number."[36] Critics, therefore, feel that Virtue Ethics has insufficient focus on the actual content of virtuous versus non-virtuous acts, especially because it doesn't provide guidance in how to act. These critics consider Virtue Ethics relativistic, in that there is no key set of virtues, so what is considered a great virtue in one country (or organization), may not be considered so in another.[37]

Some critics consider the personal, reflective nature of applying Virtue Ethics to be limiting. They point out that Virtue Ethics is very personal based, and therefore lacks a more general approach toward acting.[38]

Critical Opportunities

As has been the case, Virtue Ethics has been revived in recent decades, as human interactions become more diverse, and rigid rules and directions are more complex to implement. The precious aspect of inter-human connection and reflectivity toward a better community with more solid happiness and well-being for a larger group is not only refreshing, but also creates a hopeful picture for future generations.

Critical Threats

Over time, every theory needs to evolve, as concepts and perspectives change. Given our globalizing communities, the understanding of what constitutes

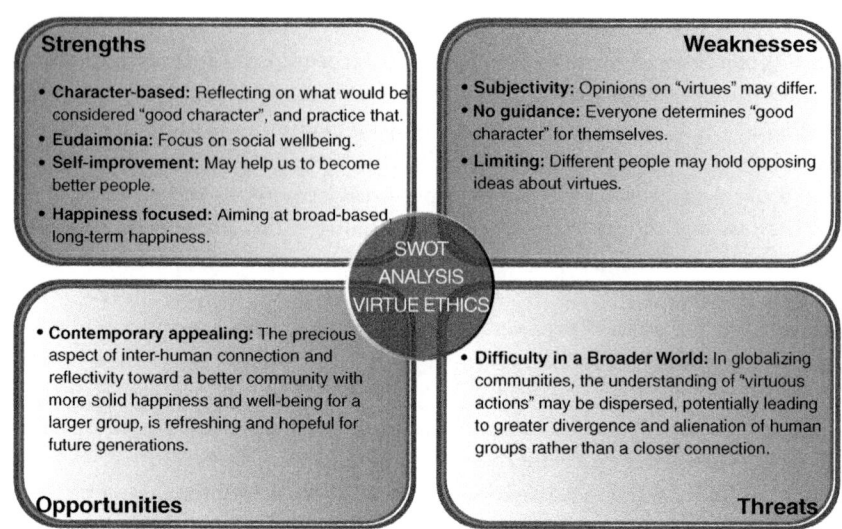

Strengths

- **Character-based:** Reflecting on what would be considered "good character", and practice that.
- **Eudaimonia:** Focus on social wellbeing.
- **Self-improvement:** May help us to become better people.
- **Happiness focused:** Aiming at broad-based, long-term happiness.

Weaknesses

- **Subjectivity:** Opinions on "virtues" may differ.
- **No guidance:** Everyone determines "good character" for themselves.
- **Limiting:** Different people may hold opposing ideas about virtues.

SWOT
ANALYSIS
VIRTUE ETHICS

- **Contemporary appealing:** The precious aspect of inter-human connection and reflectivity toward a better community with more solid happiness and well-being for a larger group, is refreshing and hopeful for future generations.

- **Difficulty in a Broader World:** In globalizing communities, the understanding of "virtuous actions" may be dispersed, potentially leading to greater divergence and alienation of human groups rather than a closer connection.

Opportunities

Threats

FIGURE 9.4 SWOT Analysis of Virtue Ethics.

"virtuous actions" may be a pretty dispersed one, potentially leading to greater divergence and alienation of human groups rather than a closer connection.

Figure 9.4 presents the above-mentioned SWOT analysis for Virtue Ethics in a nutshell.

Four Moral Theories: A Brief Comparison

As may have already become apparent, there are favorable and unfavorable sides to each theory, and some of these theories, such as Universalism and Utilitarianism, are in many cases each other's exact opposite! Where the Universalist approach focuses on good intentions and discourages using anyone as a means toward our ends, the Utilitarian approach focuses on good outcomes, which means that others may have to be used as means toward the desired end. The Golden Rule approach and the Virtue Ethics approach both focus on internal reflection before deciding how to treat another person, yet, with an important difference:

- Within the scope of the Golden Rule, a person only reflects on how she would have liked to be treated, and then applies the same treatment to the other person.
- Within the scope of Virtue Ethics, a person reflects not only on how she would prefer to be treated, but on what would be considered "good moral behavior" in the community, and bases her actions on that.

Immediately, however, we can discover some challenges here, as are also displayed in the four SWOT analyses: The Universalist approach is so focused on good *intentions* that emotions are completely disregarded, whereas the Utilitarian approach considers possible *outcomes* of different acts, and calculates which act will lead to what the decider considers to be "the greatest good for the greatest number." First, this may not work out as planned, and second, what the decider considers the best possible outcome, from her perspective, may be unattractive or even downright disastrous to others. Similarly, the reflection-based approaches in both the Golden Rule and Virtue Ethics are mainly *assumptions* of the decision-maker, and they may not necessarily lead to the most proper treatment of other parties, because, after all, people happen to have different outlooks on reality. What is considered a desirable or even socially preferred solution for one may not be for another.

The Universalist approach emphasizes consistency at all times through its universalizability foundation, but the Utilitarian approach supports flexibility based on the circumstances at hand. Within their reflective approach, the Golden Rule and Virtue Ethics also apply the flexibility of reflection, thus freeing themselves from a rigid model to adhere to. Then again, there are critics who assert that reflection and calculation (as practices in Virtue Ethics, Golden Rule, and Utilitarianism), bring their own limitations, as they are based on personal opinions, and can therefore lead to unpleasant outcomes for some people.

One common intention behind each theory, albeit not always successfully implemented, is the notion of being less selfish: each of the theories aims at greater respect and compassion for others:

- The Universalist approach prescribes treatment of every person as an end unto itself, so one should never try to take advantage of others, under any circumstance.
- The Utilitarian approach prescribes respect for the greatest number of people in any situation, which may be painful to small groups, but will be beneficial for most.
- The Golden Rule demands self-reflection, leading to treating others in ways one wants to be treated. This could, in many instances, lead to similar treatments of others as with the Universalist approach.
- Virtue Ethics prescribes good character in treating others, and doing it in such a way as to transcend personal preferences and be socially praiseworthy.

Each of the theories can be defended as promising in a world where people are, on average, more intelligent, travel more often, and get exposed to different cultures:

- Due to its focus on treating others with unconditional respect and impartiality, Universalist thinking may grow out in becoming the most gratifying and acceptable and, hence, dominant moral philosophy.

- The Utilitarian approach could also be considered promising, because it is circumstantially focused, without using any existing or preconceived rules to arrive at a solution.
- The Golden Rule, being widely honored among many cultures and religions in the world, could be seen as a common bond among different peoples of the world, thus reducing disagreements and aversions, and cultivating increased tolerance and respect.
- Virtue Ethics also has quite some contemporary appeal, as it focuses on inter-human connection and reflectivity toward a better community with more solid happiness and well-being for a larger group. This is seen by many as refreshing and hopeful for future generations.

Nonetheless, it is also important to be aware of the challenges of each theory, which is the exact purpose of reviewing them alongside one another in this chapter. While Universalism is considered too rigid and void of emotions, which is a tough act for us, emotional beings, to consistently follow, Utilitarianism is considered too calculative, and exploitative of minority groups. While the Golden Rule is considered a potential danger, because people may have questionable behavioral preferences, which they may project on others, Virtue Ethics is also considered a challenge because one can never assume that all people are aware of what good virtues entail, and even if they are, one's good virtue may not coincide with another's.

Case 9.1 Preying on the Vulnerable: Mylan's EpiPen Price Gouging

EpiPen is a pen-shaped, self-injectable medication prescribed for people with life-threatening allergies. Because EpiPens can be life-saving in cases of extreme allergic reactions that can cause swelling in airways leading to unconsciousness or even death, about 3.6 million Americans are dependent on this drug injector, and carry it with them at all times.[39] EpiPens are important because they contain epinephrine, also referred to as adrenaline, which causes muscle relaxation, re-opening of airways, and a chance to breathe again, all within thirty seconds after injecting it into the thigh of the allergic person. Since this medication wears off in 10 to 20 minutes, it is critical for the allergic person to get help within that time for physical treatment. While there are somewhat similar remedies, they do not have the same effect as EpiPen, so doctors usually don't prescribe the alternatives. A recent effort to get a true generic alternative into the market was rejected by the Food and Drug Administration.[40] In 2017, the FDA approved Symjepi, a direct generic alternative to the EpiPen, to be made available in the market before the end of 2017[41].

Since 2007, the price for a two-pack of EpiPens, as they are sold, has shot up by more than 500 percent, from about $100 to more than $600. This has placed an enormous pressure on patients with high health insurance deductibles. The company that markets the EpiPen is Mylan, and its CEO is Heather Bresch, a woman who has been ranked in Fortune's Top 50 of the most powerful women in business, and whose father is the senior US senator from West Virginia. The EpiPens must have been a true cash cow for Mylan's executives, as their salaries took an immense hike along with the price increase of the medication. Bresch, for instance, saw her annual salary increase almost seven-and-a-half times since 2007, from $2.5 million to $18.9 million.[42]

As the media started highlighting this case of severe price gouging of a life-saving medication, some interesting pieces of information surfaced. One of these is Bresch's family ties to Washington, and the immense nepotism she benefited from. In 2007, she faced accusations of falsely claiming an MBA from West Virginia University on her resume. She was promptly granted an MBA by the university, which had to be rescinded when the faculty revolted against the decision and the university's president, who was a political friend of Bresch's father, had to resign.

In regards to the EpiPen price gouging accusations, Bresch claimed that the price increase was needed to compensate for the immense marketing and lobbying campaigns that the company set up for the EpiPens. As the company came under increased media scrutiny, it started offering vouchers to reduce the price of the medication for those who have to pay it out of their own pocket. However, this resulted in yet another wave of criticism, as vouchers are not a price reduction.[43] While Mylan has thus far refused to drop the price of the EpiPens, the company saw its stocks plummeting, and got pressured into either giving in to the demand for a drastic price reduction, or finding creative alternatives to regain some of the public's trust.[44]

Sources reported that Mylan's top executives cashed in about $300 million in compensation between 2011 and 2016.[45] What makes the morality of this case even more questionable is that Bresch is not just another CEO. As mentioned before, her father is a US senator and her mother a powerful executive in the National School Boards Association, who headed a campaign to require EpiPens in schools.[46] Yet, as accusations piled up, Bresch did exactly what most business executives do when caught in the act of greed: they point the finger elsewhere. In Bresch's case, she conveniently blamed it all on Obamacare, calling it a "broken system that needed to be fixed." Her father, Senator Joe Manchin, also took the easy way out by denying any knowledge of his daughter's activities, claiming that he had little or no understanding of her industry practices.[47]

Meanwhile, Mylan has introduced a generic version of EpiPen for half the price into the market, causing the company's market performance to be corrected, with a stock price spiking due to reported adjusted earnings per share of $1.57, instead of the estimated $1.42.[48]

Questions

1. Analyze the case of Mylan's price increase on EpiPens from the lens of each of the four moral theories discussed in this chapter. What are your findings? Please explain.
2. Heather Bresch is listed as a powerful woman in business. In the not-so-distant past, she was caught in a lie, claiming a degree she did not hold. Choose any of the four moral theories to analyze this act, and share your findings.
3. Mylan has introduced a generic version of the EpiPen to the market, selling it at half the price of the EpiPen. What is your moral view on this act?

Summary

- Moral theories can be complicated and confusing. Some of them overlap, while others complement one another, and yet other completely contrast each other in the decisions and actions they recommend. Some moral theories are rather inflexible, while others provide ample room for interpretation and implementation variance.
- Moral Theories—A Brief Recap:
  - Universalism is a deontological or duty-based approach, which assumes that there is a single moral obligation, called the *categorical imperative*. The categorical imperative holds that every act we commit should be based on our personal principles or rules, or *maxims*.
  - Utilitarianism focuses predominantly on the end-result or outcome (the consequence) in any act. This theory forms a stark contrast with the Universalist approach. Utilitarianism holds the view that the action that produces the greatest well-being for the largest number is the morally right one.
  - The Golden Rule is one of the oldest known moral theories, usually articulated as, "Do unto others as you would have others do unto you." The Golden Rule calls for its practitioners to reflect on their own preferences, and refrain from treating others in ways they would not want to be treated.

- Virtue Ethics focuses on virtues, or moral character, in contrast to duties or rules or consequences of actions. Our virtues are the foundations of our personality. Being a truly virtuous person is admirable, because life presents us many challenges that create or increase the temptation to decide against virtuous acts.
- Strengths and Weaknesses of the Theories
  - Universalism
    - Most important strengths: consistency, focuses on intentions rather than outcomes, reflective, treating others as an end unto themselves instead of a means toward our ends.
    - Most important weaknesses: universalizability may be impossible to implement; the equality based approach is not very realistic in restoring existing imbalances.
    - Critical opportunities: the mind-set of Universalism may become more appealing in near-future moral considerations.
    - Critical threats: Universalism is known as a rigid, inflexible moral stance. Universalism needs to be adjusted toward contemporary needs of human society.
  - Utilitarianism
    - Most important strengths: its focus on the well-being of the majority, thus ensuring a broadminded social approach to any problem that arises.
    - Most important weaknesses: one should be willing to let the general welfare prevail, thus be ready to denounce personal moral beliefs and integrity in case these are not aligned with what is considered "the overall good."
    - Critical opportunities: its prominence may rise, due to the fact that societies are increasingly diversifying, thus in need of continuous changing considerations of what is the proper moral decision.
    - Critical threats: the perceived greatest good for the greatest number for one group, organization, city, county, state, or nation, may turn out to be disastrous for others.
  - The Golden Rule
    - Most important strengths: it grants the actor full autonomy in regards to what she or he considers to be the most appropriate treatment of others.
    - Most important weaknesses: not everyone wants to be treated the way we would like to be.
    - Critical opportunities: this rule is honored by so many different groups globally, so it could be seen as a common bond among many different peoples of the world.
    - Critical threats: what one may consider the ideal treatment for the self, may drastically conflict with what another considers so, due to diverging circumstances.

- Virtue Ethics
  - Most important strengths: it prompts us to become better people by reflecting on characteristics such as generosity, honesty, compassion, friendliness, and other admirable qualities, in spite of our own behavioral preferences.
  - Most important weaknesses: it is subjective in that not everyone agrees on what is a virtue.
  - Critical opportunities: its aspect of inter-human connection and reflectivity toward a better community with more solid happiness and well-being for a larger group, creates a hopeful picture for future generations.
  - Critical threats: the understanding of what constitutes "virtuous actions" may be a pretty dispersed one, potentially leading to greater divergence and alienation of human groups rather than a closer connection.
- Four Moral Theories: A Brief Comparison
  - Some of these theories, such as Universalism and Utilitarianism, are in many cases each other's exact opposite.
  - The Universalist approach is focused on good intentions, so emotions are completely disregarded.
  - The Utilitarian approach considers possible outcomes of different acts, and calculates which act will lead to "the greatest good for the greatest number."
  - The reflection-based approaches in both the Golden Rule and Virtue Ethics are mainly assumptions of the decision-maker, and they may not necessarily lead to the most proper treatment of other parties.
  - Common intention behind each theory is the notion of being less selfish:
    - The Universalist approach prescribes treatment of every person as an end unto itself.
    - The Utilitarian approach prescribes respect for the greatest number of people in any situation.
    - The Golden Rule demands self-reflection, leading to treating others in ways one wants to be treated.
    - Virtue Ethics prescribes good character in treating others, and doing it in such a way that it would transcend personal preferences.

Reflective Questions

1. After reading this chapter, which of the four moral theories do you identify with best, and why? Please explain.
2. Which of the four moral theories do you identify least with, and why? Please explain.

3. Engage in some additional reading on the concept of *eudaimonia*, and explain in your own words (about 150 words) what your take is on this phenomenon, and whether you consider it important in today's community.
4. Think of a situation where telling the truth would lead to greater moral problems than not. Please explain.
5. Think of a situation where the greatest good for the greatest number may not work to your advantage. Please explain.

Notes

1   Weiss, J. W. (2009). *Business Ethics: A Stakeholder & Issues Management Approach.* Mason, OH: South-Western Cengage Learning.
2   Ibid.
3   Ibid.
4   Robertson, M., Morris, K., & Walter, G. (2007). Overview of psychiatric ethics V: Utilitarianism and the ethics of duty. *Australasian Psychiatry 15*(5), 403.
5   Burton, B. K., & Goldsby, M. (2005). The Golden Rule and business ethics: An examination. *Journal of Business Ethics, 56*(4), 371–383.
6   Ibid.
7   *Virtue Ethics* (July 18, 2003, rev. Mar 8, 2012). *Stanford Encyclopedia of Philosophy.* http://seop.illc.uva.nl/entries/ethics-virtue.
8   Ibid.
9   Yang, X. (2006). Categorical imperatives, moral requirements, and moral motivation. *Metaphilosophy 37*(1), 112–129.
10 Moyaert, M. (2010). Ricoeur on the (im)possibility of a global ethic towards an ethic of fragile interreligious compromises. *Neue Zeitschrift Für Systematische Theologie Und Religionsphilosophie 52*(4), 440–461.
11 Kim, E. (2012). Justifying human rights: Does consensus matter? *Human Rights Review 13*(3), 261–278.
12 Divine Command Theory (2017). Internet Encyclopedia of Philosophy. Retrieved from: http://www.iep.utm.edu/divine-c/.
13 Ibid, p. 263.
14 Robertson et al., 403.
15 Moyaert, 440.
16 Robertson et al., 404.
17 Volkman, R. (2010). Why information ethics must begin with Virtue Ethics. *Metaphilosophy 41*(3), 386.
18 Robertson et al., 402–410.
19 LaRue, T. H. (1987). Ethical analysis and human resource management. *Human Resource Management (1986–1998), 26*(3), 313.
20 Ibid.
21 Rakhshani, Z. (2017). The Golden Rule and its consequences: A practical and effective solution for world peace. *Journal of History, Culture & Art Research/Tarih Kültür Ve Sanat Arastirmalari Dergisi 6*(1), 465–473.
22 Singer, M. J. (2012). *The Golden Rule. Wisdom and Knowledge, Issue 5,* Tehran: Etelaat.
23 Rakhshani, 465–473.
24 Ibid.
25 Goodman, J. (2014). Altruism and the Golden Rule. *Zygon 49*(2), 381–395.
26 Ibid.
27 Ibid.

28 Ibid.
29 Bruton, S. V. (2004). Teaching the Golden Rule. *Journal of Business Ethics 49*(2), 179–187.
30 Ibid.
31 Rakhshani, 465–473.
32 Randall, C. (2014). *Caudle v. District of Columbia*: The Golden Rule has no place in a courtroom. *Boston College Law Review 55*(6), 75.
33 Ibid., 73–87.
34 Roberts, S. K. (2008). Becoming the neighbor: Virtue theory and the problem of neighbor identity. *Interpretation: A Journal of Bible & Theology 62*(2), 146–155.
35 11 Virtue Ethics strengths and weaknesses (May 21, 2016). *Flow Psychology*. http:// flowpsychology.com/11-virtue-ethics-strengths-and-weaknesses.
36 Richter, D. (1999). Virtue without theory. *Journal of Value Inquiry 33*(3), 353–369.
37 Table: Strengths and weaknesses (October 9, 2008). Virtue Ethics. http://peped. org/philosophicalinvestigations/table-strengths-and-weaknesses-of-virtue-ethics.
38 11 Virtue Ethics strengths and weaknesses (May 21, 2016). *Flow Psychology*. http:// flowpsychology.com/11-virtue-ethics-strengths-and-weaknesses.
39 Ossola, A. (August 26, 2016). What you need to know about the EpiPen. Why is everyone talking about an injector? *Popular Science: Health*. www.popsci.com/ what-are-epipens.
40 Ibid.
41 Potenza, A. (June 16 2017). Cheaper alternative to EpiPen allergy shot approved by FDA. *TheVerge*. Retrieved from https://www.theverge.com/2017/6/16/15816188/ symjepi-cheaper-epipen-allergy-shot-fda-approval-adamis.
42 Ibid.
43 Ibid.
44 Ibid.
45 Ibid.
46 Ibid.
47 Ibid.
48 Mangan, D. (March 3, 2017). Mylan CEO Heather Bresch says diversification is boosting company after EpiPen controversy. *CNBC: Biotech and Pharmaceuticals*. www.cnbc.com/2017/03/03/mylan-ceo-heather-bresch-discusses-epipen-controversy.html.

10

FIVE MORAL HANDLES FOR EVERY TYPE OF DECISION-MAKING

Abstract

This chapter highlights five practical considerations that can guide decision-making under multiple circumstances: the family, friends, and role models consideration; the newspaper consideration; the self-reflective consideration; the "advice to loved one" consideration; and the win-win-win consideration. An in-depth review of these five factors will be presented. The moral handles will further be brought to life through examples.

A Moral Compass without Theories

In Chapter 9, we reviewed four established moral theories, on basis of which people frequently make their decisions. We have also discovered that each of these theories has strengths, weaknesses, and offers opportunities and threats. Some theories even contradict one another!

That said, there are still more people in the world who live a morally attuned life than not, even though they don't know the formal moral theories. In Chapter 9 it was already stated: these people go with their "gut feeling." Whether they are homemakers, entrepreneurs, employees in major corporations, or non-profit entities, they make just as many moral decisions as any other person, but use simpler parameters to do so, without worrying about the theories behind them, or even the need for an overarching unity in moral performance.

Whether any form of universal moral stance could ever be enforced remains to be seen. As matters currently stand, our global human community, while converging through social networks, increased travel, and worldwide professional shifts, still holds too much perceptual, moral, religious, and cultural divergence to seriously strive for a global ethic. And why should there be a global ethic anyway? Pluralism is the spice of life, and serves as the foundation to keep us thinking critically about the various notions of "right" and "wrong" that currently exist. As long as human beings have divergent mental models which they develop through the multiplicity of impressions they acquire throughout their lives, they will continue to differ in perspectives. Rather than developing one single moral approach that we are all supposed to honor, we should consider, within reasonable, compassionate boundaries, the healthy dialogues and the perceptional expansion that results from diversity.

In the end, there is still no stronger and more direct response to any ethical dilemma than the following five questions:

1. Would I still do this if my family, friends, or role models would know about it?
2. Would I still do this if it would be published in tomorrow's newspaper?
3. Will I be able to live with myself if I make this decision?
4. Would I still do this if my child (or another loved one) would be on the receiving end?
5. Is my decision causing any harm to others?

Let's review each of these considerations in some more detail.

The Family, Friend, and Role Model Consideration

"Would I Still Do This If My Family, Friends, or Role Models Would Know About It?"

While there is no scientifically proven theory behind this reflective question, it has a high probability of being effective for most people. While we may not have the greatest relationship with all of our family members, most of us do care what our family thinks about us, and wouldn't want our family to be mortified by our poor decisions. Most people thrive on the fact that they can make their family happy, and wouldn't want to do anything to disrupt that. Thinking of those special people in our life, our family, our truest friends, or those people we look up to and want to make proud of us, is a strong motive for most people to refrain from doing anything callous.

Interestingly, the question above has a lot to do with fear for consequences: we do not want to alienate or disappoint people we consider important, so we refrain from the act in order to avoid the consequences we dread.

Of course, there are exceptions here as well, because some people may not care about their family, or even want to embarrass the ones they formally belonged to. Some people may not care about their friends, or may, sadly, not have any friends. Other people may not have any role models, or may be disappointed in these people, whom they once considered great examples in their lives. These are all instances where the consideration above may fail.

Yet, the reflection test on important people in our lives is not a new one. Over the past decades, several authors have mentioned it as a solid and efficient moral questioning strategy. Referring to this and the next consideration (the newspaper consideration) as "spotlight questions," one author asserts, "How you would feel if family, friends and role models learn of your actions is a powerful way to test whether a decision is consistent with your ethical standards."[1]

The Newspaper Consideration

"Would I Still Do This If It Would Be Published in Tomorrow's Newspaper?"

Whether we get along with family members, or have true friends and great role models or not, most people would shy away from having their name published in the newspaper,[2] exposed to the entire community as tied to immoral behavior. The newspaper consideration has been described in several sources under several headers, such as "The Front of the Newspaper Test"[3] and "The New York Times Rule."[4] Reputation is a sensitive matter, and can hurt us personally and professionally, so the ramifications can be painful for quite some time. Questioning ourselves about wanting to see our decision in tomorrow's newspaper or not may, therefore, be an effective deterrent in making rash decisions.

There is an aspect of Virtue Ethics tied to this specific question, because it touches on the concern for good behavior in light of communal perspectives.

Within the realm of consequentialism, under which the Utilitarian approach falls, there is also something to be said for the newspaper query. There is a concept called Plain Consequentialism,[5] which prescribes the morally responsible action to be the one with the best overall consequences. In consequentialism, the consequences are actually all that matter. Since we often reflect consequences in light of what would happen to us and those close to us (as in the family, friends, and role model consideration), the newspaper question could be considered a critical consequentialist approach in that we would be concerned about the consequences of the publication of our decision in the newspaper.

An important point of caution to consider with the newspaper consideration is that people may sometimes shun morally responsible behavior *because* of the fear that it would be made public. Sounds strange? Not so much if we consider the following:

Making ethical decisions is not always appreciated by others, because such decisions require tremendous courage and, sometimes, hard choices. An example would be, rightsizing of a company in bad economic times. Regardless of the guidance a leader may want to provide employees, sometimes she will have to let some go. If a majority of these laid-off employees subsequently fall on extreme hard times, or develop mental issues, family break-ups, drug abuse, and other negative effects, the leader will be chastised in the community.

Reflecting on all of this may lead the leader to refrain from engaging in what may have been the wisest decision toward a chance of continuation of the organization, and potential regrowth in the future.[6]

Just as with the family, friend, and role model consideration, we should also keep in mind that some people are insensitive to, or even thrive on, negative publicity. Consider the case of Martin Shkreli (Chapter 8), who seemed to enjoy the negative publicity he received for his unethical price gouging on life-saving drugs. And then there are the cases of major corporations such as AIG, Citigroup Inc., Wells Fargo, Bank of America, JPMorgan Chase, and Morgan Stanley, many of which continued to use private jets for their executives to crisscross the country while at the same time asking the government for financial assistance in the financial downturn of 2008.[7]

What the above behavior demonstrates is that even publication will not always stop some people from engaging in immoral behavior, because they don't care, because they are addicted to the public's eye, or because they consider themselves above the law.

The Self-Reflective Consideration

"Will I Be Able to Live with Myself If I Make This Decision?"

The self-reflective consideration can be complicated, because it requires the capacity to look ahead and place ourselves in a more mature version of who we are today. For many people, especially younger ones, this may not be an easy task, because it is hard to imagine how and if we will think differently later. Especially younger people are oftentimes less capable of harboring emotions of empathy, guilt, or compassion than are older people, because "the medial prefrontal cortex, which is the part of the brain that is associated with higher-level thinking is often under-used in the decision-making process of teenagers."[8] It is often later in life, when we get confronted with hardship and losses, that we learn to use other parts of the brains where the softer behaviors are generated.

Yet, even at a younger age, the process of imagining ourselves as if we were at the age of our parents or grandparents may still trigger an association about the things these older ones, who invested part of their being in us, would say about the act we are about to commit. Some members of the younger generation are well in tune with their moral self, regularly attending church, spending much time with their elders, and therefore carrying within a decent level of reflectiveness. In addition, there are plenty of young people who got confronted with hardship at an early age: the loss of precious loved ones, illness, painful changes in their living circumstances, the divorce of parents, and the like. These situations cause a more rapid ripening process, enabling a greater level of reflectiveness, and deeper consideration of actions to be taken.

We should not underestimate the importance of self-reflection in making ethical choices. This goes for any stage in our lives. One thing that self-reflection can help us attain is to see our values and the things we have to decide upon in context: through self-reflection we gain a better understanding that any occurrence has its circumstances through which it should be considered, even values such as compassion, honesty, and integrity.[9] There are always many surrounding factors to be determined, which is exactly where many philosophers have a problem with the rigid, inflexible approach of Immanuel Kant's Categorical Imperative, which is the foundation for Universalism. Kant feels that what's right is right, and what's wrong is wrong, and that there is no middle path. Self-reflection sharpens our views in regard to the fact that sometimes even telling the truth may cause greater consequences and more difficulty living with ourselves afterward than would not doing so. If, for instance, we would cause an innocent loved one to be killed or severely harmed by telling the truth, we may consider other alternatives through self-reflection.

The self-reflective consideration harbors elements of both The Golden Rule and Virtue Ethics, especially the latter, because it is reflective, and leans to the intuitive practice of a person. It could be seen as the unformatted manifestation of Virtue Ethics, as it holds in regard what one may consider good character in the future, even if it is currently not completely present.

The "Advice to a Loved One" Consideration

"Would I Still Do This If My Child (or Another Loved One) Would Be on the Receiving End?"

It is amazing what we may forego if we picture a loved one in the shoes of the person(s) that will be affected by our decision. This is a difficult concept, because in business, especially, people are taught to refrain from continuously fretting about those at the receiving end of their actions, otherwise they would never raise prices, lay off people, or engage in any type of change that could even remotely inconvenience others. Admittedly, sometimes there are hard decisions to be made, which is why some people maintain that business and ethics are each other's polar opposites. Yet, hard decisions can be made in a way that still demonstrates a level of compassion: some companies have laid off people, but ensured decent severance packets or mediated in finding other employment for those who were let go. Think of it this way: even parents sometimes make hard decisions to teach their children valuable lessons and to help them understand or develop certain values. This is sometimes referred to as "tough love." Tough love may initially seem, or even feel, harsh and callous, but the intentions are positive, and hopefully the outcomes too. Making difficult decisions is a part of life, and its purpose is usually to obtain future improvement.

Doing business in an ethically responsible way may not lead to the quickest way of gaining wealth, but it doesn't have to lead to anyone's demise, either. As leaders such as Ray Anderson from Interface, one of the world's largest manufacturers of modular carpet for commercial and residential applications, have demonstrated in past decades, there are always ways to minimize suffering and damage, while still sustaining business performance, if only we reflect, think constructively, and do our best.

The "advice to a loved one" consideration could be considered complementary to the self-reflective consideration, as it predominantly pertains to mature individuals, who hold the ability to project loved ones in the shoes of the person(s) at the receiving end of their decisions. That is not to say that this consideration could not be entertained by younger people, of course. As described above, there are enough younger members of society who had to mature at an early stage due to experiences that caused them to reflect on the real important aspects of life.

Due to the fact that there is an element of reflection and substitution in this consideration, it can also be brought into the context of (a) The Golden Rule, because it considers a loved one (whom could also be the self) at the receiving end of the act; (b) Virtue Ethics, as it taps into the decency of one's character and calls for in-depth soul searching; and (c) Universalism, as it invites the actor to consider each person as an end unto himself or herself and not as a means toward anyone's end.

The Win-Win-Win Consideration

"Is My Decision Causing Any Harm to Others?"

In Stephen Covey's book *The Seven Habits of Highly Effective People*,[10] there is a habit (Habit Four) that invites us to "Think Win-Win." This concept intends to get the message across that, in mutual dealings, there is no need for one party to lose in order for the other to win. There can be an effort made for both parties to win, and constructive outcomes to be achieved. Think win-win could, therefore, be considered a character-based code for human interaction and collaboration.[11]

Inasmuch as this is undoubtedly a strong concept, our world today requires an even broader scope when we make our morally responsible decisions: we should elevate our thinking from win-win to win-win-win,[12] whereby three parties win: the two parties taking part in the negotiations, and the stakeholders who are not present at the negotiation table, but that should still be considered. The win-win-win mind-set can become second nature: it is highly reflective, in that the person who is about to make a moral decision ensures that not only the immediate stakeholders are considered, but also those that don't have a voice but still have a right to exist.

In Buddhist philosophy, there is a concept called *ahimsa*, which is Sanskrit for "Do not harm." It is one of the Dalai Lama's favorite statements, "Always help others, and if you cannot help, at least don't harm."[13] This is a powerful guideline toward making decisions that can help us to avoid feeling deep regret in the future for the things we did or decided in the past. It can also help us feel better about ourselves and the world we live in. Yet, there is also a challenge to this concept: it is rather difficult to always refrain from harming, especially when it pertains to things that harm us or endanger our existence. For instance, while it should be understood that every living organism has a good purpose for existing, it also remains a fact that we have to be cautious about swarms of dangerous mosquitoes, aggressive wasps, or other general health-affecting creatures.

The reflective nature of the win–win–win consideration can be placed within the scope of several moral theories we discussed earlier in this book, such as The Golden Rule, because it considers "others" unto whom we should not do what we would not like to have done unto ourselves, and Virtue Ethics, as it strives toward the implementation of good character and remaining in line with societal standards of general good behavior.

FIGURE 10.1 Five Moral Handles.

Case 10.1 Scott Thompson's Padded Resume

In January 2012, the future looked promising for Scott Thompson: he had just landed a dream job as CEO with Yahoo!, once the most prominent search engine and most-visited website in the world. Prior to Yahoo!, Thompson had served as the president of EBay's subsidiary Pay-Pal, where he had managed to accomplish significant company growth. His reputation was solid, and his new workforce at Yahoo! was hopeful that he would be able to turn the company in more successful directions.

Unfortunately, Thompson's lucrative opportunity fell apart when barely four months into his tenure, early May 2012, one of Yahoo's very vocal shareholders, Daniel Loeb, expressed concern that Thompson's resume included a grave inconsistency: the college degree he claimed to have did not exist, at least not at this particular institution. Thompson had claimed to hold a degree in Computer Science from Stonehill College in Massachusetts. With his suave ways and likable personality, no one really questioned Thompson's credentials, and many of the company's board members considered shareholder Loeb an immense and unwelcome nuisance. Many felt that Loeb, who was one of the company's largest external shareholders, wanted more control in the company and saw Thompson as an obstacle to doing so. Loeb, as the story went, started looking for ways to eliminate Thompson, and found the discrepancy in his degree listing.[14] Many of Yahoo's board members had experienced Thompson as a nice guy, and couldn't fathom why he would do anything wrong, most of all something as unethical and wicked as lying about his education on his resume! It did not take long to find out, however, that Stonehill College did not even offer Computer Science degrees, and that the degree Thompson had earned from this institution was in Accounting.[15]

While many of Yahoo's board members were dismayed about letting such a promising leader go, they found themselves with their backs against the wall. It became apparent that Thompson had created his own undoing with this twist of the truth for a company in the heart of Silicon Valley. The saddest part of this entire distasteful story was that Thompson did not immediately admit his wrongdoing. Instead, he tried to deny the allegations, and even became upset at the individuals who blew his cover. As the investigation intensified, Thompson tried to obtain statements of support from his employees, but none of them trusted him enough to do so.

Through his mindless act, Thompson placed himself on a list of other official document falsifiers, such as Bausch & Lomb's CEO, Ronald Zarrella, who admitted in 2002 that he did not graduate from NYU's Stern School of Business, but who managed to retain his position up to his retirement, and former RadioShack CEO, David Edmondson, who claimed that he graduated from Pacific Coast Baptist College with bachelor's degrees in Theology and Psychology, and had to resign in 2006 after admitting he didn't have either.[16]

Yahoo's board and workforce were particularly unhappy with this unsettling course of events, since the company was already in a fragile position due to a bumpy performance road,[17] and in desperate need of a positive turnaround. Just a few months prior to Thompson's appointment, Yahoo's previous CEO, Carol Ann Bartz, who had acquired the reputation of most-overpaid CEO, was removed from her position by phone, and subsequently resigned from the Board of Directors. The disappointment about Thompson's behavior became even greater when he decided to refrain from openly owning up to his mistake. There was embarrassment throughout the firm, and many highly educated employees were considering leaving the company.

Thompson tried to downplay the issue in a radio interview by explaining that his training had been in accounting and computer science, and that he always thought in terms of engineering. When the storm did not seem to blow over, Thompson finally tried to rationalize his departure from Yahoo! as being caused by medical reasons: he had recently undergone surgery for thyroid cancer, so he reasoned, and could not guarantee a steady presence in the company due to his medications, so he thought it would be better to resign. This obvious act of denial did not go over well with the Yahoo! community, and the company's lawyers made sure that he would not be eligible for any severance and wouldn't be entitled to stock grants, which, in this case, would equal about $16 million.[18]

In hindsight, it became clear that Thompson's claim of holding a degree in Computer Science dates back long before his tenure at Yahoo! In his decade-old biographical information on the PayPal website, from his days as president there, the Computer Science degree had also been included.[19] Perhaps most ironically, Thompson's existing experience with PayPal in combination with his Accounting degree would have sufficed amply in performing as Yahoo's CEO.[20]

Scott Thompson's career did not have an unhappy ending after the Yahoo! incident. He was quickly hired by ShopRunner, one of Amazon Prime's independent competitors, fulfilling the position of CEO. According to Michael Rubin, the CEO of ShopRunner's holding company Kynetic, there is a lot of excitement in ShopRunner for having attracted Thompson. He is respected for his insights and integrity, considered an absolute asset, and an attraction to investors. According to Rubin, no one would be better suited to run ShopRunner than Thompson.[21]

Questions

1. Scott Thompson got caught padding his resume, and resigned from Yahoo!, claiming health issues. Consider the ways in which you think Thompson has performed unethically, and discuss each of these acts.
2. Apply the five handles to the act of lying about holding a degree, and share the outcomes of your reflections.
3. Scott Thompson did not really need a Computer Science degree to become CEO at Yahoo! What could be some of the reasons he lied about his degree?

Summary

*   As long as human beings have divergent mental models which they develop through the multiplicity of impressions they acquire throughout their lives, they will continue to differ in perspectives. Rather than developing one single moral approach that we are all supposed to honor, we should consider, within reasonable, compassionate boundaries, the healthy dialogues and the perceptional expansion that results from diversity.
*   The family, friend and role model consideration: *"Would I still do this if my family, friends or role models would know about it?"*
    *   Most people thrive on the fact that they can make their family happy, and wouldn't want to do anything to disrupt that. Of course, there are exceptions here, as well, because some people may not care about their family, or even want to embarrass the ones they formally belonged to.
*   The newspaper consideration: *"Would I still do this if it would be published in tomorrow's newspaper?"*
    *   Most people would shy away from having their name published in the newspaper, exposed to the entire community, and tied to immoral behavior. Reputation is a sensitive matter, and can hurt us personally and professionally, so the ramifications can be painful for quite some time.
    *   An important point of caution to consider with the newspaper consideration is that people may sometimes shun morally responsible behavior *because* of the fear that it would be made public.
        *   Making ethical decisions is not always appreciated by others, because such decisions require tremendous courage and, sometimes, hard choices. Leaders may, therefore, refrain from engaging in what may have been the wisest decision toward a chance of continuation of the organization, and potential regrowth in the future.
    *   Another point of caution is that some people are insensitive to, or even thrive on, negative publicity. Those people may seek out publication of their immoral behavior for the sake of being in the limelight.

- The self-reflective consideration: *"Will I be able to live with myself if I make this decision?"*
  - The self-reflective consideration can be complicated, because it requires the capacity to look ahead and place ourselves in a more mature version of who we are today.
  - We should not underestimate the importance of self-reflection in making ethical choices. This goes for any stage in our lives. One thing that self-reflection can help us attain is to see our values and the things we have to decide upon in context: through self-reflection we gain a better understanding that anything has its circumstances through which it should be considered, even values such as compassion, honesty, and integrity.
- The "advice to a loved one" consideration: *"Would I still do this if my child (or another loved one) would be on the receiving end?"*
  - It is amazing what we may forego if we picture a loved one in the shoes of the person(s) that will be affected by our decision.
  - Hard decisions could be made in a way that still demonstrates a level of compassion: some companies have laid off people, but ensured decent severance packets or mediated in finding other employment for those who were let go.
  - The "advice to a loved one" consideration could be considered complementary to the self-reflective consideration, as it predominantly pertains to mature individuals, who hold the ability to project loved ones in the shoes of the person(s) at the receiving end of their decisions.
- The win-win-win consideration: *"Is my decision causing any harm to others?"*
  - We should elevate our thinking from win-win to win-win-win, whereby three parties win: the two parties participating in the negotiations, and the stakeholders who are not present at the negotiation table but that should still be considered.
  - In Buddhist philosophy, there is a concept called *ahimsa*, which is Sanskrit for "Do not harm." This is a powerful guideline toward making decisions that can help us avoid feeling deep regret in the future for the things we did or decided in the past.

Reflective Questions

1. Which of the five handles discussed in this chapter would *most* motivate you to do the right thing? Why?
2. Which of the five handles discussed in this chapter would *least* motivate you to do the right thing? Why?
3. When comparing the moral handles discussed in this chapter to the moral theories discussed in Chapters 2 and 9, which path toward moral behavior do you consider easier? Please explain.

4. Consider the "advice to a loved one" consideration: Why could it be difficult in business performance to place yourself in the shoes of others?
5. Think of a situation where you could have made a different decision if you had used one of the five handles discussed in this chapter. Please share your story.

Notes

1 Schermerhorn, J. A. (2011). *Exploring Management* (3rd Ed.). Hoboken, NJ: Wiley, 67.
2 Marques, J. (2015) Universalism and Utilitarianism: An evaluation of two popular moral theories in business decision making. *The Journal of Values-Based Leadership, 8*(2), Article 3. http://scholar.valpo.edu/jvbl/vol8/iss2/3
3 Craft, J. J. (2013). Living in the gray: Lessons on ethics from prison. *Journal of Business Ethics 115*(2), 327–339.
4 MacDonald, C. (December 8, 2010). Business ethics and the "New York Times" rule. *The Business Ethics Blog.* https://businessethicsblog.com/2010/12/08/business-ethics-and-the-new-york-times-rule
5 Consequentialism. *Internet Encyclopedia of Philosophy, IEP.* April 2, 2017, from www.iep.utm.edu/conseque
6 MacDonald, C. (December 8, 2010). Business ethics and the "New York Times" rule. *The Business Ethics Blog.* https://businessethicsblog.com/2010/12/08/business-ethics-and-the-new-york-times-rule
7 Wall Street still not downgrading to first class: Companies – some taking bailout money – still fly corporate jets. (Dec 21 2008). *NBCNews.com-Associated Press.* www.nbcnews.com/id/28338918/ns/business-us_business/t/wall-street-still-not-downgrading-first-class/#.WOGNwTvyuUk
8 Holt, S., & Marques, J. (2012). Empathy in leadership: Appropriate or misplaced? An empirical study on a topic that is asking for attention. *Journal of Business Ethics 105*(1), 95–105 (103).
   Blame it on the brain (October 2006). *Young Minds, 16* (*UCL Institute of Cognitive Neuroscience*). www.cypnow.co.uk/news/759494/.headlinks
9 Bashe, A., & Handelsman, M. (October 21, 2012). Self-reflection in ethical choice-making balancing values through the looking glass. *Psychology Today.* www.psychologytoday.com/blog/the-ethical-professor/201210/self-reflection-in-ethical-choice-making
10 Covey, S. (2004). *The 7 Habits of Highly Effective People: Powerful Lessons in Personal Change.* New York: Free Press.
11 Covey, S. (N/A). *Books: The 7 Habits of Highly Effective People - Habit 4: Think Win-Win.* Retrieved on April 2, 2017, from www.stephencovey.com/7habits/7habits-habit4.php
12 Marques, J. (2008). Workplace diversity: Developing a win-win-win strategy. *Development and Learning in Organizations 22*(5), 5–8.
13 Marques, J. (2015). *Business and Buddhism.* New York: Routledge (Taylor & Francis), 134.
14 Jacobs, D. L. (May 14, 2012). The little black book of billionaire secrets: The high price of career lies. *Forbes.* www.forbes.com/sites/deborahljacobs/2012/05/14/the-high-price-of-career-lies-2/2/#5745471c3633
15 Stewart, J. B. (May 8, 2012). In the undoing of a C.E.O., a puzzle. *The New York Times.* www.nytimes.com/2012/05/19/business/the-undoing-of-scott-thompson-at-yahoo-common-sense.html

16 Jacobs, D. L. (May 14, 2012). The little black book of billionaire secrets: The high price of career lies. *Forbes*. www.forbes.com/sites/deborahljacobs/2012/05/14/the-high-price-of-career-lies-2/2/#5745471c3633.

17 Pepitone, J. (May 14, 2012). Yahoo confirms CEO is out after resume scandal. *CNN Money*. http://money.cnn.com/2012/05/13/technology/yahoo-ceo-out.

18 Ibid.

19 Ibid.

20 Jacobs, D. L. (May 14, 2012). The little black book of billionaire secrets: The high price of career lies. *Forbes*. www.forbes.com/sites/deborahljacobs/2012/05/14/the-high-price-of-career-lies-2/2/#5745471c3633.

21 Carlson, N. (July 31, 2012). Why I just hired Scott Thompson, the Yahoo CEO with a fabricated computer science degree. *Business Insider*. www.businessinsider.com/why-i-just-hired-scott-thompson-the-yahoo-ceo-caught-lying-on-his-resume-2012-7.

INDEX

Page numbers in *italics* refer to figures; page numbers in **bold** refer to tables.